ANALYTICAL PSYCHOLOGY IN A CHANGING WORLD

How can we make sense of ourselves within a world of change?

In *Analytical Psychology in a Changing World,* an international range of contributors examine some of the common pitfalls, challenges and rewards that we encounter in our efforts to carve out identities of a personal or collective nature, and question the extent to which analytical psychology as a school of thought and therapeutic approach must also adapt to meet our changing needs.

The contributors assess contemporary concerns about our sense of who we are and where we are going, some in light of recent social and natural disasters and changes to our social climates, others by revisiting existential concerns and philosophical responses to our human situation in order to assess their validity for today. How we use our urban environment and its structures to make sense of our pathologies and shortcomings; the relevance of images and the dynamic forms that underpin our experience of the world; how analytical psychology can effectively manage issues and problems of cultural, religious and existential identity – these broad themes, and others besides, are vividly illustrated by striking case studies and unique personal insights that give real lucidity to the ideas and arguments presented.

Analytical Psychology in a Changing World will be essential reading for Jungian and post-Jungian scholars and clinicians of depth psychology, as well as sociologists, philosophers and any reader with a critical interest in the important cultural ideas of our time.

Lucy Huskinson, Ph.D., is Senior Lecturer in the School of Philosophy and Religion at Bangor University, UK. She is co-Editor-in-Chief of the *International Journal of Jungian Studies*, and author and editor of various books and articles on analytical psychology and philosophy, including *Nietzsche and Jung* and *Dreaming the Myth Onwards: New Directions in Jungian Therapy and Thought.*

Murray Stein, Ph.D., is a training and supervising analyst with ISAPZURICH. He was formerly president of the International Association for Analytical Psychology and president of the International School of Analytical Psychology in Zurich. His publications include *Minding the Self: Jungian Meditations on Contemporary Spirituality.*

ANALYTICAL PSYCHOLOGY IN A CHANGING WORLD

The search for self, identity and community

Edited by Lucy Huskinson and Murray Stein

Routledge
Taylor & Francis Group
LONDON AND NEW YORK

First published 2015
by Routledge
27 Church Road, Hove, East Sussex, BN3 2FA

and by Routledge
711 Third Avenue, New York, NY 10017

Routledge is an imprint of the Taylor & Francis Group, an informa business

British Library Cataloguing in Publication Data
A catalogue record for this book is available from the British Library

Library of Congress Cataloging in Publication Data
Analytical psychology in a changing world: the search for self, identity and community/edited by Lucy Huskinson and Murray Stein.
pages cm
1. Jungian psychology. 2. Psychoanalysis. I. Huskinson, Lucy, 1976– II. Stein, Murray, 1943–
BF173.A656 2014
150.19′54 – dc23
2014009544

ISBN: 978-0-415-72126-4 (hbk)
ISBN: 978-0-415-72128-8 (pbk)
ISBN: 978-1-315-75590-8 (ebk)

Typeset in Times
by Florence Production Ltd, Stoodleigh, Devon, UK

CONTENTS

FIGURES

CONTRIBUTORS

James Alan Anslow is a Ph.D. candidate at the Centre for Psychoanalytic Studies, University of Essex, UK, researching UK tabloid journalism from a post-Jungian perspective. For many years he was a national newspaper journalist and media educator, lecturing in journalism at City University London and the University of Bedfordshire. In the 1990s he was Chief Production Editor of the *News of the World* – later controversially discontinued – and oversaw its editorial output the night Diana, Princess of Wales died. He has an M.A. in Media from Nottingham Trent University.

Helena Bassil-Morozow, Ph.D., is a cultural philosopher and film scholar. Her principal interest is the dynamic between individual personality and socio-cultural systems in industrialised and post-industrial societies. She is an honorary research fellow of the Research Institute for Media Art and Design, University of Bedfordshire, UK. She edits the film section of *Spring: the Journal of Archetype and Culture*. Helena's books include *Tim Burton: the Monster and the Crowd* (Routledge, 2010) and *The Trickster in Contemporary Film* (Routledge, 2011).

Terence Dawson, Ph.D., teaches English and European literature at Nanyang Technological University, Singapore. With Polly Young-Eisendrath, he co-edited *The Cambridge Companion to Jung* (Cambridge University Press, 1997; 2nd edn 2008) and he is the author of *The Effective Protagonist in the Nineteenth-Century British Novel: Scott, Brontë, Eliot, Wilde* (Ashgate, 2004) and articles on wide-ranging literary subjects.

Isabelle DeArmond, M.D., Ph.D., is a physician specialised in immunology/allergy, trained at the University of Paris, France. After spending most of her career in clinical research, she recently obtained a Ph.D. in clinical psychology at Saybrook University, California. Her main interests in Jungian psychology are spirituality and the psychological aspects of end-of-life.

John Dourley, Ph.D., is a Jungian analyst (Zurich, 1980). He is Professor Emeritus, Department of Religion, Carleton University, Ottawa, Canada. He has written widely on Jung and religion. He is a Catholic priest and member of the religious order, the Oblates of Mary Immaculate.

Lucy Huskinson, Ph.D., is Senior Lecturer at Bangor University, UK. She is co-Editor-in-Chief of the *International Journal of Jungian Studies*, and author of *Nietzsche and Jung* (Routledge, 2004), and *Introduction to Nietzsche* (SPCK, 2010). She is editor of, and contributor to, *Dreaming the Myth Onwards: New Interpretations of Jungian Therapy and Thought* (Routledge, 2009), and *New Interpretations of Spirit Possession and Trance* (Continuum, 2010). She has also authored numerous papers on analytical psychology and philosophy.

Toshio Kawai, Ph.D., is a professor at the Kokoro Research Center, Kyoto University, Japan, and a Jungian analyst in private practice. He was educated in clinical psychology at Kyoto University, and in philosophical psychology at Zurich University. He also has a diploma from the C.G. Jung Institute, Zurich. He is author of several papers in analytical psychology, published in the *Journal of Analytical Psychology* and various Jungian anthologies.

William E. Kotsch, Ph.D., is a clinical psychologist (Vanderbilt, 1976) and Jungian analyst (Chicago, 1995) practising in Taos and Santa Fe, New Mexico, USA. A practising Buddhist, he is currently in a three-year retreat at the Vajra Vidya Center in Crestone, Colorado, under the direction of The Venerable Thrangu Rinpoche and Khenpo Jigme.

Cedrus Monte, Ph.D., is a Jungian analyst, graduate of the C.G. Jung Institute in Zurich, Switzerland. She currently resides and practises in Zurich but is a native of the San Francisco Bay Area, with both paternal and maternal Portuguese roots (Azores and Madeira). Her professional focus is on body-centred analysis, the creative process and the relationship between psyche, land and culture. For further information about Cedrus Monte, visit www.cedrusmonte.org.

Konoyu Nakamura, Ph.D., is Professor of Clinical Psychology at Otemon Gakuin University, Japan, and a Jungian-oriented psychotherapist. She has authored chapters in several books, including: *Dreaming the Myth Onwards: New Directions in Jungian Therapy and Thought* (Routledge, 2008); *Sacral Revolutions* (Routledge, 2010); *Body, Mind and Healing After Jung: A Space of Questions* (Routledge, 2010); *Jungian and Dialogical Self Perspectives* (Palgrave Macmillan, 2011).

Elizabeth Eowyn Nelson, Ph.D., is core faculty and Dissertation Policy Director at Pacifica Graduate Institute, USA, where she has been teaching courses in research design, methodology and dissertation development for more than a decade. She is co-author of *The Art of Inquiry* (Spring Publications, 2005) and author of *Psyche's Knife: Archetypal Explorations of Love and Power* (Chiron, 2012).

Yuka Ogiso, Ph.D., is a Research Fellow at the Kokoro Research Center, Kyoto University, Japan. She also works as a clinical psychologist. She was educated in the Philosophy of Education at Tokyo University and in Clinical Psychology at Kyoto University, where she received her Ph.D. in 2013. Recently she published *Jung and James: A Search for Eachness and Universality* (Sogensha, 2014).

Andrew Samuels is a Training Analyst of the Society of Analytical Psychology in private practice in London, and a founder Board Member of the International Association for Relational Psychoanalysis and Psychotherapy. He was co-founder of Psychotherapists and Counsellors for Social Responsibility in the UK, and is immediate past Chair of the United Kingdom Council for Psychotherapy. He is Professor of Analytical Psychology at the University of Essex, UK. Publications include *Jung and the Post-Jungians* (Routledge, 1985) and the award-winning *Politics on the Couch* (Karnac Books, 2001).

Guilherme Scandiucci is a Ph.D. student at the University of São Paulo, Brazil. He also works as a clinical psychologist in private practice, and as both a teacher of analytical psychology and a clinical supervisor in analytical psychotherapy at the Mackenzie Presbyterian University in São Paulo.

Marta Tibaldi, Ph.D., is a Jungian analyst of the *Associazione Italiana di Psicologia Analitica* (AIPA) and of the International Association for Analytical Psychology (IAAP). She is a Training Analyst and Supervisor in Rome and Hong Kong, a Training Supervisor of the C.G. Jung Institute, Zurich and the Liaison Person of the IAAP Developing Group in Hong Kong. Author of many articles and essays, recently she published *Oltre il cancro: Trasformare creativamente la malattia che temiamo di più* (Moretti & Vitali, Rome, 2010) and *Pratica dell'immaginazione attiva* (La Lepre, Rome, 2011).

INTRODUCTION

As Heraclitus noted over two and a half millennia ago, 'nothing endures but change'. Change is persistent and inevitable, and perhaps also one of the most difficult experiences in life to manage well. It spells the loss of what once was and heralds the new and unfamiliar. Although often painful, however, change may also excite with its possibilities and promise of renewal. Our personalities are shaped importantly by the variations, changes and transitions that we experience within and in response to our environments. Yet often we may wonder how to make sense of ourselves upon such transitory grounds. Are all attempts to establish cohesive and abiding identities within our impermanent and makeshift climates doomed to failure? Or are there other ways to think about identity, perhaps as evolving personality?

C.G. Jung sought to make sense of the personality as a conglomerate of many different aspects, each in dialogue with the other, a dynamic interplay of psychic factors and energies. According to Jung, personality evolves throughout a lifetime, and it is by engaging with the shifts and transitions we encounter that we can experience creative vitality and realise our potentials for development. On the other hand, if we deny change and seek to establish a permanently fixed identity, closed off from the possibilities that come with change, we run into the difficulties of one-sidedness, which creates neurosis, and begin to experience life as unfulfilling and lacking in meaning.

A hundred years have passed since Jung named his approach 'analytical psychology' (to differentiate it from the ideas of 'psychoanalysis' as proposed by Sigmund Freud). The face of the world has changed a great deal since then. Whereas Jung and his fellow depth psychologists spoke principally of 'the unconscious' as the driving force and foundation of the mind, scientists today refer principally to the 'brain' and its neurological functions and processes. And yet it is a testament to the abiding value of analytical psychology that Jung's ideas continue to inform and inspire theorists, scholars, professionals of many stripes, and psychotherapeutic practitioners and patients. Although regarded as a body of thought and therapeutic practice in their own right, Jung's ideas have influenced people within many academic departments and fields of study far beyond their own disciplinary origins within psychology and psychiatry. Analytical psychology continues to contribute to important debates and discussions across a multitude of disciplinary boundaries. Central ideas of analytical psychology may be found in philosophy, political thought, literature, linguistics, religious studies, education, sociology, business studies, history, film and media, fine art and art history, neuroscience, quantum physics, and environmental studies. Likewise, the therapeutic practice of analytical psychology continues to be in demand and is sought after to treat the cultural and natural traumas and upheavals of our day, and to offer interventions within a variety of relatively new fields of human care, such as HIV counselling, relief work to victims of natural disaster (such as those who have been affected by the earthquakes in China and Japan), political consultation, reconciliation within interfaith groups, treatment within terminal healthcare, ecological sustainability, and more. Analytical psychology continues to contribute to human understanding in the face of changing cultural values, and its widespread appeal and demand testify to its usefulness for making sense of these values and their manifestations within the shifts and ruptures of the world in which we find ourselves.

It was in this spirit of the roles that analytical psychology is playing in the world today that an international conference titled *Jung's Analytical Psychology in Conversation with a Changing World* was organised. It was the fourth international academic conference for the International Association for Analytical Psychology (IAAP) and third joint conference with the International Association for Jungian Studies (IAJS). Held at Universidade Católica Portuguese, Faculdade de Filosofia (Portuguesa Catholic University, Faculty of Philosophy) in Braga, Portugal, the conference represented a multiplicity of engagements with our dynamically changing world. Significantly, Braga, one of the oldest Christian cities in the world and the oldest city in Portugal (founded around 20 BCE, during a period of Roman occupation) is today at the centre of one of the fastest growing areas in Europe. It looks at one and the same time to the spirit of the past through its historical traditions, within which it is deeply steeped, and to the future by embracing the demands of a thoroughly modern and multicultural era. Braga, home to two universities where Jungian studies are actively taught, provided a most hospitable forum for a gathering of scholars in Jungian studies and professional Jungian therapists from around the world to come and debate, and to develop their ideas about how analytical psychology can participate constructively in rapidly changing environments and cultures.

The chapters in this volume represent a variety of perspectives on the conference theme. Each seeks to make sense of specific attempts to carve out identities of a personal or collective nature and to highlight some of the common pitfalls and challenges faced in these efforts. A message that underpins many of the chapters is that there is much to be gained from valuing the attempts to relate to change, not the least being the realisation that change is something one should not resist or shy away from, but something one must embrace if one is to nurture and cultivate more fulfilling identities and relationships with the world. The attentive reader will discover in these chapters the notion that transformation requires us to bear discomfort and that, paradoxically, through accepting these difficult feelings and the uncertainties they evoke we may discover a sense of stability and containment.

The reader will also find that the authors interpret the nature of present changes differently, and they also emphasise an array of different understandings of identity (or lack thereof) that are sought today around the world. They may, for instance, consider identity as individual personhood, or as social roles and community ethos, or as cultural aspiration, religious identification and expressions of faith, or as existential condition. Likewise, 'the world' may be construed as one's inner world or as the natural and cultural environments that we inhabit. Furthermore, change may refer to transitions in one's mortal life and confrontations with death, or to sudden catastrophes, ruptures or shifts in economic and social climates, or to developments within language and alterations in the use of definitions and concepts within analytical psychology as it attempts to engage with these different yet interrelated personal and social dimensions.

The volume begins with three studies that examine some of the tensions that arise when individuals seek recognition at the fringes of prescribed collective identity or have to engage with identity issues in the midst of social, political, or environmental upheavals. Helena Bassil-Morozow and James Anslow regard our current age as basically consumerist in orientation and filled with false promises and false prophets of individuation. They alert us to the dangers that befall those who seek to find answers to life's deep questions too quickly within the dazzling array of ready-to-hand personalities and ideal lifestyles prepared for consumption, which inevitably lead us astray and weaken our personal resolve and community spirit (Chapter 1). From that slippery social face of our changing world, we move to catastrophic changes of nature and attempts to engage effectively with them. Toshio Kawai reflects upon the devastation caused by the 2011 tsunami in Japan and considers the ways in which the narratives created by victims may heal individuals and community, thereby enabling transformation and positive growth from out of the sudden upheaval and devastation of change. Kawai argues that therapeutic relief is signalled when the focus shifts from the 'large story' of collective trauma experienced within society at large and the overarching Japanese social 'worldview' to the 'small story' of personal problems expressed by victims (Chapter 2). Next, Andrew Samuels offers some timely political advice on ways in which the individual can have an impact within society by facilitating social and political solidarity and ultimately enabling collective change. In this conversational piece, the traditional conception of the individual as a rebellious and marginalised figure in political discourse is given new energy and revealed to be the means to social and political action, not an obstacle to it (Chapter 3).

With chapters by Guilherme Scandiucci (Chapter 4) and Lucy Huskinson (Chapter 5), attention turns to the urban environment and its structures in order to ascertain how we utilise our constructed environments to enhance and shape our identities and to make sense of our pathologies, our shortcomings and ourselves. Scandiucci addresses this through his insightful commentary on the social upheavals within adolescent communities in São Paulo, Brazil, as this is expressed in graffiti and street art. He argues that graffiti is both symptomatic of the pathology of the urban psyche and also a remedy for its healing. In contrast to this, Huskinson critiques the pervading views in the humanities that extol the romanticism of nature one-sidedly and to the detriment of the aesthetics of urban life. She deconstructs three categories of experience traditionally associated with architecture – the uncanny, the sublime, and the numinous – in order to trace the psychodynamic processes that underpin them and to argue that the humanly constructed environment is no less a site for psyche than the natural world, and that our experiences of buildings are no less therapeutic than experiences with living forms of nature.

Issues of cultural, religious and existential identity are investigated within the three studies that follow. Konoyu Nakamura examines the social disquiet of gender inequality in Japan, and she asks to what extent analytical psychology as a method of therapeutic intervention needs to change and adapt if it is to manage these social issues effectively (Chapter 6). Following this, William Kotsch offers a different kind of possibility for facilitating our well-being in the midst of the continual changes that affect our lives by postulating therapeutic methods within Buddhist thought (Chapter 7). By opening up a dialogue between concerns of analytical psychology and Buddhist thinking, Kotsch puts forward the notion that life is fulfilling only when we engage with it in a way that refrains from appropriating it to our own ends. He also critiques the notion of identity as an ideal to aspire to or to desire. John Dourley's study continues the theme of quest for a meaningful life (Chapter 8). Again, we find it to be a quest that is both challenging and troublesome for the ego. Dourley shows how the very awareness of our mortality and subjectivity brings with it a great deal of existential anxiety and dissatisfaction, a condition that is exacerbated when we experience the world as fleeting and unstable. Dourley considers the only meaningful response to a radically changing world to be a spiritual one, which is expressed most aptly by Paul Tillich's notion, 'courage to be', an approach to life that requires us to accept our existence and identity as individuals and members of a community with trust in an ultimate ground of being.

The theme of identity within a changing world is then carried forward into an area of investigation where our attention turns to the relevance of images and the dynamic forms that underpin our experience of the world. Elizabeth Nelson examines James Hillman's desire that we start to notice (*notitia*) properly the images of the world as they appear to us, so as to engage their soulful nature (Chapter 9). This applies not only to mental forms, nor merely to the natural world, but also to manufactured objects and built environments that are otherwise regarded as mundane and lacking in soul. Marta Tibaldi similarly calls for an engagement with our imagination and the images it unfolds, and she evaluates specific therapeutic approaches that may help us to do so (Chapter 10). After describing her own tried-and-tested methods of therapeutic intervention, inspired by Hillman, she argues in terms that resonate with the Buddhist approach expounded by Kotsch, that psychological transformation is a matter of engaging with images that press upon us in such a way that we are able to 'see through them' and harness the autonomous energy that they reveal to us. Following this, Yuka Ogiso revisits Jung's visions of a flood extending over Europe as an image or symptom of the inner turbulence and feelings of uncertainty he felt about his life at the time of the visions (Chapter 11). She goes on to explore how Jung's attempts to make sense of his visions led him to theorise about the nature of opposites and their role both within his developing ideas about typological theory and his own personal typological disposition.

The volume concludes with three chapters that regard the spirit of change and its place and situation within the world. Isabelle DeArmond considers what is perhaps the most potent symbol of change – namely, death – by reflecting on the spirit of the unconscious and its capacity to heal and transform us through our apprehension of mortality. Her fascinating study investigates the experiences of those who are inevitably forced to confront death in their care for the dying (Chapter 12). Finally, the volume returns to the spirit of place in which the ideas and reflections of these chapters were aired, discussed and developed, to Portugal, and specifically to the great poet, Fernando Pessoa, one of its most celebrated writers. Cedrus Monte (Chapter 13) and Terence Dawson (Chapter 14) present Pessoa as one who proclaims the changing world as a nourishing source for transformation. Here we hear Pessoa's call to experience our multiple selves and to discover ourselves anew within the changing world of forms that we can readily perceive within and around us. By embracing change in this way, we discover a renewed capacity to connect meaningfully to the discord, anxiety and longing that we may otherwise try to escape.

The committee formed for selecting and assessing the chapters submitted for this publication included, in addition to the editors, Axel Capriles (Venezuela), Angela Connolly (Italy), Terence Dawson (Singapore) and Luke Hockley (UK), to whom the editors are thankful for their help and thoughtful comments.

Lucy Huskinson and Murray Stein

1

FAKING INDIVIDUATION IN THE AGE OF UNREALITY

Mass media, identity confusion and self-objects

Helena Bassil-Morozow and James Alan Anslow

It has become a commonplace to call postmodern culture fluid, traditionless, lacking in stable identities and meanings. It is characterised by a sense of 'unreality', identity confusion, and lack of psychological unity and completeness. In the ever-changing, fluid post-industrial world, with its endless consumer and personal choices, the only thing that is not on offer is the absolute truth, wholeness, meaning. However, even now that psychological fragmentation is the psycho-cultural norm, and the quest for wholeness has long been relegated to the 'mytho-religious' domain, the question of identity remains as acute as ever.

'Stable' identities grow in stable cultural environments with fixed meanings. In the absence of a fixed order, or *habitus,* to use Pierre Bourdieu's term, mass media has begun to perform some of its functions. Television, newspapers, the Internet offer alternative identities (or, rather, fragments of identities), which lead to the confusion between truth and fiction. In this liminal atmosphere, in the absence of permanent identity-inspiring role models, mass media reflects, embraces and contributes to the brokenness of culture. It acts as a kind of identity pimp providing the insatiable public with a rotation of inspiring public figures.

However, due to the speed of news rotation, identities thereby procured are often shallow and superficial. The entire cultural framework can be seen as narcissistic in the sense that it relies on the individuals *not* having, or sometimes not even *seeking* a stable individual character core. Not only mass media, but consumer capitalism in general does not support the concept of stable identity. Instead, it manipulates consumer demand by introducing multiple choice and uncertainty.

The individual inhabiting such a culture does not feel psychologically safe; his or her sense of identity remains fluid and shaky, always keeping pace with the fast-moving life, always prepared to change direction of individual or professional development. Marshall Berman highlights one of the principal dialectical features of modern existence: alongside the great emptiness of values ('God is dead') there exists 'a remarkable abundance of possibilities' (1983, p. 21). The psyche of the modern individual – and of society in which he or she inhabits – consists of fleeting, flying, metamorphosing elements. Its very ephemeral character constitutes its anxiety – its neuroses and psychoses.

This chapter combines postmodern theory, Jung's concept of individuation and Heinz Kohut's notion of selfobject in an attempt to outline the trajectories of personal evolution in the dynamic and unpredictable world.

Identity and individuation in post-traditional contexts

In post-industrial contexts individuals are responsible for their own development, and they are not expected to rely on community, tradition and ritual for providing them with a sense of identity. Anthony Giddens argues in *Modernity and Self-Identity* that in pre-modern contexts

> tradition has a key role in articulating action and ontological frameworks [and that it] offers an organising medium of social life specifically geared to ontological precepts. [. . .] In addition, tradition creates a sense of the firmness of things that typically mixes cognitive and moral elements. The world is as it is because it is as it should be.
>
> (Giddens 1991, p. 498)

Identity transitions and any reorganisations of the self in pre-modern cultures usually have predetermined character:

> Transitions in individuals' lives have always demanded psychic reorganisation, something which was often ritualised in traditional cultures in the shape of *rites de passage*. But in such cultures, where things have stayed the same from generation to generation on the level of the collectivity, the changed identity was clearly staked out – as when an individual moved from adolescence into adulthood.
>
> (Giddens 1991, pp. 32–3)

By contrast, identity in post-traditional order is fluid. The self becomes a do-it-yourself, reflexive project. This constant redefinition and recollection of the self from fragments is the norm in post-traditional societies and is not confined to life's crises. It is, Giddens argues, a feature of modern social activity in relation to psychic organisation (1991, p. 33).

Despite psychological fragmentedness being the norm in post-industrial societies, the individual still regards it as unsettling. In the absence of 'instructions', people are left directionless and looking for leaders and role models. Giddens writes:

> Modernity, it can be said, breaks down the protective framework of the small community and of tradition, replacing these with much larger, impersonal organisations. The individual feels bereft and alone in a world in which she or he lacks the psychological support and the sense of security provided by more traditional settings.
>
> (1991, pp. 33–4)

Individuating in the Jungian sense – i.e. defining yourself in relation to your surroundings; gradual self-fulfilment through inner internal and external psychological conflict – in post-traditional societies is invariably bound with the question of lifestyle and the dilemma of choice. It is also closely linked to the projective–introjective character of mass culture assisted by contemporary media structures. Jung defines the individuation process as driven by the self – the centre of the personality. He writes in *Psychological Types*:

> In general [individuation] is the process by which individual beings are formed and differentiated; in particular, it is the development of the psychological *individual* as a being distinct from the general, collective psychology. Individuation, therefore, is a process of *differentiation*, having for its goal the development of the individual personality.
>
> (Jung 1921, para. 757)

However, the weakening of *habitus* (the collective aspect of life) did not in any way enhance individuals' ability to 'individuate' – it only gave them more choice; it presented them with the right to build their lives from a wider variety of bricks. Choosing from a variety of options and constructing one's identity from an array of available building bricks requires a high degree of self-knowledge and self-reflection. Giddens argues:

> Lifestyle is not a term that has much applicability to traditional cultures, because it implies choice within a plurality of possible options, and is 'adopted' rather than 'handed down'. Lifestyles are routinised practices, the routines incorporated into habits of dress, eating, modes of acting and favoured milieu for encountering others; but the routines followed are reflexively open to change in the light of the mobile nature of self-identity. Each of the small decisions a person makes every day – what to wear, what to eat, how to conduct himself at work, whom to meet with later in the evening – contributes to such routines. All such choices (as well as larger and more consequential ones) are decisions not about how to act but who to be. The more post-traditional the setting in which the individual moves, the more lifestyle concerns the very core of self-identity, its making and remaking.
>
> (Giddens 1991, p. 81)

A fixed order, or *habitus* (to use Pierre Bourdieu's term) can be both a good and a harmful thing for the individual. Culturally prescribed norms tend to swing the individuation process in the direction of the collective. By contrast, lifestyle choices characterising post-industrial societies are supposed to assist individuals in discovering their new – and unique – identity. This does not mean, however, that each and every individual is equally capable of assembling this unique identity from a variety of fragments offered by the capitalist system and mass media. Moreover, mass media makes the differentiation of the personal from the collective difficult due to the powerful character of mass projections. Often projection on to public figures, assisted by mass media, takes the place of true self-reflection. Objectification is firmly integrated into contemporary individuation process and often replaces true, live, problematic, uncontrollable human relationships.

Mass media provides its customers with self-definitions, which, in their quality and disposability, differ from the relatively stable identities characteristic of community-based societies. It ensures rapid rotation of celebrities, borrowed and appropriated by consumers for the purposes of self-understanding. In doing so, individuals hope to restore their relationship with their inner wholeness on the one hand, and their connections with the outside world on the other. With the help of these artificial identities urban individuals gain a false feeling of being at one with the (Jungian) Self, as well as being connected to one's community.

Heinz Kohut's selfobject: towards artificial individuation

When relationships and people are replaced with objectification and objects, the vision of oneself – of one's personality core – becomes blurred and destabilised. Heinz Kohut's concept of selfobject can clarify the main mechanisms, as well as explain personal and cultural aspects, of objectification.

In his book *Individuation and Narcissism* (1985) Mario Jacoby argues that Jung and Kohut are ideologically close and compatible despite the fact that their sets of terminology differ significantly. He notes that 'modern psychoanalytic research on narcissism, especially that of Heinz Kohut, shows a clear convergence with the Jungian position' and Jung's concept of the individuation process 'may be paralleled with the lines of maturation in narcissism as postulated by Kohut' (Jacoby 1985, p. 6). For instance, their views on individual development are not conflicting and can even be used to complement and enrich each other. Kohut's concept of selfobject, coupled with Jungian individuation, can illuminate the contemporary individual's struggle for identity and self-definition.

Selfobjects are 'people or objects that help the self regulate affect and feel whole and competent, but cause frustration if not there when needed' (Fromme 2010, p. 201). The self in Kohut's psychology is self-representation rather than the totality of the psyche. Self-representation is the way in which 'I-as-a-person am represented in my own mind – in contrast to representations of persons and things that are not myself – i.e., objects' (Jacoby 1985, p. 59). In this sense, the concept of the self as self-representation is ideologically close to the Jungian ego – its subjective and introspective experience (ibid.).

Jung defined the ego, the conscious part of the personality, as the complex of representations that constitutes 'the centre of the field of consciousness and possesses a high degree of continuity and identity', is strong and solid enough to expose and confront evil (Jacobi 1973, p. 7). Meanwhile, the Self in his psychology is the totality of the psyche, embracing both its conscious and unconscious aspects. As Mario Jacoby notes, the Self is an experiential fact that is far superior to ego consciousness: 'for Jung the self is at the same time an irrepresentable psychic centre, the central archetype, which affects psychic development, change and balance' (Jacoby 1985, p. 70).

By contrast, Kohut theorised the self as being split into the True and False parts. Jacoby notes that the concepts of the split self – its False and True parts – correspond to Jung's concepts of persona and the personal ego/transpersonal self structure (Jacoby 1985, p. 70). False Self is an external and largely artificial structure (very much like the persona) that 'behaves' in a way that brings social benefits. In narcissistic disturbances, when the True Self is damaged, the False Self is particularly well developed as its overgrowth serves to protect the fragile personality core. The genesis of the disorder, Kohut argues, can be insufficient mirroring of the child's self by the mother. As a result, the child's self cannot

> establish itself securely (the child does not build up an inner sense of self-confidence; it continues to need external affirmation). [. . .] But . . . we do not see merely fixation on a small child's need for mirroring – the traumatic frustration of the normal need intensifies and distorts the need: the child becomes insatiably hungry for mirroring, affirmation, and praise. It is this intensified, distorted need which the child cannot tolerate and which it therefore either represses (and may hide behind pseudoindependence and emotional coldness) or distorts and splits off. [. . .] In the narcissistic transference, the infantile need for selfobject is remobilized.
>
> (Kohut 2011, p. 558)

Kohut's analysis of narcissism and immature relationships that rest on mirroring and manipulation is applicable to cultural analysis. The psyche of the urban individual is living with a very old trauma – inflicted by industrialisation, social alienation, the weakening of community and intensification of city life – which was already apparent in the middle of the nineteenth century but became particularly acute at the start of the twentieth century. The trauma – of which Jung was a faithful historiographer – was catastrophically deepened by the two world wars. The individual of today is suffering from a traumatic identity crisis brought about by the profound and irreversible changes in the social and relational structures of society.

The individual, torn from his or her roots, grows up thinking that the most responsible way of dealing with problems is trying to solve them on your own, without the involvement of your immediate or wider environment. The society of independent individuals, self-reliant and stoical, barraged with identity and lifestyle choices, separated from fellow human beings and isolated by the specifics of the urban environment, feel fragmented and broken. They feel out of control, insecure, lost. Anthony Giddens projects the loss of 'the early sense of ontological security' (characteristic of narcissistic disturbances) on to contemporary culture and concludes that

> trust is a crucial generic phenomenon of personality development as well as having a distinctive and specific relevance to a world of disembedding mechanisms and abstract systems. [. . .] Trust in this sense is basic to a 'protective cocoon' which stands guard over the self in its dealings with everyday reality. It 'brackets out' potential occurrences which, were the individual seriously to contemplate them, would produce a paralysis of the will, or feelings of engulfment.
> (Giddens 1991, p. 3)

Trust and the desire to take control of one's destiny go hand-in-hand. A broken identity is always on the look-out for reparation and completion, for ways to achieve the mythical wholeness. The American historian Christopher Lasch famously theorised in his book *The Culture of Narcissism* (1979) that narcissism can be used as a metaphor to explain the contemporary individual's fascination with fame and celebrity as well as the widespread 'fear of competition, the inability to suspend disbelief, the shallowness and transitory quality of personal relations, the horror of death' (Lasch 1991, p. 23). The contemporary narcissist lives for himself and only for the moment: 'To live for the moment is the prevailing passion – to live for yourself, not for your predecessors or posterity' (ibid., p. 5). Meanwhile, this man, 'the final product of bourgeois individualism', is permanently haunted by inner emptiness and anxiety as well as 'doubts the reality of his own existence' (ibid., p. xvi). The contemporary narcissistic individual feels lonely, angry and out of control; he is constantly on the look-out for inner peace and meaning. He still seeks intimacy and mirroring – but in post-traditional cultures both are fleeting and impermanent.

This is when mass media comes to the rescue by offering artificial means of control and other escapist and superficial solutions to identity brokenness. It offers the individual a variety of safe replacements – celebrities, cars, brand clothes – for the all-too-real and emotionally unsafe messiness of human connection and human relationships. Identities are produced, advertised and consumed in limitless quantities; they are offered in all shapes and sizes.

Famous people are ready-made personality samples, complete with distinguishable lifestyles, beautiful faces and bodies, fashionable wardrobes and interesting, eventful lives. Caught in the eternal consumption process, participants are pushed into further destabilising their selves, deferring the process of maturation, of self-formation. One no longer knows what one wants – the only thing knowable, verifiable and, in fact, real – is the never-ending process of *wanting*.

The non-stop mirroring and copying process – the postmodern reaction to the trauma of modernity – has become obsessive-compulsive. Individuals caught in this process cannot stop consuming because constantly buying new things and altering their identities numbs the inner emptiness – the narcissistic lack of a genuine identity. The obsessive-compulsive element of shopping lessens the pain, dissolves the anger, and numbs the acute awareness of the trauma.

According to Kohut, immature relationships with selfobjects often turn into love or hate alliances that are either defensive – attempts to

> ward off, through an exaggerated experience of love or hate relations, the loss of the archaic [parental] selfobject, which would lead to fragmentation of the self – or they are not expressions of object-love or object-hate at all, but of the need for self-objects in lieu of self-structure.
>
> (Kohut 2011, p. 557)

Because relationships of this kind are superficial, any individual development resulting from them can be considered fake. Deep down, under the Persona (Jung) or the False Self (Kohut) there is nothing – there dwells and broods the ubiquitous phenomenological emptiness; the anger, the fear of non-existence. To use the Jungian analytical matrix, there is no pronounced ego and no hope for the totality of the psyche (the Self). The impermanence, the high turnover of generated and debased objects effectively fuels the system – but also destabilises it. Media's typically tricksterish habit to impulsively (and unpredictably) debase and replace the objects of its manipulation is essentially self-destructive because it accelerates the whole process to dangerous proportions.

Consumers and the system of objects

Objectification is probably the easiest, and most psychologically accessible, type of relationship based on projective (less frequently – introjective) identification. By introducing mass production, the capitalist system encouraged objectification of the outside world and fostered dependence on selfobjects. Contemporary hectic lifestyles are not suitable for fostering long-term or authentic relationships but gravitate instead towards a rotation of partners, friends and role models. The contemporary individual expects objects in his or her environment to be easily governed and predictable. There is simply no time for studying – or entering into – complex interactions with the objects that are too unpredictable. The individual of the machine age expects things to happen at the touch of a button.

In his first major work, *The System of Objects* (1968), the French cultural critic Jean Baudrillard points out the fact that the contemporary individual's relationship with the outside world is both immature and manipulative. Technology, Baudrillard argues, only supports us in this immaturity and dependence on immediacy. We are no longer prepared to wait; we want things to happen quickly – we want things *here and now*. Only then do we feel in control – because quick satisfaction of our needs remind us of the omnipotent uroboric state of early childhood. This illusion of control, carefully orchestrated by consumer capitalism, keeps the individual in the constant state of dependency on the immediate availability of objects. This kind of manipulation makes consumers feel in control of many aspects of their lives; in a way, it also empowers them, but only temporarily, and only as long as they are prepared to pay for new products and devices.

Industrialisation made it possible for us to exercise our right to change the objective environment. For instance, one feels at one with the car when one is driving. The car becomes our narcissistic extension, our ideal object. Thus, driving becomes a particularly attractive form of projective identification. Baudrillard writes:

> When it comes to material objects, however, and especially to manufactured objects complex enough to lend themselves to mental dismantling, this tendency has free rein. With the automobile, for instance, it is possible to speak of '*my* brakes', '*my* tail fins', '*my* steering wheel'; or to say '*I* am braking', '*I* am turning' or '*I* am starting'. In short, all the car's 'organs' and functions may be brought separately into relation with the person of the owner in the possessive mode. We are dealing here not with a process of personalization at the social level but with a process of a projective kind. We are concerned not with *having* but with *being*.
>
> (Baudrillard 2005, p. 109)

The contemporary Western consumer-citizen, Baudrillard also points out, can be metaphorically seen as a 'collector' with a tendency to objectify everything, including people and relationships, and expecting obedience, mirroring and silent appraisal from his or her environment. The practice of collecting is based on the narcissistic illusion of control over the world. For instance, for children 'collecting is a rudimentary way of mastering the outside world, of arranging, classifying and manipulating' (ibid., p. 93). Collecting is a form of obsession; as an activity, it is both regressive and sublime, and is based on 'serial intimacy' (ibid., p. 94). Obsession with objects presupposes impermanence and fear of genuine, long-term intimacy. The collector only loves his objects 'on a basis of their membership in a series' while 'human relationships, home of uniqueness and conflict, never permit any such fusion' (ibid.).

By contrast, old-fashioned forms of communication and forming relationships involved *limited* choice, or did not give any choice altogether. In the traditionalist, socially rigid world of pre-individualism in which the fragmenting trickster of freedom had limited power, people lived in communities, which they could escape only if they were very lucky. People in pre-industrial societies had jobs to which they were bound for life. Their freedom of movement was restricted both socially and technologically. Any attempt to manipulate the world and/or change one's destiny involved confrontation with the social order.

Interaction with one's objective reality was not a form of aggressive mirroring – or the process of relishing and exercising the right for unlimited choice – but more of a fight for the right to have any choice at all. In the words of Giddens, 'tradition or established habit orders life within relatively set channels' whereas 'modernity confronts the individuals with a complex diversity of choices and, because it is non-foundational, at the same time offers little help as to which options should be selected' (Giddens 1991, p. 81). Life with multiple lifestyle choices turns into a hall of mirrors; identities become mere reflections. In these circumstances, connecting with the outside world becomes an exercise in objectification. But how to pick the right object? What to collect now? How to determine ways of connecting with the object(s)? What is in fashion today? Unfortunately, the absence of a rigid traditional framework does not automatically create independent thinking. Freedom of choice does not magic unique identities out of thin air. This is when mass media and the advertising industry become useful.

There is a difference between 'I am this' and 'I want to be this'. The first presupposes knowing your personality and its boundaries; the second stands for aggressive mirroring of one's surroundings in the absence of this knowledge. These two notions are often confused by the contemporary individual, and mass media and advertising do everything to keep this confusion working. Mirroring in the absence of stable identity foundations is a form of instant gratification. The advertising industry supports the magical thinking of instant gratification. Baudrillard writes:

> Whether advertising is organised around the image of the mother or around the need to play, it always fosters *the same tendency to regress to a point anterior to the real social processes*, such as work, production, the market, or value, which might disturb this magical integration: the object has not been bought by you, you have voiced

> a desire for it and all the engineers, technicians and so on, have worked to gratify your desire. [. . .]
>
> And even as it separates the producer and the consumer within the one individual, thanks to the material abstraction of a highly differentiated system of objects, advertising strives inversely to re-create the infantile confusion of the object with the desire for the object, to return the consumer to the stage at which the infant makes no distinction between its mother and what its mother gives it.
>
> (Baudrillard 2005, pp. 190–1)

Today's Western individual would see this socially determined inability to control *most* objects and phenomena in one's surroundings as a form of madness, as a severe form of psychological impairment. Individuals in industrialised and post-industrial societies expect non-stop availability of objects suitable for projective identification. Lack of mechanical, dismantlable bodies is seen by the consumer-collector as a breach of contract; as if god(s) failed to supply them with (temporary) sources of (disposable) identities. The individual would therefore perceive this as unfair and cruel.

For instance, Baudrillard compares the car to the horse in his discussion of the failure of projective identification. Projection on to non-manufactured 'objects' and manipulation of these objects becomes extremely difficult. The behaviour of natural (non-manufactured) entities is disturbing for the consumer-collector because of their non-controllable qualities such as temper and character:

> With the horse, despite the fact that this animal was a remarkable instrument of power and transcendence for man, this kind of confusion was never possible. The fact is that the horse is not made of pieces – and above all, that it is *sexed.* We can say 'my horse' or 'my wife', but that is as far as this kind of possessive denomination can go. That which has a sex resists fragmenting projection and hence also the mode of appropriation that we have identified as a perversion. Faced by a living being, we may say 'my' but we cannot say 'I' as we do when we symbolically appropriate the functions and 'organs' of a car. That type of regression is not available to us. The horse may be the recipient of powerful symbolic cathexes: we associate it with the wild sexuality of the rutting season, as with the wisdom of the centaur; its head is a terrifying phantasy linked to the image of the father, yet its calm embodies the protective strength of Cheiron the teacher. It is never cathected, however, in the simplistic, narcissistic, far more impoverished and infantile manner in which the ego is projected onto structural details of cars (in accordance with an almost delusional analogy with disassociated parts and functions of the human body).
>
> (Baudrillard 2005, p. 109)

In other words, we as consumers prefer the world to be as psychologically uncomplicated as possible because establishing a system of relationships with this kind of world – mechanical and two-dimensional – is not emotionally taxing. However, as Jung pointed out, individuation cannot happen outside of one's society or community – one cannot 'individuate' on his own or using psychological prostheses to replace real-life relationships. 'Collecting' assisted by media and advertising does not lead to genuine individuation.

Celebrity culture, fed and shaped by mass media, cannot be seen as assisting individuals in finding themselves, in discovering their 'true selves'. Celebrities are treated by their makers and consumers as collectable and disposable prosthetic selfobjects created for the purpose of temporarily filling the gaping hole, of numbing the pain of brokenness. They are but pictures, images, two-dimensional things to be idealised, copied, manipulated, devalued, deposed, punished, shamed, stalked and projected upon in the endless repetition of the cycle. The hunger for compulsive collecting is a sign of the great emptiness within. Neither quality nor quantity of prosthetic selfobjects make any difference as far as achievement of internal wholeness or freedom is concerned. To quote Baudrillard once more:

> The possession of objects frees us only as possessors, and always refers us back to the infinite freedom to possess more objects . . . [. . .]
>
> There is no prospect of a model entering a series without being simultaneously replaced by another model. The whole system proceeds *en bloc*, but models replace one another without ever being transcended as such and without successive series, for their part, ever achieving self-transcendence as series. [. . .] This perpetual cycle of aspiration and disillusion, dynamically orchestrated at the level of production, constitutes the arena in which objects are pursued. [. . .] Everything is in movement, everything shifts before our own eyes, everything is continually being transformed – yet nothing really changes.
>
> (Baudrillard 2005, p. 167)

The biggest tragedy for the object is to realise that it has been used and abused – merely employed to temporarily fill the gap where the ego is supposed to be. The hapless objects who believed themselves to be genuine – and genuinely loved and accepted – eventually realise to their own horror that they have been deceived by the system and the former admirers. However, celebrities are not the only victims of the cycle of collecting and discarding. The consumer-spectator remains unhappy at every stage of the cycle and because the great emptiness remains unchanged, and unchallenged, it cannot be healed or helped by the ever-proliferating stream of images.

Case study: Princess Diana

A prime example of prosthetic selfobject is Diana, Princess of Wales (1961–1997), known popularly as Princess Diana or Princess Di, she was one of the most notable 'celebrity martyrs' of modern times in Britain, the USA and throughout many other parts of the world. In November 1997, shortly after her death in a Paris car crash, the *American Journalism Review* recorded:

> USA Today's total circulation for the week after Diana's death was several hundred thousand above normal. The Washington Post sold more than 20,000 additional copies of its Sunday editions the day Diana died and the day after her funeral. Television news ratings also increased. CNN reported 'a dramatic surge in viewership,' and the highest ratings ever for its Sunday night newsmagazine, 'Impact', which aired the night Diana died. More than 15 million people watched the August 31 60 Minutes' devoted to the princess, according to Nielsen Media Research . . . two weeks after Diana died broadcast networks devoted more time to the princess and the British monarchy than any other story, according to The Tyndall Weekly. 'We over-dosed on Diana,' says Steve Geimann, immediate past president of the Society of Professional Journalists.
>
> (www.ajr.org/article.asp?id=785)

The media object labelled 'Diana' was both real and celestial, ego and the self, reality and wholeness, and therefore an ideal prosthetic representation of the ego-self axis; the individual's sense of selfhood – what I am now and what I am aiming to be ideally. For the postmodern consumer of public identities, she was not just a celebrity – she was the perfect celebrity. Christopher Hauke identifies this media phenomenon as indicative of a fractured, post-religious, postmodern world in which self-identity is increasingly fragile, mobile and untrusted, and where what consumers 'seem to be grasping for is contrast and change, differences and disjunctions' (Hauke 2001, p. 26).

To analyse the euphoric adoration that swept Britain after her death, Hauke uses a combination of Fredric Jameson's ideas and Jungian psychology:

> Diana, the epitome of a postmodern cultural icon enshrined and known almost entirely through the photographic image, seems to have attracted to her image aspects of the human self (not in Jung's sense, but self as in the subject's sense of selfhood) which became embodied and personalised, in the individual known as 'Princess Diana'. These aspects of self range from her kindness and love towards unfortunate others, her challenging of taboos around 'contamination' such as those towards leprosy and AIDS, her exposure of personal vulnerability in revealing her bulimia and low self-esteem, her willingness to maintain

> her individuality against a background of establishment protocol, and her public valuing of her role as a mother being the first that come to mind.
>
> (Hauke 2001, p. 58)

Mass media reassembled these fragments into a powerful image; it created and maintained a seductive picture charged with affect. Tina Brown explains that often this creation was achieved with the expert connivance of Diana herself:

> Her relationship with the image makers who had helped create her had become a love affair in its nasty death throes, a cycle of dependency and combat. On the one hand, she was a master at providing striking images to dramatise the success of her philanthropic missions or to make a point to (and frequently against) Charles. Photographers would be tipped off when there was a prospect of heart-warming pictures of Diana with the kids . . . showing what a great mother she was.
>
> (Brown 2007, pp. 431–2)

However, Hauke argues that

> despite appearances there was never any real 'knowing' but rather the experience of another simulacrum. No original has ever existed but the postmodern subject 'discovers' affect through the image, imagining that they are feeling for a person 'behind' the image. In fact, this person does not exist, only the image exists; moreover, the image functions as a location for affects unavailable to the postmodern subject or individual.
>
> (Hauke 2001, p. 69)

Diana was the supreme example of a tabloid running story: a personality is chosen and converted into a news object whose adventures, loves, conquests and defeats are related to an eager, paying audience. These stories, like fairy tales, archetypally reinforce and affirm for their readers meaning of the human condition shattered and dispelled in the postmodern tumult of secular relativism. The numinosity of the news object, Diana, was apparent from the moment she stepped on to the tabloid stage in 1981. A shimmering photograph in *The Sun* shows the virgin Diana carrying a young child and holding the hand of another with the light shining through her dress, inadvertently making it see-through and appropriately diaphanous.

From then on Diana served as a succession of tabloid news objects to feed a readership depressed by war (Falklands, 1981) and bewildered by the 'greed is good' financial explosion of the 1980s. She became the fairytale princess marrying her prince (Charles), then the doting 'Madonna' mother of sons William and Harry, then the victim of a scheming royal family nicknamed 'the Firm' who wanted her to 'shut up and disappear' (Brown 2007, p. 406). Cinderella had it easy by comparison! However, the public enjoyed and cheered her fight-back as portrayed mainly in the pages of the tabloid press. Even her multiple affairs in the face of her husband's ongoing relationship with his now wife Camilla, were excused, even lauded, by an eager, paying readership, much as the sacred prostitutes were admired in classical times as described so well by Qualls-Corbett (1988). Renos Papadopoulos puts it thus: '(Diana) admitted to adultery, to suffering from eating disorders, even to self-harming behavior. These revelations had a paradoxically opposite effect: instead of bringing her down from stardom, they made the public love her more . . .' (Papadopoulos 1998, p. 63).

Diana's final, and most dramatic, role in this tabloid ritual was as 'sacrifice' in her subterranean death in the Pont d'Alma underpass in Paris in the early hours of Sunday, 31 August 1997; the spot was eerily marked by a pre-existing 'flame of freedom' statue. The death led to an explicit outpouring of public grief that Britain had not witnessed since the late Middle Ages. J. Haynes notes: 'One of the most extraordinary facets of this national mourning process has been the declaration of the People that they felt, not *as if* but that they *concretely* knew Diana' (1998, p. 26). Public fury at the death of this goddess was aimed at the establishment, particularly the Royal Family; the Queen was 'forced out of Balmoral to London for a public walkabout amid the grief and the flowers outside Buckingham Palace; she was obliged to make her first ever live TV broadcast to the nation, expressing an empathy she almost certainly did not feel . . .' (Brown 2007, p. 563).

In 1995, with public relations honed by years of media combat with the Firm, and perhaps intuiting its mythic resonance, Diana had crowned herself 'a queen of people's hearts' (*Panorama*, BBC1). This distinctly postmodern intertwining of classes and the final 'sacrifice' of the media goddess, Diana completed a meaning-making modern ritual of the kind described by the cultural anthropologist Victor Turner in his book *The Ritual Process: Structure and Anti-Structure* (1969). The elimination of such social distinction and the binding of participants 'concretely' (to use Haynes's word) is noted by William Beers in his commentary on *The Ritual Process*. Beers observes:

> Turner notes two interrelated consequences of liminality and the liminal period in ritual. First, liminality has the effect of eliminating (literally, 'from the threshold') previous social identity and distinctions in order to prepare the participants for their new station in social life. And second, such elimination has the consequence of drawing the participants closer together. That is, with the social structures (e.g., kinship, status) gone, the participants share a common identity, purpose and space. This liminal community is unstructured and more

> or less undifferentiated. Turner defines the liminal experience of the participants as 'communitas'.
>
> (Beers 1992, p. 46)

Beers then notes how Turner identifies a class-crossing 'communion', which, we suggest, precisely reflects the tabloid allure of Diana. He continues:

> (Turner) distinguishes communitas from structure. Indeed, communitas is 'anti-structure' (96–97). The social purpose of communitas within liminality is to allow the participants, no matter what their social status, to experience the reality that all are in communion, that the higher need the lower, and that the opposites, as it were, constitute one another and are mutually indispensable. The effect of communitas is to allow the ritual process to proceed to reaggregation. Then, returning to the four-part social drama, the reintegration of the participants into the larger society is finally able to take place.
>
> (Beers 1992, p. 46)

Jung himself understood sacrifice as a ritual by which the ego is subordinated to the self. He emphasised: 'A gift only becomes a sacrifice if I give up the implied intention of receiving something in return. If it is to be a true sacrifice the gift must be given as if it were being destroyed' (Jung 1954, para. 390). To the tabloid reader the gift of Diana – 'England's rose' as she was dubbed by her friend Sir Elton John singing at her funeral – was a ritual sacrifice for which there could be no recompense.

Conclusion

Mass media has only replaced the stable, traditional systems that used to provide the individual with identity and belonging. The individual, who longs for the lost communal connection, finds its replacement in mass communications. This is his way of interacting with society. But the post-industrial individual is fooled into thinking that he or she has attained a degree of maturity or a sense of belonging. It is as if the media says: 'We will provide you with meaning; we will give you role models. We will also change them every day – because we need to make money. And, in doing all this, we will be lying to you because our real aim is to keep you broken.'

Making independent decisions is laborious; attaining maturity is hard work. One has to relinquish the illusion of omnipotent control of the world. Or, as Jung puts it:

> Everything good is costly, and the development of personality is one of the most costly of all things. It is a matter of saying yea to oneself,

> of taking oneself as the most serious of tasks, of being conscious of everything one does, and keeping it constantly before one's eyes – truly a task that taxes us to the most.
>
> (1931, para. 24)

Alternatively, you can ask the media to do that for you.

References

Baudrillard, J. ([1968] 2005) *The System of Objects*. London and New York: Verso.

Beers, W. (1992) *Women and Sacrifice: Male Narcissism and the Psychology of Religion*. Detroit, MI: Wayne Staye University Press.

Berman, M. (1983) *All That Is Solid Melts into Air: The Experience of Modernity*. London: Verso.

Brown, T. (2007) *The Diana Chronicles*. London: Arrow Books.

Fromme, D.K. (2010) *Systems of Psychotherapy: Dialectical Tensions and Integration*. New York: Springer.

Giddens, A. (1991) *Modernity and Self-identity: Self and Society in the Late Modern Age*. London: Polity Press.

Hauke, C. (2001) *Jung and the Postmodern*. London: Routledge.

Haynes, J. (1998) 'A Princess "More Sinned Againgst than Sinning"' in J. Haynes and A. Shearer (eds) *When a Princess Dies: Reflections from Jungian Analysts*. Trowbridge: Harvest Books, p. 26.

Jacobi, J. ([1942] 1973) *The Psychology of C.G. Jung* (8th edn), trans. Ralph Manheim, New Haven, NJ and London: Yale University Press.

Jacoby, M. (1985) *Individuation and Narcissism*. London: Routledge.

Jung, C.G. Except where a different publication was used, all references are to the hardback edition of C.G. Jung, *The Collected Works* (CW), edited by Sir Herbert Read, Dr Michael Fordham and Dr Gerhardt Adler, and translated by R.F.C. Hull. London: Routledge.

—— (1921) *Psychological Types*, CW 6.

—— (1931) 'The Secret of the Golden Flower', CW 13.

—— (1954) 'Transformation Symbolism in the Mass', CW. 11.

Kohut, H. ([1978] 2011) *The Search for the Self*. London: Karnac.

Lasch, C. ([1979] 1991) *The Culture of Narcissism: American Life in an Age of Diminishing Expectations*. New York: W.W. Norton & Co.

Papadopoulos, R.K. (1998) 'A Moving Star: The Diana Phenomenon: Collective Masks of Individuality and Virtual Spirituality' in J. Haynes and A. Shearer (eds) *When a Princess Dies: Reflections from Jungian Analysts*. Trowbridge: Harvest Books, p. 63.

Qualls-Corbett, N. (1988) *The Sacred Prostitute: Eternal Aspect of the Feminine*. Toronto: Inner City Books.

Turner, V. (2001) *From Ritual to Theatre: The Human Seriousness of Play*. New York: PAJ Books.

—— (1969) *The Ritual Process, Structure and Anti-Structure (Foundations of Human Behaviour)*. London: Routledge & Kegan Paul.

Online sources

www.ajr.org/article.asp?id=785, *American Journalism Review*, downloaded 27 August 2012.

www.bbc.co.uk/news/special/politics97/diana/panorama.html, downloaded 28 August 2012.

2

BIG STORIES AND SMALL STORIES IN THE PSYCHOLOGICAL RELIEF WORK AFTER THE EARTHQUAKE DISASTER

Life and death

Toshio Kawai

Outreach model and collective task

As the strict setting of psychoanalysis typically shows, psychotherapy has been based on the free will and decision of patients to visit psychotherapists and pay the fee for sessions. However, recently more and more psychotherapists have been engaged with work in hospitals (HIV counseling, terminal care, genetic counseling etc.), schools and even in places hit by natural disaster and social crisis. Psychotherapy is used for crisis intervention. In such cases people can get psychological help as a service offered on site, sometimes without paying a fee. Although the conventional model of psychotherapy is still widely used, this new type of psychotherapy may bring about a fundamental change in the idea of psychotherapy.

Analytical psychology is not an exception in this trend. There is no statistical data available for what percentage of Jungian analysts work outside of their own private practices. However, analytical psychology's involvement with various kinds of trauma work and activity after the earthquake in China (Shen & Lan 2012) seems to prove its engagement with new needs and working models for psychotherapy. This change effects not only the working style from the analytical setting to an outreach model, but also the theoretical framework. As Jung's work, *Symbole und Wandlungen der Libido* (1912), which inaugurated the school of analytical psychology, typically shows, analytical psychology has tried to investigate the collective psyche through work with individual persons. However, especially in the case of crisis intervention a collective problem stands in the foreground while in a normal and conventional analysis the collective dimension is hidden in the background and elucidated only as interiority. In this sense, analytical psychology is faced with a new situation, which is caused by the changing needs of people and society.

I would like to discuss how analytical psychology and psychotherapy confront collective problems and tasks in the new working model by mainly referring to my involvement with the psychological relief work after the unprecedented earthquake disaster in March 2011 in Japan. Unlike in normal psychotherapy, there is a clear assumption in this psychological relief work that psychological problems are caused by the shock of the earthquake. How can analytical psychology cope with the collective problem of an earthquake disaster? Moreover, I have to point out that there is not only the concrete collective problem, but also that of the worldview. In the case of this earthquake, it was not only a natural but also a national disaster. The whole of Japan was physically and psychically hit by the disaster. The way of living, the trust placed in technology, and the responsibility of political officials have all come into question. So people have to face the collective dimension not only as a concrete problem but also as worldview problem. In this chapter, I will mainly focus on the practical aspect, but I will refer finally to the metaphorical aspect.

Listening to stories

Let me describe briefly the devastation caused by the 2011 earthquake off the Pacific coast of Tōhoku, which occurred on the afternoon of March 11, 2011. It was the most powerful earthquake ever to be recorded in Japanese history, with the extremely strong energy of a magnitude 9.0. About 16,000 people died and 3,000 are still missing. More than 350,000 houses and buildings were half destroyed or totally destroyed. More than 22,000 ships were lost. The huge tsunami, following the earthquake, triggered at the epicenter about 70 km off the coast, caused unprecedented damage and victims. More than 90 percent of the victims were swept away by the tsunami and were drowned. Moreover, the shock and the tsunami destroyed several nuclear power plants in Fukushima, which led to the secondary disaster of radiation leakage from the plants. There is still ongoing danger and after-effects from the nuclear accidents. Given the nature of the series of tragic events that occurred, this disaster is appropriately called 'the Great East Japan Earthquake.'

Immediately after this tremendous disaster, not only rescue parties and relief supplies but also psychological relief teams were sent to the stricken areas. Many volunteer psychotherapists and psychiatrists and those sent by public services travelled to the region in order to support refugees psychologically. At the beginning it was almost impossible to differentiate psychological help from practical help. Many volunteer psychotherapists helped to dispose of rubble and mud, or they simply stayed with depressed and despairing refugees.

Afterwards, psychological relief work was mainly organized by the Association of Japanese Clinical Psychology, which has more than 20,000 members. The Association of Jungian Analysts Japan (AJAJ) and the Japanese Association for Sandplay Therapy (JAST) also organized a joint working committee for psychological relief work for earthquake victims. (Sandplay Therapy is very popular in Japan, and the JAST has more than 2,000 members. This is probably because Japanese people still partly live within a pre-modern worldview in which experience is not primarily situated within the human subject but in things or in nature. In this sense, Sandplay Therapy fits nicely into the worldview of Ikebana and the Japanese garden tradition (Kawai 2010).) I was Chair of this joint working committee and our activity has been reported in part on the IAAP website (http://iaap.org/).

Our project had several focuses. One important concept was the care of caregivers such as psychotherapists, nurses, teachers and firemen. The reason for this type of indirect intervention was that our team came from a distance and could not be on site permanently. Such caregivers are supposed to be able to endure psychological difficulties for a certain period of time and wait for psychological help. Our second focus was to send a school counselor to the stricken areas, since sandplay is suitable for children. This project led to care of people based at the school because not only children but also their teachers and parents came to consult the school counselor in the course of time. From the standpoint of the government, equality is of absolute importance, which very often leads to a scattering of money and persons. With our limited resources, we tried to use the chance to have contact with victims and to deepen our quantitatively limited work, which could contribute to creating a new model for psychological relief work in the future.

The caregivers have to contain the difficult experiences and stories without any outlet for a period of time. This can become an unbearable burden for them, so it is important that those stories are shared in a protected circle. In this sense, the care of the soul means the care of stories. Stories should be listened to, respected and shared. Our project does not try to teach the caregivers or to impose new methods to cope with psychological difficulties. Rather, we try to make protagonists out of people who suffer and to learn from them as well. Indeed, many caretakers are overwhelmed by various new methodologies and offers given to them. There are many courses for psychological coping and relief work organized by the government.

We did not go to the Tōhoku region immediately after the earthquake but waited until there was a need from the victims to reflect on what was happening. The first set of emails and fax inquiries about the damage and situation among members of both associations in the Tōhoku region met with very few replies. However, the second set of inquiries that were sent out resulted in many responses, indicating how our members experienced the disaster and how they were struggling for professional help. So we decided to visit the site at the end of April for the first time, just after the partial recovery of Sendai Airport.

Life and death, coincidences

On arriving at Sendai Airport and observing the area from the plane, we were shocked by the piles of destroyed cars that had been swept away and crushed by the tsunami. Observing the wiped-out trees and buildings, we saw that the tsunami came right up to the airport building and destroyed everything around.

On arriving at the city center of Sendai by bus a short while later, I had another strange feeling because I expected to find a heavily damaged city like Kobe after the Great Hanshin Earthquake of 1995. At least seen superficially from outside, almost no sign of the earthquake disaster was noticeable. People and cars were moving on the streets without any trace of damage from the earthquake. The contrast to the condition of the area near the airport was signficant. Later, we visited the area directly hit by the tsunami near the coast. On one side of the highway there were ruins of buildings, destroyed cars, fallen trees, personal belongings, etc. On the other side of the highway, however, there was almost no damage to be seen because the highway bank blocked the tsunami. Because most of the damage was caused by the tsunami in the case of this earthquake in Tōhoku, there was a clear contrast of damage along the path of the tsunami versus areas outside the tsunami's path. Very often, the damage on one side versus the other side of a road was completely different.

This is why there were so many stories about life and death. Some people could narrowly escape with their lives, while others unfortunately died. Some schools had no victims, while others had several or many victims. More than 20,000 people were killed, most of them because of the tsunami.

Concerning these dramatic stories of life and death, I would like to report only one story told by my colleague, Yasuhiro Tanaka, who was a member of our psychological relief work team. His mother-in-law who lived in Ishinomaki, a port town devastated by the tsunami, was missing for a week after the earthquake, so we were afraid the worst might have occurred. However, luckily she was found alive in a high school. Two days before the huge earthquake, there was a relatively big earthquake of magnitude 7.2 in the same area. This was later regarded as a major foreshock of the main earthquake. Her neighbor who was Korean and had not experienced a big earthquake before was terribly upset and visited her to ask what the matter was. His mother-in-law explained that this was an earthquake. Her neighbor thanked her for the explanation and promised her to escape together in his car when a big one should come since she did not have a car. When the big earthquake really occurred in the afternoon of the 11th of March, her neighbor came up to her after the first long shake and suggested to escape with him by car. They went by car to the nearest elementary school to take refuge, but they were refused entry because it was already full of people. This school, which was regarded as safe and a refugee spot, was hit by the tsunami afterwards and many people died there. So a seemingly unfortunate rejection turned out to be fortunate for them. They went on by car, but the road was crowded because many people tried to go up the hill by car. The tsunami was already coming from behind. The Korean neighbor did not know the roads, but my colleague's mother-in-law did. She suggested to her neighbor to make a right turn on the next street. Because of this decision, they were narrowly able to escape the tsunami and arrive at a high school that was used as a refugee camp, where they stayed for a week. Coming back home, she found her house totally devastated, full of water, and a corpse of an unknown person floating inside.

This story shows how my colleague's mother-in-law was saved by several coincidences. Without these coincidences she might very well have died. If there was no preliminary earthquake, if her neighbor had not come up, if they had been accepted by the first school, if they had not turned right on the road . . . This story is dreadful enough. But there are many stories about how a person lost a partner, children, parents, friends or pupils. The principal of the school to which we sent a school counselor told us that four pupils were picked up by their parents right after the earthquake and killed by the tsunami afterwards while other pupils remained at school and were saved.

If one's fate was decided by sheer coincidences, how did one feel and react in the face of such a fate? Did a person who suffered nothing but slight damage only feel lucky and relieved, while a person who suffered a serious loss such as death of family members was left with a great sorrow and agony? Psychological pain is not simple and does not correlate with the objective gravity of damage. This experience of the earthquake let us know how the human psyche is complicated, connected with others and sharing the sufferings. A counselor told me that those firemen who had to wait for an order to dispatch and stayed in the station experienced more suffering and psychological problems than those who actually did the hard rescue work and were confronted with many corpses. The imagination and guilty feelings caused more psychological problems. In a workshop for nursing teachers concerned with psychological relief work for the earthquake disaster, some teachers said that they had been suffering from guilty feeling because their schools were relatively safe and had less damage. Because the human psyche is connected, this can lead to a positive and negative result. On one hand, we can be sympathetic to other people and share their sufferings. This earthquake reminded us of human solidarity and produced the key word 'Kizuna' (solidarity). But on the other hand, because of the connectedness of the human psyche, we can have unnecessary pain that has in truth nothing to do with us. The point in psychological relief work seems to be to find out how to relate to and at the same time separate from the issue.

Telling and listening to a story also has these two aspects. Telling one's own story of suffering can bring back the fear and agony, but it may also provide relief from the suffering. In this regard, I would like to point out that Jung emphasized the dialectics of union and separation in his late works on alchemy (Giegerich 2007). The subtitle of his late work *Mysterium*

Conjunctionis is 'An inquiry into the separation and synthesis of psychic opposites in alchemy'. In analytical psychotherapy, the aspect of integration and union is stressed as a successful result of therapy: one should integrate the shadow, or relate to anima/animus. But the moment of separation and the dialectic relation between union and separation seem to be crucial in the psychological relief work after the earthquake.

Experience sharing: psychological time

During our psychological relief work, we noticed that stories about life and death are not told soon after a disaster. Our team does not consist of trauma and crisis intervention specialists, so we stay with the victims and observe without presumption what happens in the course of time. Very often victims of a disaster need a certain lapse of time before they are psychologically ready to tell their personal stories of their experiences. However, this timing is very often not respected by the mass media, which are eager to find and report dramatic stories immediately following any disaster. And in these days of communication by Blog and Twitter, people tend to ignore their psychological timing and disclose their stories too early. Because we visited the area hit by the tsunami regularly, we noticed that there is a general flow of psychological time. When we visited in July, four months after the disaster, we had many reports from school counselors that children begin to talk about their nightmares. I am not of the opinion that psychotherapists should focus on and 'work out' technically these nightmares and trauma experiences in such cases. How, then, can we understand such nightmares and their timing?

In the case of therapy with schizophrenic patients, it is reported that they begin to have dreams related to their delusions and hallucinations when the condition is a little stable. A Japanese psychiatrist, Hisao Nakai (1974), who is famous for therapy of schizophrenics, interpreted this change as absorption of delusions into dreams. Delusions can now be objectively experienced and placed in the framework of dreams. In the analogy with this process, experiencing and telling nightmares should not be interpreted as a revival of the traumatic events. It rather means that they cease to have overwhelming power and are no longer so threatening. It revives the memories, but also helps them to disappear. The person can now be connected to the experience and the story, but also be separate from them. Here again is a dialectical play of union and separation in the sense of Jung's alchemy study, so it is important simply to listen to the story without working it out too much and trying to relieve the person from the story.

In a school we visited regularly, one teacher told us in July that he had recently dreamt about the earthquake and tsunami and wondered why this timing. And the principal of the school we had met several times before told us for the first time his experience of the tsunami in detail. Maybe his experience could be digested in ways that he could talk about it only after it was not so overwhelming for him. His story was as follows. After the earthquake, he led first all the teachers and pupils into the sports hall, but as he felt that the hall might not be resistant enough against a possible tsunami, he wanted to evacuate them from the hall to the rooftop of the main school building. He went there with the vice principal to check it. Then on the way back to the first building the tsunami came all of sudden. The vice principal behind him was swept away, and the principal walking ahead could barely escape and run up the stairs to the rooftop. From the rooftop he observed a scene like hell where many broken houses, cars and people were being swept away. He was desperate because he was afraid that the hall was destroyed and children were killed. Luckily, the vice principal could hold on to something and was saved. Also, the hall remained intact, somehow, against the tsunami so that no child was injured or killed.

I think such critical stories are told when they are no longer too overwhelming for the person telling of their experience. Our experience with the children at the school supports this hypothesis. In one of the first-grade classes, children freely drew a picture in February by chance, so that was just before the earthquake (Figure 2.1). Then the teacher let them draw a free picture in April again, just after the tremendous earthquake (Figure 2.2). Most of pictures indicated a negative effect of the earthquake and tsunami. It is especially impressive that the structure of the picture was very often destroyed, which seemed to mean the psychic structure of the children was fundamentally shaken by the earthquake and especially by the tsunami.

According to picture-drawing test and therapy, such disturbances of structure in drawings is equivalent to that which is symptomatic of a psychotic crisis.

Figure 2.1 Painting in February (just before the quake)

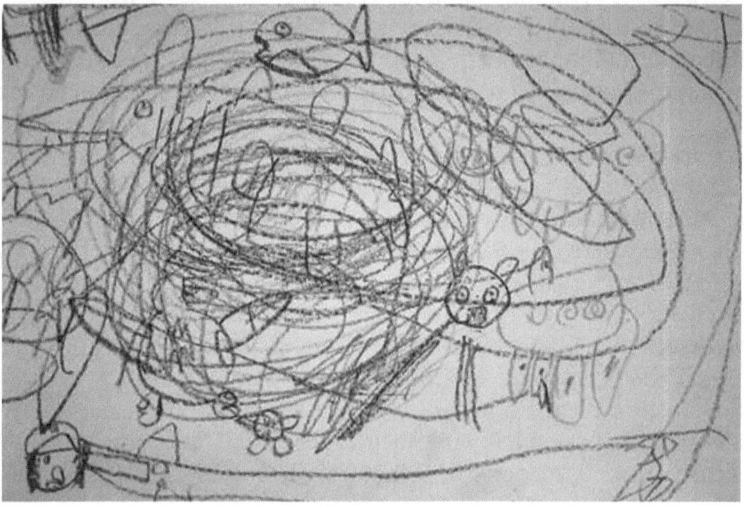

Figure 2.2 Painting in April (just after the quake)

In the pictures drawn in June, a clear recovery was already noticeable (Figure 2.3). The structure of pictures no longer showed any disturbance, so we may conclude that the experience of an earthquake and tsunami leaves indeed a tremendous influence on the psychic structure of people for a short period. However, most children, and indeed most people generally, seem to be able

Figure 2.3 Painting in June (three months after the quake)

to recover from it if there is a sufficiently good protecting environment. So the frequent reports of so-called traumatic experiences and nightmares in July, four months after the disaster, do not necessarily reflect the onset of traumatic complications. This means rather that the first psychological crisis is over. Although those nightmares and fearful stories are told after the earlier stories become less overwhelming, it is still very important that those stories are shared by a receptive person and in a protective atmosphere.

Psychotherapy and small stories

The reader can imagine how often memories of traumatic experiences of earthquake and tsunami are recounted in psychological relief work. However, as we have experienced in many psychological interventions after other natural and social disasters such as typhoons, criminal attacks and suicides, most people usually begin to talk about something other than the traumatic events after a while. As I explained before, it took about four months after the earthquake disaster for people to overcome their initial shock. Very often adults and children start at some point to speak about other problems, like difficulties in their family relationship or conflicts in school and the workplace. So the traumatic experience of disaster falls away into the background and improvement in psychotherapy is brought about by dealing with more immediate problems like family relationships or conflicts in school.

Our working committee sends a school counselor once a week to an elementary school that was hit by the tsunami. After a while, according to the counselor's reports, the earthquake and the tsunami as such are no longer the theme of counseling. There are various problems that have very little to do directly with the earthquake, although they might be caused indirectly by the earthquake disaster. We also have some reports from teachers that they are anxious about some children and suspicious about the negative effects of the earthquake. Children's psychological and behavioral problems are worth handling, but they have very little to do with the earthquake directly.

So psychotherapy may start because of the earthquake, but its theme does not necessarily have to do with traumatic experiences related to it. In this connection, I would like to introduce very briefly sandplay therapy in the Pediatrics Department of the Red Cross Hospital of Ishinomaki. The following cases were presented in a supervision session offered by our working committee. (I would like to thank our colleagues for permission to use the material.)

The first case (Case 1) was a 10-year-old girl reported by Takehiro Tanaka. She was already in therapy because of a physical complaint before the earthquake. When she lost her sister in the tsunami, her condition deteriorated. In the first sandplay (Figure 2.4), which was made several months after the earthquake, she put many animals in the box. Some seemed to be climbing up the tree, so a tendency toward height was noticeable. In the next session,

Figure 2.4 Case 1: 10-year-old girl, No. 1

she made a big mountain and thrust a paper stick in the center (Figure 2.5). Afterwards she leveled the ground and separated the tray into two lands (Figure 2.6). So in this process a clear centering and separation were achieved, which indicated the establishment of her self. After this session, her condition became much better. Her mother, by contrast, made a literal copy of the tsunami scene in her sandplay in the same session, and seemed to stick to the big and literal story of the disaster (Figure 2.7).

Another case of a 10-year-old boy, reported by Akiko Sasaki-Miura, shows a nice psychological development. He took refuge on the rooftop of his school right after the earthquake and watched the tsunami from there. Afterwards he was nervous, bit his nails and could not change into his pajamas at night. The first sandplay (Figure 2.8) was a mixture of woods and water, which may have been to do with the effects of the tsunami. In subsequent sandplays, the work of separation and establishing height was expressed. In the next sandplay (Figure 2.9), there is already some order. In the last sandplay (Figure 2.10), butterflies are at the top of trees. The need for dependence seems to turn into a feminine quality. The boy felt better and was able to leave therapy.

We may conclude that the success of psychotherapy consists in the shift of stories, from the big story of the traumatic event to stories about small, personal problems, or personal psychological development. The big story is repressed and replaced, to use the Freudian term, by small stories. As the

Figure 2.5 Case 1: 10-year-old girl, No. 2

Figure 2.6 Case 1: 10-year-old girl, No. 3

Figure 2.7 Case 1: mother's sand play

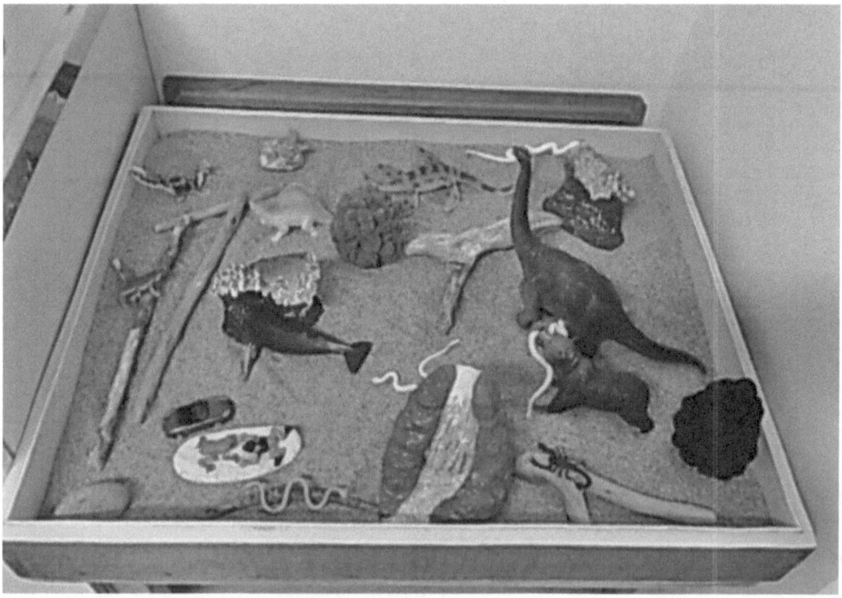

Figure 2.8 Case 2: 10-year-old boy, No. 1

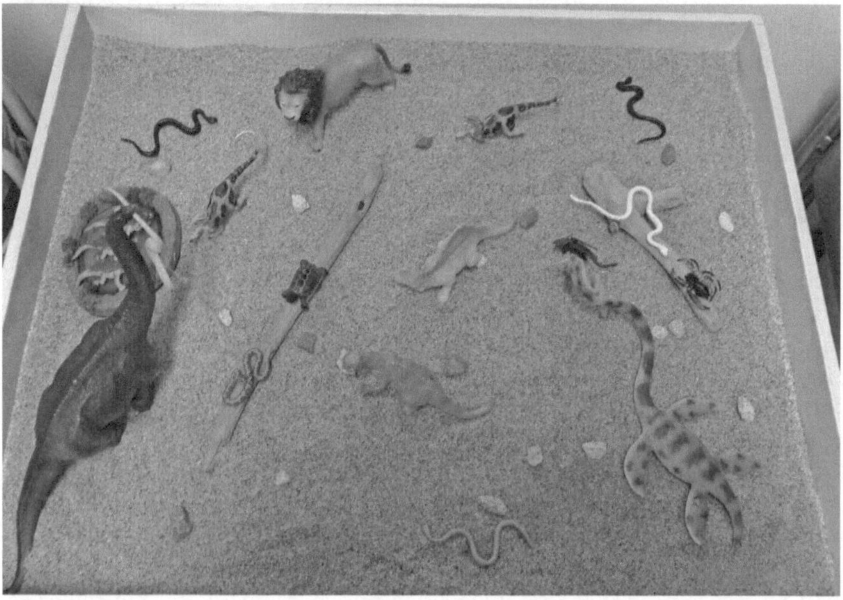

Figure 2.9 Case 2: 10-year-old boy, No. 2

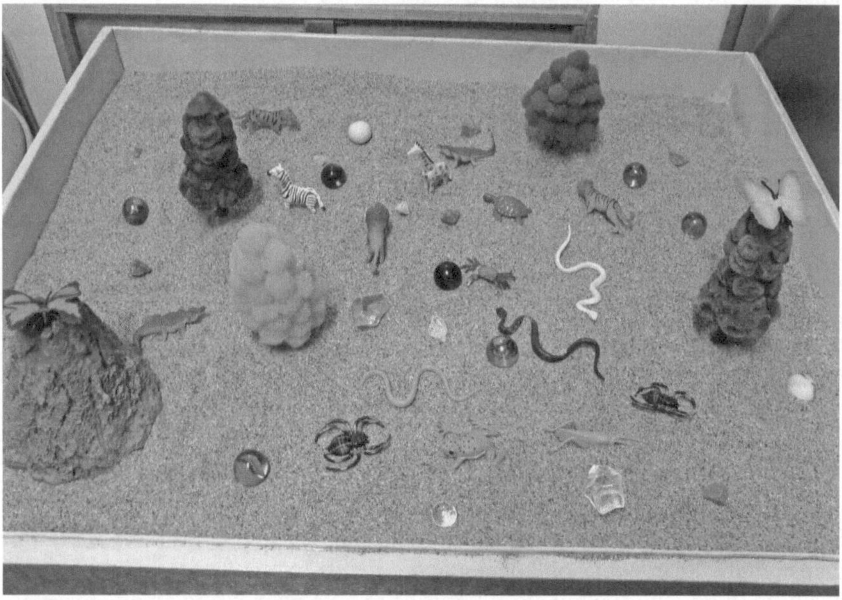

Figure 2.10 Case 2: 10-year-old boy, No. 3

sandplay of the mother of the girl shows, psychological recovery is difficult if the patient sticks to the big story of earthquake and tsunami.

The relationship between the big story and small stories is also valid for the psychotherapy of so-called psychosomatic symptoms. I work as a psychotherapist in a hospital specializing in thyroid diseases. If a medical doctor there diagnoses that psychological factors play a signficant role or it is difficult to cure a patient by medical treatment alone, he or she sends the patient to psychotherapy. Also in this case, if the patient talks only about physical problems and complaints, there is no chance of improvement. But psychotherapy and even physical recovery can be facilitated if the patient starts to talk about, for example, her mother-in-law, discontent for her husband, and so forth in the therapeutic session. In this case there is also a shift from the problem of physical complaint to small personal stories.

In psychological relief work after an earthquake disaster I would like to suggest that some victims can make use of the disaster experience for psychological development. In the two sandplay cases mentioned above, both children could achieve the psychological task of separation, height and centering, which are appropriate developments for their ages. A very impressive paper on a psychological work with a boy after the earthquake in Northridge reported by Taki-Reece (2004) can be understood not as trauma work, but rather as psychological development using the crisis of the earthquake. The separation from his parents and the establishment of his psychic center was the theme of the story expressed by his sandplay. Psychotherapy cannot cure the big story, but rather has to do with the small stories.

The importance of small stories should also be stressed outside psychological relief work. The Internet is full of small—and I am inclined to say even unnecessary—stories in the form of personal blogs and twitter postings. 'I get up . . . I am now eating . . . I am now in a bus heading to . . .' But just after the earthquake all such stories disappeared from the Internet. People were compelled, or at least felt compelled, to make a headline message: 'I feel deepest sympathy for those hit by the earthquake . . .'. They refrained from reporting daily, trivial events. One big story could dominate and suppress the small stories, which can be unhealthy. Control of mass media by the government was a critical theme after the earthquake, especially concerning the nuclear plants, but we have to be aware that we must have hidden self-control.

Psychotherapy and big stories

As our psychological relief work with victims of the earthquake disaster indicates, psychotherapy has less to do with the collective problem of earthquake trauma than with small personal problems. In this sense, psychotherapy has little to do with the big story but tries to help people find small stories to live and cope with. When a big story is brought up during therapy as a social and collective problem, it is very often a sign that a victim still sticks to the old story and avoids change. Sometimes this could be interpreted as resistance to therapy. The exact reproduction of the tsunami scene in a sandplay made by the mother of one of our patients shows that a fixation on the trauma experience is counterproductive for psychotherapy. This may suggest that psychological relief work, which focuses too much on the trauma experience, could be problematic. Various kinds of methods specializing in trauma work were used on this occasion. Such methods could draw too much of the victims' attention to the trauma experience as a big story. According to our support activity in schools, the earthquake and the tsunami really did cause recognizable psychological shocks that, however, became somehow endurable and controllable after several months in a normal and protected process. As we analyzed the meaning of nightmares and the telling of dreadful experiences, the dialectic relationship between integration and separation, between remembering and forgetting, seemed to be psychologically important concerning a collective problem and the big story.

In the big story, it is important to differentiate between the level of concrete problems and that of the worldview. The Tōhoku earthquake in 2011 caused not only real damage but also brought a tremendous shock in the worldview to many Japanese people. It totally destroyed their trust in technology and recalled their relationship to nature. The previously believed big story became meaningless. Following the disaster of the earthquake, the Japanese seem to be in search of a new worldview. In the face of concrete collective problems, psychological relief work suggests that the process of dialectical separation is crucial. In this sense, psychotherapy has nothing to do with the collective dimension, but what about the worldview?

The power of nature: fear and fascination

In *Memories, Dreams, Reflections*, there is a famous inner conversation about myth. Jung asks himself: 'But in what myth does man live nowadays? In the Christian myth, the answer might be 'Do *you* live in it?', I asked myself. 'To be honest, the answer was no. For me, it is not what I live by.' 'Then do we no longer have any myth?' 'No, evidently we no longer have any myth.' 'But then what is your myth – the myth in which you do live?' 'At this point the dialogue with myself became uncomfortable, and I stopped thinking' (Jung 1963, p. 195).

In this conversation, Jung manifested his clear concern about his worldview after the loss of the Christian myth. Similarly, analytical psychology is interested in the big story, not as a social problem but as a worldview on the metaphorical level. However, we have to distinguish psychology from psychotherapy. Psychology does have to do with the discussion of the worldview and the big story, but very seldom does a psychotherapist encounter a creative big story, which seems to be left for artists and novelists. In this case, the big story tends to be symbolized and metaphorized in a work of art or a novel instead of being replaced by small stories. In the form of psychological interpretation and investigation, psychology does have to do with such big stories. There are some stories in the past and new ones that should be taken into consideration, but in this chapter I would like to remain in the field of psychotherapy.

Although sandplay therapy has to do with an individual problem and solution, there are some signs of the collective dimension as well. In the first case of a girl reported above, a lot of animals were put in the sand box. It is striking that many animals were gathered in some other cases of sandplay. For example, in one case reported by Chie Yoshinari (Figure 2.11), who works as a school counselor in the area hit by the tsunami, a girl made a sandplay in which many animals were coming forward. In another one, presented by Akiko Sasaki-Miura (Figure 2.12), many animals were gathered in the center of the box. Such animals do not necessarily mean confusion or something overwhelming because there is some kind of order among the animals. Rather, they give the impression that the power of life is returning and approaching us, and this indicates the recovery of life.

In the case of a natural disaster, very often there is both the aspect of fear and the feeling of power derived from it. For example, on the coasts hit by the tsunami this time there are hundreds of Shinto shrines. This is because people are both afraid of and thankful for the power of the water, the power of the ocean, which provides fish and other products. People are afraid of nature but, at the same time, grateful for its richness, which is why people built many shrines along the coast.

Figure 2.11 Case 3 by Chie Yoshinari

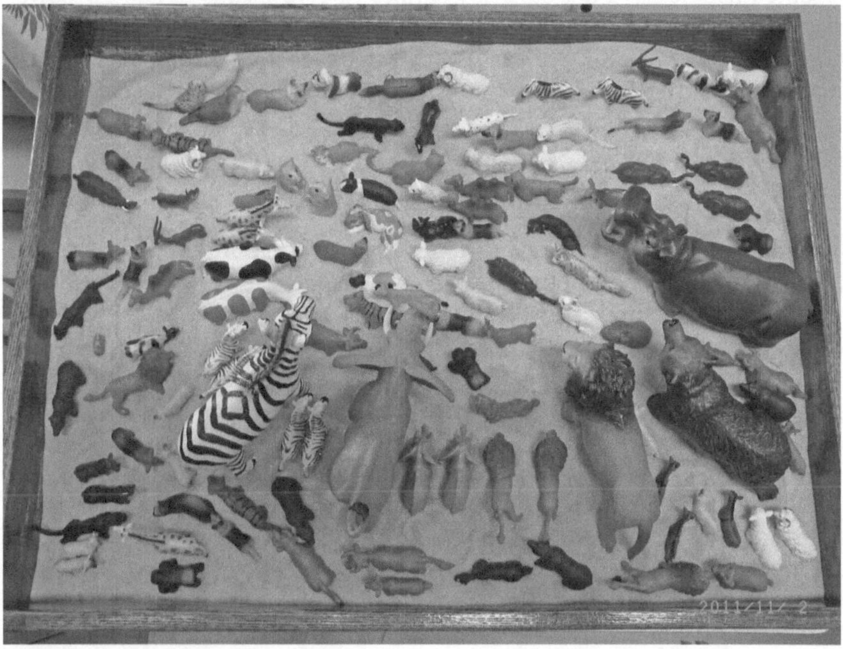

Figure 2.12 Case 4 by Akiko Sasaki

These two attitudes are somehow equivalent to the feeling of *tremendum et fascinosum* that Rudolf Otto described as feeling toward the 'holy'. Both aspects belong to our attitude toward the holy and nature, and were historically noticed in other rituals in Japan. After many natural disasters and epidemics around the ninth century in the Heian period in Japan, a festival was created to drive away bad spirits. This was Gion Matsuri, the most famous festival in Kyoto. However, according to historians, it was important for people at that time not only to drive away bad spirits, but also to gain power over them, so there is both a moment of fear and of fascination. Bad spirits were not feared and hated, but welcomed because they could bring power to the people. Seen from this context, many animals in the sandplay box seem to indicate the power of nature in the positive sense after victims experienced the negative side of the power of nature. Thus it is psychologically problematic if victims are only afraid of an earthquake and tsunami and try to defend themselves from them.

If we go further and analyze people's attitude toward the nuclear power plant in Japan from this point of view, I have to say that it is totally outside of this worldview of fear and fascination, fear and gratitude. Nuclear power does not belong to environmental order and is outside nature. No wonder

Japanese people have not built any shrines to give thanks to nuclear power plants and want to discard them now without any gratitude for such powers. Is it a failure to build nuclear plants, which do not belong to Japanese cosmology? Do we have to establish a new relationship with the nuclear plant? These are open questions.

Psychotherapy and psychology

In this chapter, I have remained within the standpoint of psychotherapy and tried to show the aspect of the big story and small stories in the psychological relief work for victims of the earthquake disaster. The psychotherapy consists in the shift from the big story of collective suffering to small stories of personal problems. But as a collective image, the feature of coming-back-to-life power is suggested as a counterpart to the negative natural power of the earthquake.

For psychology, it is also important to think about big stories as a worldview expressed in the novels and works of art both in the past and present day. I cannot go into the subject here, but there are a number of good ideas in past and modern literature (Nakazawa 2011). One legend concerning a tsunami from Kunio Yanagita's *Legends of Tono* (1910) gives an important hint, and Haruki Murakami's stories in *After the Quake* are very suggestive, but it is premature to speak about a new story concretely. It is important now to accept and carry the loss as loss. Because of the earthquake of March 11, 2011, many people lost loved ones, precious property and a place to live. As a psychologist and a psychotherapist, I would like to respect the loss of the old story and worldview so that the emptiness may become a place for the birth of a new story.

References

Giegerich, W. (2007) 'Psychology – study of the soul's logical life'. In A. Casement (ed.) ([1963] 1995) *Who owns Jung?*. London: Karnac Books.

Jung, C.G. ([1912] 1976) *Symbols of Transformation*. Princeton, NJ: Princeton University Press.

Jung, C.G. ([1963] 1995) *Memories, Dreams, Reflections*. Recorded and edited by A. Jaffé. London: Fontana Press.

Kawai, T. (2010) 'Jungian psychology in Japan: Between mythological world and contemporary consciousness'. In Stein, M. & Raya, A.J. (eds.) *Cultures and Identities in Transition*. Routledge: London and New York.

Murakami, H. (2003) *After the Quake*. New York: Vintage.

Nakai, H. (1974) 'Seishinbunretsubyou jyoutai karano kankaikatei' ('Recovering process from schizophrenic conditions'). In Miyamoto, T. (ed.) *Bunretsubyou no seishinbyouri* 2. Tokyo: Tokyo University Press.

Nakazawa, S. (2011) *Nihon no Daitenkan* (*Big change of Japan*). Tokyo: Shueisha.

Otto, R. (1917) *Das Heilige*. Breslau: Trewendt und Granier.

Shen, H. and Lan, G. (2012) 'The garden of the heart and soul: Psychological relief work in the earthquake zones and orphanages in China'. *Spring Journal.*

Taki-Reece, Sachiko (2004) 'Sandplay after a catastrophic encounter: From traumatic experience to emergence of a new self'. *Archives of Sandplay Therapy*, 17.

Yanagita, K. ([1910] 2008) *The Legends of Tono*. Trans. R. Morse, Lanham, MD: Lexington Books.

3

MAKING A DIFFERENCE?

When individuals take personal responsibility for social and political change

Andrew Samuels[1]

Introduction

When presenting this material in lecture or workshop format, I begin by playing Ennio Morricone's theme music from the 1966 spaghetti western *The Good, the Bad and the Ugly*. The Man with No Name – the Clint Eastwood character – is the consummate individual. He needs no name. Readers could perhaps go now to YouTube to listen (again?) to the music: www.youtube.com/watch?v=LQGGQ-FCe_w. The interactive vein of the chapter is also maintained by a series of experiential exercises with which it is peppered.

I am careful to say that I am sure that this chapter could only have been written by a man in his sixties, enabled by time and its ravages to be less cautious and correct. And the music is also a bit of self-mockery, ironic and suggestive, I hope.

It may seem perverse to call for a return to the notion of the individual in progressive political theorising at a time when so many bemoan the collapse of social and communal ties in Western societies. Families don't go bowling any more. And you (Andrew) want more individualism when everyone is already looking after Number One, in an ethos of *sauve qui peut* ('every man for himself')?

But I hope I may seem less weird if I say that, in a nutshell, I am wondering if there is a place still in radical politics for individualism and the idea of the individual. I need to confess that it was very hard to write this chapter, which came from an inner place, quite contrary to what I usually think in my roles as political consultant, activist and academic. In those situations, how many times have I explained that there is no such thing as an individual? I still think the political world and individual inhabits are vitally important, including the ecological world. However, it is the experience of being an individual that interests me at the moment.

Beyond context

In academic discourse (and also in politics, whether mainstream, progressive or reactionary) the idea of the individual *tout seul* ('by himself') simply does not pass muster these days. Context is all – family, community, society, culture, nation. The contemporary discourse stresses that individuals are embedded in social relationships, communal networks, task-oriented groups and ecosystems. This isn't wrong, of course, but has the potential of an individual to contribute to social and political change been underestimated by this set of assumptions?

The psychoanalytic writer who foregrounded the question of the relations between the individual and the collective was Jung. My proposal is that, if Jungian psychology could refashion its approach to the individual, then we could become a source of support and inspiration to embattled citizens whose experience of their battles is often that they are in it on their own. Jung was one of the first to explain that 'there is a human desire to "belong", to conform, to relinquish individual responsibility and find a king, a dictator, a boss who will tell you what to do' (Jung 1935, para. 326).

Exercise 1

> We can all think of individuals who have 'made a difference'. Sometimes, you may feel you have yourself made a difference. Think of times when you personally as an individual have made a difference in some situation or other, whether an important situation or something relatively less important. What happened?

So – has the academy gone too far in stressing the contingent and context-bound nature of an individual person? Are the professors saying 'there's no such thing as an individual'? What does it mean when there is a book entitled *Constructing the Self, Constructing America*? (Cushman 1991). Is the consensus that the idea of individuals is just another bit of constructivism? Is Levinas right, with the ethical stress on alterity, on the other, on someone other than the individual?

I think it is important to explore these questions because many of the horrid conformist features of contemporary Western societies rest on the idea that 'you belong'. This becomes 'you should belong' and, then, 'you belong to us'. Society does its bit to get us all to stay in context – even the bankers! Joining the system is more or less compulsory – in Durkheim's terms, mechanical solidarity not organic solidarity.

The opposites of constructionism and contextualism are essentialism, universality and eternity. As some Jungian commentators have noted, these can lead to a sort of 'archetypal determinism', which, in its own way, can be massively damaging to the idea of the individual who Jung says he values so much.

Here's a bit of self-criticism. I have written about and done a workshop exercise called 'Where did you get your politics from?' We look at parents, family, ethnicity, class, nationality and all imaginable other influences. But what about the accidental, or even the constitutional factor? The individual factor? Some ineluctable and irreducible piece of chance or fate that enters into the realm of political choices and actions? Something that cannot be explained by context. Just thinking about what we could call political style or political type enables us to recuperate the idea of the individual with regard to social responsibility. Anyway, the conventional wisdom is that we are always in groups, networks, contexts. By now, this may have become banal – and, without critique, destructive. Where has the individual gone in progressive discourse?

In the spoken versions of this, I sing as follows, to the tune of 'Where have all the flowers gone?': 'Where have all the individuals gone, long time passing? Where have all the individuals gone, long time ago? Where have all the individuals gone? Professors have banned them every one. When will they ever learn? When will they ever learn?'

Of course, economic and ethnic factors form part of 'subjectivity'. Of course, we are relational beings. And it is important to assert that we are not atomised, split up entities sitting in empty space. OK, already! But the shadow aspect of this is that it plays into the ever-increasing centralisation of society. It is all about central control. Individuals are coerced into neighbourhood groups and societies. Join or die! Your society needs you!

By the way, as a sort of aside, all of this adherence to 'the context' is the Zeitgeist for the industrialisation of psychotherapy that is going on in many countries. They want to legislate, regulate, manualise, standardise us. They want to get the power to decide which individuals are Fit to Practise and which are not. And the clinical encounter itself seems to exclude individuals. Everyone is 'relational' nowadays. 'It's the relationship, stupid!' was seriously proposed as the banner headline for a campaign in favour of the 'talking therapies'.

Relational intersubjectivity may undermine or exclude individual subjectivity. 'The therapy relationship' is supposed to take the strain, not the sweating individuals who compose it. It's all about dyads, dialogue, communication, attachment, attunement, rupture and repair, transference–countertransference. This refusal of one-person psychology has gone too far. The therapy relationship has become an oppressive, conventional, moralistic norm. But that is a topic I've addressed in other chapters recently (Samuels 2010), so I will get back to the main thrust of this one now.

I hope my argument becomes clearer: it is that the shadow of understanding ourselves as group beings in context is that we unwittingly support many of the things we hate. We norm, we conform, but we very rarely storm.

Solidarity becomes a curse as well as a blessing, a cul-de-sac, not the way ahead. Although I am a supporter of ecopsychology and wrote about it at length in 1993 in *The Political Psyche*, I think this shadow groupishness and enforced belonging stalks many ecosystemic approaches to politics. Where's the individual when the discourse is planetary? Can the Earth really be so hostile to the individual?

Let's explore the old liberal idea of the individual, the individual subject, and root it in a new critical anti-relational discourse. Let's see if we can refresh our idea of political action by engaging with the individual and individualism a bit.

Classical individualism stresses the moral worth of the individual who is its focus. The fundamental premise is that the human individual is of primary importance in the struggle for liberation. Individualism is thus also associated with artistic and bohemian interests and lifestyles – self-creation and experimentation as opposed to tradition or mass opinion. (This is what analysis and psychotherapy used to be before they became bourgeoisified and subjected to *deformation professionelle.*) I'd like to suggest that we can revise this monolithic and over-solid approach to take in the idea of the individual as fractured. The fact that an individual is fractured is not an obstacle to radical politics, rather it is a source of them. The individual is a bridge: between inner and outer, between the personal and the political, between introverted solitude and being in a network. An individual who is more of an uprooted anti-hero than a hero – a bum, a schlemiel, a nomad . . . . Clearly, there is more to psychology than the isolated individual human being, and much has been usefully done to get rid of that idea. But academics have set up a false situation. If we simplistically equate the idea of the individual with the conscious ego, or with sentimental Jungian, romantic ahistorical trumpeting of the supremacy of the individual, then hurrah for the intellectuals who've got rid of a dangerously misleading conception. However, this unthinking and reactionary version is not the only possible playing out of the notion of the individual. The individual who needs our attention today has never been like that, never been solely the product of Puritanism, nor snowy-white, nor a romantic cliché, nor a humanistic ideal, nor the unified being of orthodox psychology, nor Jungian Self, nor Freudian ego. Do those pristine creatures, who certainly deserve critique, really exist?

No. I suggest that the individual who stalks contemporary culture and who is trying to return to its politics, has always been a decentred subject, an actor performing many roles in many scripts, characterised by lack, somewhat faded as well as jaded, jerky, marginalised, alienated, split, guilty, empty, imaginary. The individual has always been a trickster in his or her practice of politics. I think there is something we can do with this deidealised, putrefied, violent and marvellously rebellious individual. The internally pluralistic individual is the means to an engagement with politics and culture, not an obstacle to it.

Make no mistake, individuals in the West are today in agony. It is an agony that politics is so broken. It is also an agony how political language has collapsed. George Orwell was prescient in *1984* when he tells us that Ingsoc and the Thought Police had a project to reduce the size of the dictionary, hence banishing the nuanced conversation needed for intimate and political life alike (Orwell 1949).

The body of the individual bears this agony just as much as mind and psyche (*agon* means to writhe). Today's body is always armoured against attack or loss; people cannot breathe because of pollution; there's a constant state of adrenalisation; consumerist pressures tyrannise us into thinking we are either too fat or too thin; we are obsessed with medications that we know will fail us.

Recuperating the Jungian individual

By now, you may be thinking 'What's this got to do with us Jungians? Don't we have a coherent theory of the individual firmly in place?' Doesn't Jung firmly link the idea of individuation to the collective? I have to say that I am not convinced about it given the way the theory is at the moment.

When Jung writes about 'the individual', the academics turn away and snigger. The Jungian individual doesn't cut the intellectual (and political) mustard. The way in which Jung positions the individual in relation to society, and the way in which society is reduced to 'the mass' or 'the masses', simply assumes that societies and individuals are inevitably antipathetic. Never mind that, at times, Jung seems to suggest that a society or a nation is simply made up of the individuals in it, and there is nothing more to be said.

In 1956, Jung wrote of:

> the agglomeration of huge masses in which the individual disappears anyway . . . the individual [is robbed]of his [*sic*] foundations and his dignity. As a social unit he has lost his individuality and becomes a mere abstract number in the bureau of statistics. He can only play the role of an interchangeable unit of infinitesimal importance.
>
> (Jung 1957, par. 501)

It's hardly surprising, then, that he continues in a sardonic, sceptical and depressive vein:

> Looked at rationally and from outside, that is exactly what he is, and from this point of view it seems positively absurd to go on talking about the value or meaning of the individual. Indeed, one can hardly imagine how one ever came to endow human life with so much dignity when the truth to the contrary is as plain as the palm of your hand.
>
> (Jung 1957, par. 501)

I think that this sense of the impossibility of the individual in relation to society represents a premature concession by Jung; it is just too pessimistic and melancholic, although the rhetoric is splendid: 'an interchangeable unit of infinitesimal importance'.

Can we recuperate the Jungian idea of the individual? To do so, would involve critiquing the relationship between individual and society as Jung sets it out. Recently, David Tacey (on-line, 29 June 2012) succinctly summarised Jung in *The Undiscovered Self* (from which the extract above was taken) as making 'a romantic defence of individuality and a warning against collectivism', but it makes for an odd kind of sociology if Jung sees the social mass only as something that wants to swallow the individual. Tacey is correct, it is an odd approach to the social – something picked up by Ira Progoff in his doctoral thesis that was eventually published as *Jung's Psychology and Its Social Meaning* in 1953. When a friend of Progoff's went to see Jung to hear his comments on the thesis, one can see from the comments Jung made that Progoff got it right when he summarises Jung as saying that 'the individual in society may be understood as a piece of the archetype, a piece that has been differentiated out of the collective representation' (1978, p. 211).

The way I see it, in the same essay Jung also gets a lot of it right – specifically, the way in which the individual is ruined and controlled by the state: 'it is small wonder that individual judgement grows increasingly uncertain of itself and that responsibility is collectivised as much as possible, i.e., is shuffled off by the individual and delegated to a corporate body' (Jung 1957, par. 503).

Unfortunately, there is more than Jung's 'odd sociology' to hold back the evolving of links between his ideas and a progressive, humane politics. Jung's ideas on the individual are aristocratic, elitist and supercilious. I am referring now to his awful reference to 'stunted individuals'. Here's the 1921 quote:

> It is obvious that a social group consisting of stunted individuals cannot be a viable and healthy institution; only a society that can preserve its internal cohesion and collective values, while at the same time granting the individual the greatest possible freedom, has any prospect of enduring vitality. As the individual is not just a single, separate being, but by his very existence presupposes a collective relationship, it follows that the process of individuation must lead to more intense and broader collective relationships and not to isolation.
> (Jung [1921] 1971, par. 758)

I want to go head to head with Jung here.

> Look, C.G., the stunted individual is the only bloody individual that there is. Just as you taught us about alchemy, we begin political struggle with base materials – citizens who are far from individuated, who inhabit a world you've told us does not want them to individuate.

Or try this quote, from the 1916 paper 'Adaptation, Individuation, Collectivity': 'Whoever is not creative enough [to individuate] must re-establish collective conformity with a group of his own choice, otherwise he remains an empty waster and a windbag' (Jung 1916/1964/1976, par. 1098).

So we have stunted individuals here, wasters and windbags over there, and truly individuated people in the first-class cabin. No wonder Sonu Shamdasani summarises Jung as saying: 'individuation was for the few' (Shamdasani 2003, p. 307). But there are many people in the world, not just 'the few', not just the Jungian 1 per cent.

Jung is like Marx here – the Marx who considered that the lowest of the low, the *Lumpenproletariat*, were incapable of making a revolution. We should join the liberation theologians in their challenge to this Marxian elitism. For Boff, it is the poorest, most downtrodden, most out-of-it who will make the revolution: 'God is in the poor who cry out. And God is the one who listens to the cry and liberates, so that the poor no longer need to cry out' (Boff 1988, p. 166).

Orwell got it too: 'If there is hope, it lies in the proles', he wrote in *1984* (1949). So did the Psalmist: 'The stone that the builders rejected has now become the cornerstone' (Psalm 118: 22).

Rebels and individuals

This chapter is a bricolage of suggestions and ideas about 'the individual'. Up to now, I have wondered whether contextualism and constructivism have gone too far. Then I discussed the 'fractured individual', one who is 'stunted' always already. I also looked at the advantages and disadvantages of Jung's conception of the individual for a progressive politics. I could at this point have turned to Otto Gross, who was the very first to state in 1913 that you can't have individual transformation without social change – and that there's no social change worth speaking of without something happening at the individual level. However, instead, I want to turn to Albert Camus and his working out of the intricate connections between existence, oppression, freedom, action – and the individual. I draw for the most part on Camus's *The Rebel,* a book I first read at school, aged 16, and used as a base for numerous attempts to get out of my cage.

Succinctly, Camus states that rebellion and revolt are critically important to the making of meaning, and hence to what we could call the birth of an individual. He reaches no conclusions about the purpose and meaning of life. He is relentlessly sceptical. Hence, his position is that there is a fundamental absurdity to life and that attempts to create meaning, which are innate and valuable, are also – crucially – attempts to avoid the unavoidable absurdity of existence. Camus is like Beckett here, but he is also, suggestively, very like Jung, too, as this quote from *The Red Book* shows: 'Meaning is a moment and a transition from absurdity to absurdity and absurdity only a moment and a transition from meaning to meaning' (Jung 2009, p. 242).

The Rebel is a history of humanity in revolt. Over time, humans have displayed a basic rejection of injustice. Hence they rebel. All one can believe in is the value of protest and the protester's life. Crucially, for Camus, the impulse to rebel is inborn. 'To breathe is to judge' (Camus 1953, p. 8). The act of rebellion is a primary given of human life. Revolt creates dignity and the ethical life – and solidarity. Individuals who rebel against an oppressive state are transformed into a collective force: 'I rebel, therefore we are' (Camus 1953, p. 111). The rebellious individual is the progenitor of the social movement.

If the impulse to rebel is inborn and hence archetypal, then any idea that Jung and Camus are total opposites may not be accurate. Camus's default position is that human nature is made by decisions and acts, whereas Jung's conception of human nature is different – but Jung is not only about archetypal determinism either. Remember, 'every confrontation with the archetype is a moral confrontation'– and there are many references to 'free will' in Jung's *Collected Works*.

I find Jung and Camus rather similar as writers. Neither Jung nor Camus is rational or linear, both use metaphor, and both are interested in psychological experience. Both write in the face of the catastrophes of the twentieth century, but Camus rejects the collective as a given; for him, rebellion creates whatever is more-than-personal.

What I take from Camus for this discussion on 'the individual' is that, while the original motivation to rebel may be inborn and individual, rebellion leads to joining others in solidarity. Camus admits that people have a longing for something social but also for something in the spiritual area. He calls it 'religion' or 'philosophy' (Camus 1953, p. 237), but I think it is more accurately termed 'social spirituality'. In social spirituality, individuals come together to take action in the social sphere, doing this in concert with other people. When this happens, something spiritual comes into being. Being actively engaged in a social, political, cultural or ethical issues, together with others, initiates the spiritual. This is a very different perspective from one that would see social spirituality as being something done in the social domain by spiritual (i.e. individuated) people. To the contrary, there is a kind of spiritual rain that can descend on individuals who get involved in politics and social issues with others – hence 'social' spirituality (see Samuels 2001 for a full discussion).

The difference from Jung's elitist conception of the individual should be clear: this is by no means an elitist perspective. Social spirituality embraces people who get involved with other people in political and social action – for example, the Occupy Movement or the protests against global capitalism that our young people are getting into. What they're doing when they get involved in the anti-capitalist movements and the environmental and ecological movements is to participate in a general resacralisation of culture (Samuels 1993). To play on the word 'politicised', many of them are becoming 'spiritualised'. When one gets involved in idealistic politics, sometimes – not always – one gets spiritualised. And so the anti-capitalist movement is creating its own spirituality and, in turn, is being informed by the spirituality that it creates in a feedback loop. Political action leads to spirituality of some kind and spirituality informs political action. Of course, eventually it all falls to pieces. Either the police wreck it or people grow up. But there is a basic resacralising tendency worth recognising.

Exercise 2

Think of times when you feel someone or something was trying to prevent you from being an individual – family, society, peer pressure, shame – whatever. Did you rebel – or not? What happened in either case?

The limits of individual responsibility

What is the scope of our individual responsibility for others and for the world? The roots of the word 'responsibility' lie in *spondere*, to promise or pledge. But what happens if we promise too much? In politics (as in life), there is a problem of people being too demanding of themselves. If they cannot live up to these demands, their idealism and energy goes underground and becomes self-supressed. They seem apathetic but, secretly, they are not – secretly, they are in touch with their 'inner politician'.

Let's think about how this banishing of political energy and idealism affects *Tikkun Olam*, Hebrew for the repair and restoration of the world. We are back to the problematic of 'the stunted individual'. If one tries to do *Tikkun* from too perfect a self-state, it won't work, because the only possible way to approach and engage with a broken and fractured world that one is a part of is surely as a broken and fractured – stunted – individual. I call the broken and fractured the 'good-enough individual', using Winnicott's epithet out of context but not overlooking his interest in how the parent helps the baby to steer a path between idealisation and denigration of the parent. Here, we are talking of the individual's own path between self-idealisation and self-denigration.

Winnicott says that 'the mother will fail the baby but in the baby's own way' (1971, p. 46). The individual will fail him or herself, but in his or her own way. Failure to make a difference in the world to the extent one hopes becomes much less shameful. One becomes less self-denigrating. This is important because shame at failure is what leads to depression and guilt, and so destroys the impulse and the capacity for action.

Individuals need a different attitude to their failure, particularly the failure of their political hopes and aspirations and projects. They need to adopt attitudes akin to those professed, for instance, by T.S. Eliot, who told us that every time we attempt a new start we attempt a new kind of failure (1944); by Samuel Beckett, who called upon us to keep on failing and to fail better each time (1989); and by Bob Dylan who, in his song 'Love Minus Zero/No Limit', equates success with failure (1965).

Perhaps this is the kind of thing Camus meant when he wrote: 'The rebel can never find peace. He (*sic*) knows what is good, and despite himself, does evil. The value that supports him is never given to him once and for all – he must fight to support it, unceasingly' (1953, p. 113).

Exercise 3

Think of times when you yourself made a difference and also of times when you wanted to but failed in the attempt.

Before we pack up in despair let's recall that the official politicians and the governments of the world, with all possible resources at their disposal, have not done such a terrific job of managing things. Governments constantly try to improve things in the political world, usually by redistributing wealth or changing legislative and constitutional structures or defusing warlike situations. It is not that nothing is being tried to make things better, but a materialist approach deriving exclusively from economics, or one that depends solely on altering the structures of the state, will not refresh those parts of the individual citizen that a psychological perspective can reach. There is disappointment at societies that fail to deliver the spiritual goods and a sense of meaning and purpose. We can change the clothes, shift the pieces around, but the spectre that haunts materialist and constitutional moves in the political world is that they only ruffle the surface. They do not (because, alone, they cannot) bring about the transformations for which the individual political soul yearns.

Note

1 An earlier and longer version of Andrew Samuels's chapter appeared in *Psychotherapy and Politics International* (12: 2) under the title 'The role of the individual in political and social change processes: Jung, Camus and the question of personal responsibility'.

References

Beckett, Samuel (1983/1989) *Worstward Ho*. London: Calder & Boyars.
Boff, Leonardo (1988) *When Theologians Listen to the Poor*. San Francisco, CA: Harper & Row.
Camus, Albert (1951) *L'homme revolte* (The Rebel. London, Hamish Hamilton (1953); London: Penguin (2000)).

Cushman, Phillip (1991) *Constructing the Self, Constructing America*. Cambridge, MA: Harvard University Press.
Dylan, Bob (1965) Love Minus Zero/No Limit. *Bringing it All Back Home*. Columbia Records.
Eliot, T.S. (1944) *Four Quartets*. London: Faber & Faber, 2001.
Gross, Otto (1913) Zur Ueberwindung der kulturellen Krise. *Die Aktion, III* (14).
Jung, C.G. (1916) 'Adaptation, individuation, collectivity'. CW 18.
Jung, C.G. (1921/1971) 'Definitions'. In *Psychological Types*, CW 6.
Jung, C.G. (1935) *The Relations Between the Ego and the Unconscious*. CW 7.
Jung, C.G. (1957) *The Undiscovered Self*. CW 10.
Jung, C.G. (1978) *C.G. Jung Speaking: Interviews and Encounters*. McGuire, William and Hull, R.F.C. (eds). London: Thames & Hudson.
Jung, C. G. (2009) *The Red Book*. Sonu Shamdasani (ed.). New York and London: Norton.
Orwell, G. (1949) *1984*. London: Secker & Warburg.
Progoff, Ira. (1953) *Jung's Psychology and its Social Meaning*. New York: Julian Press.
Samuels, Andrew (1993) *The Political Psyche*. London and New York: Routledge.
Samuels, Andrew (2001) *Politics on the Couch: Citizenship and the Internal Life*. London: Karnac.
Samuels, Andrew (2010) 'Shadows of the therapy relationship'. *European Journal of Psychotherapy and Counselling*, 12: 3, pp. 207–15.
Shamdasani, Sonu (2003) *Jung and the Making of Modern Psychology: The Dream of a Science*. Cambridge: Cambridge University Press.
Winnicott, D. (1971) *Playing and Reality*. London: Tavistock.

4

THE SOUL AND PATHOLOGIZING IN THE (MULTIPLI)CITY OF SÃO PAULO

Guilherme Scandiucci

Cities, psychology with soul, and the *anima mundi*

Cities have been with us (and we with them) for thousands of years, but now there is a sense of uneasiness that these enchanting creatures of ours may be getting out of control and that deep-rooted urban problems could become our collective downfall. The city has always been various things to various people. It might be a center for trade, economic opportunity, and production of technology, or it might be a gathering place for arts, sports, religious cults, research, and entertainment. It could also be seen in another light, as a set of collective problems to be solved: traffic, garbage collection, sewage, poverty, and so on.

> All cities are collections of structures and systems, an urban fabric that often appears dreary and monotonous, sometimes becoming wildly diverse and interesting, occasionally even inspiring . . . The city as a phenomenon can also be understood as a primary archetype of human experience; man and woman in community, with all the diversity, contradiction, tension, and exuberance that implies . . . The city has become our hope and our prison.
>
> (Jones 2003, p. 1)

Informed by the post-Enlightenment paradigm, we tend to understand cities in terms of physical forms and structures – that is, as literal and concrete things. Literalism and materialism are implicit in the dominant Western worldview (Jones 2003).

Carl Jung treats the psyche as an independent factor, thus not 'subject to the caprices of our will,' and he clearly separates the psyche into subjective and objective spheres. The former is related to conscious processes and to what he would call the personal unconscious and its contents; the latter is fulfilled by archetypal and mythological themes, and thus to the impersonal or collective unconscious.

Jung draws attention to an aspect of the psyche (or soul, since they can be seen as synonymous here), best described as the imagination – an aspect that James Hillman would later greatly invest in. The starting point of this aspect of soul is the basic idea mentioned above, in which the contents of the unconscious, prior to their modern interpretation (that is to say, prior to them being reduced to abstract, rational terms, with the mind being regarded as an apparatus) were projected onto matter, creating a phenomenon perceived as part spiritual and part physical. In this way, the act of imagining can be thought of as a kind of physical activity: 'imagination is therefore a concentrated extract of the life forces, both physical and psychic' (Jung 1959/1980, par. 394). Thus, the psyche has a powerful tendency to imagine, or make reality. After all, in 1920 Jung had already alerted us to the fact that 'the psyche creates reality every day' (Jung 1921/1976, par. 78).

Like that of Jung, James Hillman's approach to the soul is far from metaphysical. He thinks of the soul as 'a perspective rather than a substance, a viewpoint toward things rather than a thing itself' (Hillman 1975/1992, p. xvi). It has some basic characteristics, such as a deepening of events into experiences, a relationship with death, and imaginative possibility within us – that is to say, reflective speculation, dreams, images, and fantasy. To Hillman, everything we can encounter is derived from psychic images. He borrows from Jung, the idea of *fantasy-image* as a kind of synthesizing term to develop his own psychological proposal, where imagination is a process of psyche, and the *poetic basis of mind.*

Hillman is faithful once again to Jungian texts when he criticizes psychologies that are distant from the soul, and when he observes that they do not even use the word 'soul' any more to refer to a person, but use instead 'self' or 'ego.' 'We have all been de-souled,' he says (Hillman 1975/1992, p. 3). Psychology can be too worried about its conceptualizations and understandings. Hillman demands instead a psychology of personification, and the ability to personify. Imagination is a kind of aliment for the soul, according to Hillman: 'To live psychologically means to imagine things; to be in touch with soul means to live in sensorial connection with fantasy' (Hillman 1975/1992, p. 23). Besides, 'the autonomy of fantasy is the soul's last refuge of dignity, its guarantor against all oppressions' (Hillman, 1975/1992, p. 39). According to Hillman, in the seventeenth century, imagination was already being condemned in a certain way – this is not a privilege of our times, or even something that began in the nineteenth century.

The *anima* is intimately related to the soul or psyche, even though it occupies another place in Jungian conceptualization. Hillman frequently refers to the important concept, 'soul-making.' For both Jung and Hillman, one cannot actually make a soul. The *anima*, as Jung understands it, cannot be made. *Anima* is, he says, 'always the *a priori* element in [our] moods, reactions, impulses, and whatever else is spontaneous in psychic life. It is something that lives of itself, that makes us live' (Jung 1954/1981, par. 57). Soul for Jung is a work on *anima* through images, while soul-making for Hillman is nothing more than psychologizing of a kind that is as powerful as a religious engagement, because it is dependent on faith. However, it shouldn't be confused with a monotheistic faith or doctrine; it is a faith that lives in the 'promiscuity' of images in the polytheist psyche (Hillman 1971).

Taking a radical stance, Hillman places the soul in a freestanding position, where one cannot control or possess it. Soul-making is, then, an alternative to transference. 'For it is not the therapist or any actual person whatever who is the keeper of my soul beyond all betrayals, but the archetypal persons of the gods to whom the *anima* acts as a bridge' (Hillman 1975/1992, p. 51). In this sense, our personalities are like personas through which the soul speaks. Here Hillman makes a far-reaching affirmation: 'Not I personify, but the *anima* personifies me, or soul-makes herself through me, giving my life her sense' (Hillman, 1975/1992, p. 51). The soul uses us to express itself; it 'invades' us and carries the gods together; it has 'inhuman reaches,' (Hillman, 1975/1992: 173) since much of it extends beyond the nature of man.

James Hillman (1982/2006) discusses a significant idea in his article '*Anima Mundi*: Return of the Soul to the World'. He affirms that 'each and every thing of our constructed urban life has psychological import' (Hillman 1982/2006, p. 27). By recapturing Platonic and Neo-Platonic ideas and confronting them with philosophical systems – as we find in Aquinas, Descartes, Locke, and Kant – external things gain their souls back. Consequently, we discover that the world is not just material and lifeless, or 'merely a backdrop in and around which subjectivity appeared' (Hillman 1982/2006, p. 29); the world is not waiting for our projections, as psychoanalysis usually conceives it to be. The world is ensouled.

Hillman wants psychology to leave its exclusive viewpoint on the subjective. Therapeutic focus is normally intrapsychic (individual problems) or inter-psychic (issues of family, groups, and society). But, for Hillman, the world should not be psychologized in this manner. He argues:

> As expressive forms, things speak; they show the shape they are in. They announce themselves, bear witness to their presence: 'Look, here we are!' They regard us beyond how we may regard them, our perspectives, what we intend with them, and how we dispose of them. This imaginative claim on attention bespeaks a world ensouled . . . To call a building 'catatonic' or 'anorexic' means to examine the way it presents itself, its behavioral display in its skinny, tall, rigid bare-boned structure, trimmed of fat, its glassy front and desexualized coldness and suppressed explosive rage, its hollow atrium interior sectioned by vertical shafts . . . To interpret the world's things as if they were our dreams deprives the world of its dream, its complaint.
>
> (Hillman 1982/2006, pp. 33–36)

In summary, *anima mundi* is a way of perceiving, sensing, and imagining. With this proposition, Hillman suggests that psychology should change its point of view as a whole – 'from mental reflection toward cordial reflex, . . . moving as well the seat of the soul from brain to heart and the method of psychology from cognitive understanding to aesthetic sensitivity' (Hillman 1982/2006, p. 37). The threat of destruction of the world and the pathologized image of our planet in the last decades seem to revive recognition of the soul in the world. 'For where there is pathology there is psyche, and where [there is] psyche, [there is] eros' (Hillman 1982/2006, p. 47). But to really take a response from the heart seriously, radical shifts of orientation should be made, and only then can one 'value soul before mind, image before feeling, each before all, aesthesis and imagining before logos and conceiving, thing before meaning, noticing before knowing, rhetoric before truth, animal before human, anima before ego, what and where and who before why' (Hillman 1982/2006, p. 48).

Cities have souls, too. They are not merely quantities of concrete and steel, material constructions, sinks, roads, bus ways, or school systems.

> Cities, too, have repressed memories. They have forgotten ancestors. They come with a case history. They have potentials for development and suffer the pains of past failures, past violence. Cities have ambitions and destinies, periods of latency, flowering and stagnation, and they have faces, habit, and styles. Also, cities exhibit classic syndromes of psychopathology.
>
> (Hillman 1987/2006, p. 298)

Pathologizing, soul *in extremis*, and the body of the city

Another important idea introduced by Hillman is the concept of pathologizing. Pathological states are what he calls a soul *in extremis*. These are suffering and abnormal states of mind, or the fantastic conditions of the psyche. 'Each soul at some time or another demonstrates illusions and depressions, overvalued ideas, manic flights and rages, anxieties, compulsions, and perversions' (Hillman 1975/1992, p. 55). In this perspective, psychopathology does not refer to pathologies in the medical sense.

Hillman identifies some attempts to understand psychopathology; above all, there are two 'classic' ways of interpreting it: through medicine and through religion. If we suffer, it is either because we are sick or because we committed sins, and the cures call for science or faith. In both forms of comprehension, pathology is a stance of something that is wrong.

Pathologizing, in Hillman's definition, is 'the psyche's autonomous ability to create illness, morbidity, disorder, abnormality, and suffering in any aspect of its behavior and to experience and imagine life through this deformed and afflicted perspective' (1975/1992: p. 57). From an archetypal viewpoint, pathology is neither wrong nor correct, but merely necessary. It is not something foreign to us or secondary, because this neglects the reality that pathologizing is a foundation, 'a strand in all our being, woven into every complex' (Hillman 1975/1992, p. 57).

The psyche does not exist without pathologizing. Since the unconscious was discovered as an operative factor in each soul, pathologizing was recognized as an inherent aspect of interior personality. Freud affirmed this concisely: 'We can catch the unconscious only in pathological material' (cited in Hillman 1975/1992, p. 70). Pathologizing is present not only in special moments of crisis, but also in the daily lives of all of us.

The city strongly affects the psyche. The city is the psyche. It took a long time for the field of therapy to learn that the body is the psyche. Later, the field of therapy began to learn that the psyche exists entirely in relational systems, not as a self-determined monad. The next step would be to realize that the city, where the body lives and moves, and where the relational network is made, is also the psyche.

The collective unconscious is the world, as Jung said, and the psyche is not in the person, but the person is in the psyche. This unconscious would extend to beyond the great symbols of our dreams or the repercussions of the history of our ancestors. It includes the waves of flux and reflux in the city, fashion, language, tendencies, and the choreographies that orchestrate our moving souls, just like images orchestrate our souls (Hillman and Ventura 1993).

This chapter is concerned, in various senses, with the relationships, interactions, and mutual exchanges between the people and the physical body of a city. It must be noted that the former, initially subjects, can become objects in the day-to-day of urban living – that is, beings disengaged from the life of the polis and from the participation enabled by it. Whereas the latter, the city, an object in principle, may become a subject – that is, a being endowed with a soul under the perspective adopted here. The city can kill the subjectivity of a citizen, that which is potentially conferred by collective action; however, the citizen can also kill the 'subjectivity' of a city by seeing it as nothing more than rigid, functional, lifeless concrete.

The Italian anthropologist Massimo Canevacci points out the interesting consideration:

> A building 'communicates' through many languages, not only to the observer but mainly to the city itself in its complexity: the task of the observer is to try to understand the speeches that are 'pent' in the architectonical structures, which are alive by the changing of perceptions that bring together, in an uneasy interaction, the many spectators and the many roles performed by them.
>
> (Canevacci 2004, p. 22)

However, Canevacci is coming closer to a gaze upon us from the city itself, thus approaching Hillman's ideas and enabling us to make some comparisons.

The experience of the foreigner (in this case, an Italian who lived in São Paulo for a period of time) is meaningful. Others observe him, and he is noticed because he is different, as often happens with a person who is revealed as being an 'outsider.' Furthermore, the 'others' who notice him are also (concrete) elements of the city. Canevacci declines to consider the urban shapes of the Brazilian city as texts to be interpreted by the observer. Thus, he relates:

> Frequently, I myself feel observed, as if I had been dragged and taken by the 'looks' that these many subjectivities from some buildings throw upon me. It is possible that the attraction exerted by some areas of the city, or by some of its architectural forms, arises from a feeling of being observed by these urban sequences. From that results a discomfort, but also a feeling of choice, or rather of options. Sometimes I find it difficult to conclude (or remember) if some choices made regarding certain places of the city . . . were 'really' made by me or by them.
>
> (Canevacci 2004, pp. 23–24)

To look when one finds oneself looked at is an important perspective of the researcher of urban space. This is not a paranoid delirium, for we are situated in the field of the metaphor and the 'literary,' and not the 'literal.' It involves us allowing ourselves to be enclosed by the city and the soul that is simultaneously created there.

From images and imagination, things of the city tell us about themselves:

> Palaces, streets, squares, supermarkets, or even little shops are treated as 'behavioral fragments,' pent in its architectonical construction, or stirred by the metropolitan flows – the *cronotopo* – even if they appear to remain in the same spot. They 'talk' to us, even at the base of their interaction – made of symmetries and contrasts – with other 'fragments' of architectonical behavior. Between two buildings, even when they are not contiguous, a dialogic relationship can exist. They 'speak' to each other, and the researcher must uncover their dialogue and penetrate it.
>
> (Canevacci 2004, p. 140)

It is worth noticing that Canevacci concerns himself with the history of São Paulo in order to listen to this dialogue between buildings. The anthropologist begins with historical research enriched by individual observations entangled in the fragmentary body of the metropolis. The architectonical history of the estates observed by him – and which observe him at the same time – contributes meaningfully to this space narrative. If he ignored this kind of research, his narrative would be impoverished, in similar terms to the patient unable to access his childhood memories.

By developing a perspective and a method, Canevacci seeks to make familiar what is seen as strange, and strange what is considered familiar, while still asserting his work as an 'art of interpretation,' a decoder of urban messages, an hermetic art (related to the god Hermes) and an ethnographic one, starting from the '*neighborhood that must be distanced*' (Canevacci 2004, p. 30). Canevacci proposes the interesting and curious idea of an 'observative observation,' no longer simply 'participating' in the action, but also observing himself as a subject who observes the context, as a meta-observation. Or, further still, '*the visual becomes in this way the polymorphic center that must be interpreted and the means of interpretation. The visual is the target and the method*' (Canevacci 2004, p. 44).

Coincidentally, one of Hillman's definitions of 'soul' is making everyday events into experiences (Hillman 1992). As mentioned earlier, the soul is not a substance, but a relationship, whereby the soul is related to the way of viewing, and not to that which is viewed. Soul-making can take place virtually anywhere and in any situation, even though there might be places, according to Hillman, that offer better possibilities for it. Even so, archetypal psychology seeks a kind of foreign view on our neighborhoods; insofar as the ordinary can be seen poetically, the community (belonging) asks for an aesthetic that collaborates continuously with the soul, in case we are not too solitary in the metropolis and focused on the production that it also demands of us all the time.

The image – in this case, presented by the city as a spray-painted building, for example – boosts the *esse in anima*; the imagery conveyed by the architecture and the urban landscapes 'construct' the *anima mundi*. The psychological experience consists in an encounter between the city inhabitants and the city itself; in this place and during this encounter, an opportunity of soul-making is opened up. Here we have something like a psyche per se, 'independent' from the subject, or better put, beyond the 'personal' in relation to the 'object.' The city offers itself by soul-making, imposing itself as a psychological space independent from the observer.

The look that lays the foundation of the soul must be subversive. For instance, city spaces can invoke impressions that are different from their original purposes. When entering other spaces made for a particular activity, our expectations can be 'frustrated' if we are faced with other meanings and messages – as in dreams, which subvert 'by nature' the meanings longed for by the conscious mind. As Canevacci (2004) points out, if we go to a football stadium, for example, we no longer know if it is a foundation or a rite of passage; on the other hand, if we occasionally enter a church to attend an actual 'rite,' we may be shocked by the lack of transcendence in the mass service.

As an example, Hillman and Ventura affirm that the car is a private space that can go in any direction at any time. The hotel room assures that wherever you go, there will be a space for you – something peculiar to modern life and alien to every previous society. 'But the fact that there's a room for you anywhere makes the place where you are less substantial. Thus you are a transient, without having chosen to be' (Hillman and Ventura 1993, p. 118).

The archetypal perspective insists upon the idea that we live in an animated world (or a world 'ensouled'). Things are no longer just lifeless materials or objects. Thus, Hillman supposes that

> we are being harmed as much by the form of things as by their material, where form means their aesthetic quality. For instance: styrofoam cups, fluorescent lights, bad doorknobs, unpleasant chairs, K-Mart fabrics and their colors, the hollow loud clack of objects set down on fake wood tabletops. Enough. The soul, which has classically been defined as the form of living bodies, could be affected by the form of other bodies (design, shape, color, innate idea or 'image') in the same way as the matter of our bodies is affected by the matter of other bodies (pesticides, additives, preservatives).
>
> (Hillman and Ventura 1993, p. 125)

Hillman then radicalizes his 'psychotherapy' project, suddenly realizing that there are not many differences between depth psychology and design. He argues that people have been trying to dissolve depth psychology back into religion by saying that patients go to the analyst as they would go to a priest or confessor; and, further, that they have taken analysis and dissolved it into Asian wisdom philosophy (where the analyst is in the form of a guru), into education (the analyst is in the form of a tutor, mentor, or coach), and even into mythmaking, where the analyst is a mythmaker who rewrites, or reframes, our life story. This is not to mention other dissolutions into wet-nurse, mother, pseudo-lover, guide, or midwife. Hillman brings up still other ways of 'dissolving therapy into something else: interior decorator, architect, urban planner, product designer' (Hillman and Ventura 1993, p. 126).

Graffitti and *pixação* in São Paulo

According to Bynoe (2006), graffiti can be defined as messages written and images drawn in public spaces. The act as outlined here is an ancient art, present at sites such as Pompeii from the time of Emperor Nero, Hadrian's villa at Tivoli, and the Mayan site of Tikal in Mesoamerica. It also influenced mainstream modern art; Dubuffet and Picasso, for example, were attracted to graffiti from other cultures and outsider art (Rahn 2002), and the graffiti in Brazil dates back to indigenous Amazonian rock carvings (Manco *et al.* 2005).

However, 'graffiti' as referenced in this chapter is associated with twentieth-century urban environments. Continuing with the definition, we learn that more contemporary, political activists have applied graffiti 'as a means to protest government policies and actions. Gang members have also used graffiti to mark their territory. Graffiti writing that uses spray paints is also known as aerosol art and became the visual component of Hip Hop' (Bynoe 2006, p. 157). In the 1970s and 1980s, through painting, graffiti 'writers "made a place" for themselves in the city's public network, claiming a "right to the city" as a valuable and necessary part of its social and cultural life' (Austin 2001, p. 4).

In general, the involvement of the graffiti artist in his activity is enormous, and frequently compared to a sort of addiction. Since it is a prohibited activity most of the time – this is the genuine graffiti, or 'keeping it real' as some graffiti writers say – taking risks is part of the daily life of a graffiti artist. This includes running away from the police, stealing spray cans, and being in dangerous places in terms of height, risk of electrical shock, or violence. The more visible the piece, the more respect the writer gains for the risk taken. In Brazil, where this phenomenon is common (with the city of São Paulo being one of its main stages), there is a clear distinction between *pixação* and graffiti. The former generally consists of a certain way of writing that only those involved in the *pixação* action can read, and is usually regarded as vandalism (Figures 4.1 and 4.2). The latter presents colorful drawings, and is usually viewed as an art form (Figure 4.3). And sometimes *pixação* and graffiti compete for space, sharing the same wall (Figure 4.4). It is not uncommon that city councils reserve some public spaces for graffiti artists, organizing the activity and endorsing it.

Graffiti and *pixação* express important aspects of the soul of a city, especially in big cities. People who create either of them can reveal parts of this soul

Figure 4.1 A building full of *pixações* in São Paulo (author's archive)

Figure 4.2 A wall with different letters, typical of the *pixação* in São Paulo (author's archive)

that are normally hidden in the daily routine of life. These 'revelations' can be pleasant for some, and a horror for others; this is the internal conflict of any psychic system, as analytical psychology shows. When the soul appears, the last thing we can expect is tranquility.

Here, it is interesting to bring in some principles of Jungian clinical work, since this clinical perspective is being used to make observations about the city. Hillman (1974) draws attention to differentiation – that is, the need to

Figure 4.3 Graffiti over an external wall of a house in São Paulo (author's archive)

make a distinction between the component parts of personality, or to know the different collectivities that speak through the ego. This is essential in Jung's thought too, and is clearly present in his theory of complexes. Complexes are fragmented and autonomous parts of a personality, which is multifaceted by nature. Complexes can even possess the ego; this occurs, for example, in the neurotic dissociation of the personality, a common clinical phenomenon.

Neuroses and complexes can be seen in the city as much as in individuals. The city can be considered an image and elaborated in the same way as a personal dream is elaborated. The city is a collection of forms and dynamics that can reveal meanings beyond superficial interpretations. We can say it has a persona, the face it shows to the world. A city that lives constantly illuminated ignores or marginalizes what it cannot see – blurring the 'invisible' multiplicity, leaving the obscure in the shadows. It is sufficient to think about the suburban districts and their inhabitants: the former are frequently forgotten by the public administration, the latter (the inhabitants) tend to become invisible when they interact with those who inhabit the upscale, central parts of the city.

Figure 4.4 Graffiti and *pixação* sharing the same wall in São Paulo (author's archive)

If differentiating oneself is also being different in the same way that individuality implies being unique (peculiar), Jungian analysis is focused on what is different, eccentric, and non-adapted – usually evident in psychopathological abnormalities. Instead of these being seen as weak points to be excluded, they should be seen as 'seeds of individuality.' The idea is to reconnect the various parts (supposedly in equilibrium or healed) with their bizarre aspects, so that they are not avoided (or suppressed) (Hillman 1974).

Urban diseases such as suburban expansion, traffic jams, street crimes, abandoned neighborhoods, anorexic architecture, excessive consumption, and air and water pollution are everywhere. We understand them as obstacles to evolution, problems to be solved, and duties in the hands of specialists with technical knowledge. However, these problems can also be considered symptoms that can be worked through for deeper layers of meaning.

Hillman emphasizes the erotic imagination that pervades the city and its life: 'We love [cities] because they hold us in their bodies, excite us, exhaust us, don't let us leave. Or, we quit them as from a lover because we can't take it anymore' (Hillman 2003/2006, p. 19). In another essay, Hillman makes a brief reference to graffiti, writing:

> The soul wants its images, and when it doesn't find them, it makes substitutes: billboards and graffiti, for instance. Even in countries where ads are not allowed, slogans still are written large on walls and placards posted. Spontaneously, the human hand makes its mark, insisting on personalized messages, as human nature everywhere immediately chalks its initials on monuments.
>
> (Hillman 1978/2006, p. 24)

So, let us think about this phenomenon of making a mark through tags and pieces, 'bombing all city,' as graffiti writers say. In these images painted everywhere, the city seems also to declare its strange game of being known and hidden at the same time, a game played by the graffiti writers; they know some mysterious, conspiratorial secrets of the big city, some dark subway passages that few people know; they discover walls and corners almost left behind. The secrets they know are like little confessions of odd habits made by a lover, or occasional behaviors that only those who have real intimacy can know. They love the city in their own way, and vice versa. It is a complicity in the dark. As the graffiti writer Claw says about the moments she walks through New York in the night looking for a place to tag or paint: 'It's like a private little world. It's a wild feeling of really being connected with your surroundings' (Cihlar *et al.* 2005). Gene speaks of 'bringing a dead space to life,' like rekindling a relationship. Shana declares her need to 'just make the city more of my own place' (Rahn 2002, p. 168). The body of the city is the body of the lover: unfamiliar enough for sexual curiosity, intimate enough to be touched without fear.

There is no doubt about the importance of the *pixação* in São Paulo. If looking at the city helps us learn a bit more about the people who spray the *pixação*, looking at the people also helps us understand a bit more about the city.

Although graffiti and *pixações* are now considered very different forms of expression, they maintain a connection in their relationship with the city. In Brazil, as pointed out by Franco (2009), by considering graffiti as illegally created, artists of graffiti are more accepted in their act (while something quite different occurs in New York, for example, where both practices are equally prohibited).

In São Paulo, it comes to a point where there is even a conflict between graffiti and *pixação* practitioners. The dispute for space is generally the main reason for these conflicts, as the *pixações* are frequently removed and turned into walls on which graffiti is painted, in a way of 'sanitizing' the environment, since graffiti artists often act in collaboration with public authorities, as well as with advertising (with this obviously not being the case for the *pixação*). 'Therefore, the *pixadores* (the *pixação* practitioners) used to come back to these places and paint over the work of graffiti artists, as a way to demonstrate their dissatisfaction' (Lassala 2010, p. 74).

One of the most relevant aspects of *pixação* – which has driven many anthropologists to study this phenomenon – is its group dimension; it is a 'group practice,' as pointed out by Franco (2009, p. 20). The practitioners are rarely seen working alone, and the occasions when it does happen, they usually highlight the name of the gang, followed by the initials of the author and the year it was made in smaller letters. It is also possible to pay tribute to a member of the gang that died or is in jail, painting the year of his death or a penal code number relating to the crime committed. In some cases there can be a reference to an association of groups (or a *grife*, or 'label,' as the *pixadores* call it). 'However, an isolated name or pseudonym is not considered a *pixação,* for example' (Franco 2009, p. 23).

When considered as visual texts, the *pixações* can be contemplated within the logic of post-modernity. However, it is important to observe that this kind of communication differs itself, by its own nature, from the prescriptive form of warnings and machines. The *pixação* answers to them, provoking the imperatives to which we submit ourselves every day by using, ironically, the same language and the same communicative rush. *Pixação* is one of the languages of the soul of the city.

It is relevant to observe that transgression is the fundamental element in such urban expressions. According to Franco (2009), transgression creates the driving force for the expansion and dissemination of this practice, since it is necessary to leave the signature of the gang in non-authorized places, visible to any citizen. Consequently, the activists of the *pixação* (and of non-authorized graffiti) will risk themselves and will be bold in their practice.

Different authors from different times put urban and physiological organisms together (there are analogies between the city and the human body). For example, the artist Celso Gitahy (2006) writes:

> While there is all this controversy about pixação, private property, and graffiti, I feel compelled to compare the origin of such languages in São Paulo to a huge gastritis that the city contracted, in which the inflammation, rather than being on the mucosa lining of the stomach, could be on the walls and public spaces of the city. Any inflammation will do to signal the organism about some type of dysfunction or disturbance from the external environment. I will go even further: graffiti wouldn't only be the inflammation that shows the symptom of a corrupted urbanity, treated tritely by the contemporary media, but also the curative balm itself, presenting its own art on the streets for everyone.
>
> (Gitahy 2006, pp. 48–49, my translation)

Gitahy seems to regard graffiti as a kind of *pharmakon*, simultaneously a poison and a medicine, as the Greek word indicates. The comparison is interesting since it exposes a paradox present in the *pixação*; we can see the polarizations in this scenario and in the depositions of those who make them: life and death, art and destruction, solidarity and competition. At first sight, the *pixação* provokes certain disgust since it 'spoils' digestion of the urban scenario. If we look closer, however, it gives certain humanization to a mechanized city.

The connection with the outskirts of the metropolis is an identity category of the *pixadores*. Belonging to a periphery is not just a geographical or a class issue, but the adoption of particular ways of behavior and interaction with peers. The *pixadores* are extremely territorialized; even when gathering at the meeting point downtown, the issues at stake are those conceived about and in the periphery (Pereira 2010).

The suburban area becomes a symbol. In the light of analytical psychology, it is possible to think that this peripheral body offers concrete expression to a complex – devised as a character with a certain set of traits, a way of being – bonded to the psychical polytheism (the city). Even considering the constant presence of an ego (center), which is essential to the linkage and a certain 'organization' of the nuclei of affection (complex), these are the very nuclei we go through all the time.

It is very important to observe that, according to the Brazilian anthropologist Alexandre Pereira (2005), there is a great number of *pixação* of images related to dirt, criminality, marginality, and altered states of consciousness (caused by drugs or by madness). These are examples of the names of some *pixação* gangs: Mafia, Arsenal, Fugitives, Illegal, Bastards, Marginal, Shower of Bullets, Vandals, Dejects, The Dirty Sleepers, Rags, Vomits, Adrenaline, Crazies, Doped, Lunatics, Mad, Psychopathic, Psychoses, and Vicious. Once more I reinforce the idea that the *pixação* expresses the pathologizing of the city of São Paulo in the aggressive communication made by such black and straight letters, or by the identities assumed by these metropolitan beings. Such identities are related to the darkest and most feared parts of the autonomous life of the psyche. Like insistent, autonomous, possessive complexes that challenge the order given by the ego, the *pixadores* print their terrible marks in the multifaceted conglomerate that is called polis/psyche.

The person who makes the *pixação* is a city explorer. If we think about the places where the *pixação* is found, we soon realize that the 'destroyers' seem to fly like birds or escalate walls like spiders, in addition to wandering like rats through the holes of the city. The *pixação* screams from the fifteenth floor of a downtown building, from the metal door of a small shop in the suburban area, from the symbolic monument of the big city, from the bar, from the cemetery wall, from the sidewalk, from the square bench, from the mailbox, from the trash bin, and even from the sewer, literally the underworld of the city. There are no limits to the *pixação*; even death does not kill it, and even pain does not forbid it to speak through urban multiplicity. On the contrary, the possibility of pain and death gives more life to the *pixação*, defies even more radically the common citizens of the polis who are unable to understand it. They don't understand what leads someone to do it, not even in what language it is written.

However, if the city does not understand it through reason, at least the city makes itself understood through the *pixação*. It is impossible to ignore the *pixação*, impossible to erase it, impossible to overcome it. The same thing could be stated about pathologizing. We cannot ignore the symptoms of depression or panic. They insist and flourish from life and death, like spontaneous displays from the psyche.

In a given deposition, Djan Cripta, a graffiti activist (*pixador)* from São Paulo, points out the notoriety that the *pixação* gives to someone. The point is to show up in the city and to show through it, as if the city were to speak his name or that of the gang (or family) to those who walk through it. 'The wall is in my way, so I will put something personal on that wall, it came across me while I did my stroll, after all' (D.I. Silva, personal communication, 28 July 2011). The feeling of belonging to something and the access to a psychological experience that leads to social inclusion seem to be fundamental. The intimacy between space and inhabitant of the polis is shared, as if the *pixadores* said to one another: 'I understand this merging into the space, it is a concrete love, an expansive one, painted in very bold letters for those who wish to see it. That makes us special, even if I work my ass off the whole day, delivering stuff and hearing crap from my boss. Here, we are someone, and it is just us and the eternal, infinite city, above, under, everywhere, surrounded by the strong scent of paint, we're greater than ourselves, we satisfy the destructive and original appetite of the polis. We speak through it, and it speaks through us, inside us, entwined, unable to back down.'

We can consider the archetype of the *puer aeternus* to understand the *pixação*. Bernardi (2008), following Hillman, says that *puer* and senex presents two opposing qualities of time. There is the chronological time of senex, represented by Chronos, the devouring father, and there is also the time of the unexpected, the venture, the right instant to act when we face an opportunity (the Greek *kairós*).

The cautious, planned, or calculated actions are not always the most interesting or even the most efficient ones. On the contrary, according to Bernardi (2008), an irresponsible or even inexperienced action can be regarded as the most authentic and would move a process on, if it were obstructed for some reason. In this situation, the excess of caution had been restraining an action, and the irresponsible or inexperienced behavior removed the restraint. Enthusiasm moves the *puer*, this is the god inside him. Hillman (2005) also makes interesting comments on verticality, seeing it as something that breaks up regularity. This is related to the core of the creativeness of the *puer*. The spirit must ascend, Eros must radiate, the insight must produce the global vision. The encouragement of the *puer* is to overcome the father, to meet again the order from the sky downwards: it is the *puer*'s presumption. Hillman observes that 'the puer-man can go to the extreme of sacrificing himself to the cause. Not the ego sends his spirit so high, but the spirit sends his ego there' (2005, p. 163).

Taking it to account, I would like to think about the 'attacks' of the *pixadores* to the high buildings of São Paulo. Frequently, we can observe the *pixações* done on the top of the buildings in the central area of the city. The majority of the *pixadores* are very young, many are teenagers – and the verticality of adolescence (or the body in erection) is an important image of the *puer*. But what most interests me in the approach to the archetype of the *puer* is not the age itself, but the audacity and the transgressions made by a real *pixador*. He needs to climb, run, risk himself, infringe rules, penetrate into the night, and challenge authorities (of both the police and those of art itself). Verticality is one of the great potentials in this reverie, where black seals the white wall. The *pixador* tends to be arrogant; he or she marks the rich regions of the metropolis, and does not care about his or her social and geographical origin (where the majority are poor citizens from the peripheral areas of the city).

If we put aside the moral criticisms of their work as acts of 'vandalism,' we can see the acts of *pixação* are strong attempts to defy what they perceive to be dominant regimes. Ambiguity arises as a thin layer that divides the creative act from one of delinquency. Hate and love come close to each other within this ambiguity, as a mixture of enchantment, vitality, and fascination for the height, whether it is literal or symbolic. Ambiguity surrounds what it means to become famous among the *pixadores* of the city and beyond it. The image of the *pixação* found all over the buildings in São Paulo is therefore a great image of the *puer* in the life of the psyche and the city.

Obviously, the *pixação* displeases, disturbs, and exceeds what we consider to be acceptable, intervenes in a devastating way, and disposes of things black and white. Once more, it is just like pathologizing and the soul *in extremis*. We can even clear it up, but it eventually comes back again, much like our symptoms that pay us a visit after years of therapy and/or medical treatment. In the middle of the night they show up, and we repeat certain attitudes we thought were under control.

However, messages from the soul can be deciphered in some way. The symptom can be deliteralized or metaphorized, reimagined, and viewed from different perspectives, or it can compose our fictions with passages of suspense, adventure, horror, and especially drama. And the *pixação* can do it, too. What does the city say through it? If we could see through, according to Hillmanian expression, we can see many things beyond ugliness and dirt that should be disposed of. This does not mean wanting to see it as a pleasant beauty (we would never approach the paranoid delirium in that way, for example), but we can find young people that create a complex world with diversified speeches. We can find the city attesting its own violence, exclusion, injustices, and darkness, a city whose foundation is the monotonous and gray concrete, a city guided by money and private property.

The *pixação* is at the same time ugly and extraordinary. It pollutes and breathes life into the city. It makes people angry, but gives meaning to the lives of some. It is trash, and it is art. It haunts and captivates. It drives people crazy. After all, it is transgression, with all the elements a real transgression entails, including fear and fascination. It is the pathologizing of São Paulo the city in deep shades, the soul *in extremis*: we have to fear it, but without withdrawing ourselves from it.

Acknowledgments

To the Institute of Psychology of the University of São Paulo, that shelters my Ph.D. studies. This chapter is part of the research in process at the moment. To the *Coordenação de Aperfeiçoamento de Pessoal de Nível Superior* (CAPES), institution of the Brazilian Government that provides a grant to my Ph.D. studies.

References

Austin, J. (2001) *Taking the Train: How graffiti art became an urban crisis in New York City*. New York: Columbia University Press.

Bernardi, C. (2008) 'Visão geral. Senex-et-*puer*: esboço da psicologia de um arquétipo' ['Overview. Senex-et-*puer*: outline of an archetype's psychology], in D.M.R. Monteiro (ed.) *Puer-Senex: dinâmicas relacionais* [*Puer*-Senex: relational dynamics], Petrópolis: Vozes.

Bynoe, Y. (2006) *Encyclopedia of Rap and Hip-Hop Culture*. Westport, CT: Greenwood Press.

Canevacci, M. (2004) *A cidade polifônica. Ensaio sobre a antropologia da comunicação urbana* [The polyphonic city. Essay on the anthropology of urban communication]. São Paulo: Studio Nobel.

Cihlar, G., Cihlar, N. (Producers) & Pray, D. (Director) (2005) *Infamy. A graffiti film* [Motion picture]. United States: Paladin Entertainment.

Franco, S. (2009) *Iconografias da metrópole: grafiteiros e pixadores representando o contemporâneo* [Iconographies of the metropolis: graffiti writers and pixadores representing the contemporary] (Master's thesis). Retrieved from www.teses.usp.br/teses/disponiveis/16/16136/tde-18052010–092159.

Gitahy, C. (2006) 'O graffiti ocupando seus primeiros espaços' ['Graffiti occupying its first spaces'], in S. Poato (ed.), *O graffiti na cidade de São Paulo e* sua vertente *no Brasil: estéticas e estilos* [Graffiti in the city of São Paulo and its strand in Brazil: aesthetics and styles], São Paulo: Instituto de Psicologia da Universidade de São Paulo.

Hillman, J. (1971) 'Psychology: monotheistic or polytheistic?' *Spring*, 1971: 193–208.

—— (1974) 'Archetypal theory: C.G. Jung', in A. Burton (ed.), *Operational Theories of Personality*. New York: Brunner/Mazel.

—— (1992) *Re-visioning Psychology*. New York: HarperPerennial (original work published 1975).

—— (2005) 'Notes on verticality: creation, transcendence, ambition, erection, inflation', in G. Slater (ed.) *Senex & Puer* (uniform ed., vol. 3). Putnam: Spring Publications.

—— (2006a) '*Anima mundi*: Return of the soul to the world', in R.J. Leaver (ed.), *City & Soul* (uniform ed., vol. 2, pp. 27–49). Putnam: Spring Publications (original work published 1982).

—— (2006b) 'Pittsburgh: City as patient', in R.J. Leaver (ed.), *City & Soul* (Uniform ed., vol. 2, pp. 298–311). Putnam: Spring Publications (original work published 1987).

—— (2006c) 'City', in R.J. Leaver (ed.), *City & Soul* (uniform ed., vol. 2, pp. 17–19). Putnam: Spring Publications (original work published 2003).

—— (2006d) 'City and Soul', in R.J. Leaver (ed.), *City & Soul* (uniform ed., vol. 2, pp. 20–26). Putnam: Spring Publications (original work published 1978).

Hillman, J. & Ventura, M. (1993) *We've Had a Hundred Years of Psychotherapy – and the World's Getting Worse*. San Francisco, CA: HarperCollins.

Jones, P.F. (2003) 'City and Psyche: an exploration into the archetype of city' (doctoral dissertation). Retrieved from Proquest database (AAT 3119796).

Jung, C.G. (1976) *Psychological Types (Collected Works of C.G. Jung, Volume 6*). Princeton, NJ: Princeton University Press (original work published 1921).

—— (1980) 'The psychic nature of the alchemical work', in C.G. Jung (ed.), *Psychology and Alchemy (Collected Works of C.G. Jung, Volume 12*) (2nd ed.). Princeton, NJ: Princeton University Press (original work published 1959).

—— (1981) 'Archetypes of the collective unconscious', in C.G. Jung (ed.). *The Archetypes and the Collective Unconscious (Collected Works of C.G. Jung,* Vol. 9 *Part 1*) (2nd ed.).Princeton, NJ: Princeton University Press (original work published 1954).

Lassala, G. (2010) *Pichação não é pixação: Uma introdução à análise de* expressões gráficas *urbanas* (Pichaçao is not pixaçao: An introduction to the analysis of urban graphic expression). São Paulo: Altamira Editorial.

Manco, T., Art, L. & Neelon, C. (2005) *Graffiti Brasil*, London: Thames & Hudson.

Pereira, A.B. (2005) De rolê pela cidade: Os pixadores em São Paulo [Taking a walk in the city: Graffiti writers in São Paulo.]. (Master's thesis). Retrieved from www.bdae.org.br/dspace/handle/123456789/1556.

—— (2010) As marcas da cidade: A dinâmica da pixação em São Paulo (The marks of the city: the dynamics of graffiti in São Paulo). Lua Nova, 79: 235–244. doi: 10.1590/S0102-64452010000100007.

Rahn, J. (2002) *Painting Without Permission: Hip-hop graffiti subculture*. Westport, CT: Bergin & Garvey.

5

PSYCHODYNAMICS OF THE SUBLIME, THE NUMINOUS AND THE UNCANNY

A dialogue between architecture and eco-psychology

Lucy Huskinson

Introduction

In Jungian and post-Jungian studies, the terms 'numinous' and 'sublime' (and also but perhaps to lesser extent the term 'uncanny') are often used interchangeably.[1] Recently, I read in a well-regarded, scholarly book on Jungian studies about how a university lecturer inspires numinous experiences within her classroom on a seemingly regular basis.[2] We find a similar use of these terms in popular culture. Thus, a broadsheet newspaper article described the England football team's recent victory over Sweden in the Euro 2012 championship as 'sublime' (*The Times*, June 16, 2012). And ladies today are privileged enough to be able to 'spray on' the sublime with a variety of ready-to-hand cosmetic products ('Because' they're apparently 'worth it!')[3] But can a lecture really be numinous? And can a cosmetic product or a footballer[4] be sublime? Perhaps my scepticism is unwarranted, but the important question I wish to ask is, do we gain or lose insight and meaning when we use the terms 'sublime' and 'numinous' (and 'uncanny') interchangeably when we wish simply to denote something that is profound, unusual, and deeply meaningful to us?

Later I shall give a brief history of the development of the terms 'sublime' and 'numinous', and how, together with 'uncanny', they underpin Rudolf Otto's (1917) theoretical account of the dynamics of religious experience – the account that inspired Jung in his own theorising about the unconscious and its affects. For now it will suffice simply to define the terms loosely – as we might expect to find in many works of Jungian studies. Thus, crudely put, the uncanny (*das Unheimliche*) connotes that which is eerily familiar and uncertain, while both the sublime and numinous denote elevated, higher states that can inspire awe, fascination, and terror.

In this chapter I turn my attention to the numinous and what is often conceived as its sister-concept, the sublime, in order to ascertain whether their conflation within a Jungian theoretical framework is warranted, or whether these terms designate different types of experiences or psychodynamic processes.[5]

As we shall see, it is not easy to clarify the difference between theoretical terms that seek to define something ineffable or unfamiliar to our everyday rational sensibilities; subsequently, their juxtaposition often seems warranted. Therefore, in order to tease out the differences among the sublime, the numinous, and the uncanny, within the context of the dynamics of the Jungian psyche, I shall call on the help of architectural discourse, which has traditionally adopted these terms to describe the powerful affects buildings can generate in us. By turning to architectural discourse, I will attempt to spotlight how these terms have, by contrast, been embezzled within post-Jungian studies and in the so-called 'green' psychologies that are beginning to converse in Jungian ways of thinking. What I am concerned about is how supposedly 'sacred' or 'profound' terms such as 'numinous' and 'sublime' are pressed all too quickly into arguments that seek to prioritise the natural world over and above the humanly constructed or built environment, on the assumption that nature is the more valuable resource for our psychological and spiritual health.

The idealised natural world

The natural environment is often idealised within Jungian studies as something intrinsically valuable, something to protect, cultivate and venerate. To counteract our desire for the metaphysical realm, which is out of touch with our instinctual, embodied selves, Nietzsche's Zarathustra proclaims the 'death of God' and teaches us to '*remain true to the earth*' (Nietzsche 1883, prologue, 3). According to Nietzsche, we are creative only if we reflect nature's own rhythms of death and rebirth. We find echoes of this within Jungian and post-Jungian studies. There we are often told that it is within the *natural* world that we find ourselves better off, more relaxed, and more in 'tune' with life. It is apparently beneath the night sky, within the sublime forests, hilltops, uncanny deserts and cascading waterfalls that we encounter the numinous and find ourselves spiritually replenished.[6] The city, by contrast, is more often than not regarded as a place of corruption, trauma and disturbance to psychic life. The city, we are told, has even created its very own anxiety disorders, such as 'agoraphobia' (the fear of the marketplace). From city to nature we must flee,[7] and the natural land we must save from the encroaching infections of the building site. Yet, is it fair to prioritise the natural landscape in this way? Can we not also find our 'true' selves reflected in urban cityscapes? After all, didn't Jung himself discover the very 'healing function' of the psyche within the city square at the centre of the filthy, dark city streets of a dream-place called Liverpool (Jung 1961, pp. 223–4)?

It is within the rapidly developing 'green' discourses of environmental concern – known by such various names as ecopsychology, green psychology, spiritual ecology, environmental aesthetics, and so on – to which post-Jungian reflection is aptly positioned to contribute, that we find a tendency to promote an unhelpful split between the natural and the built environments.[8] We are often told that the natural world, in its all its spiritual green glory is being vanquished, raped and appropriated by urbanisation and human-orientated, power-hungry interests. Theodore Roszak, in his celebrated work of ecopsychology, *The Voice of the Earth* (2002), implements Wilheim Reich's phrase 'body armour' in his description of the city. Body armour is, Roszak says, a 'neurotic defense mechanism that cuts us off from spontaneous vitality and sensuous intimacy'. He goes on to describe the city as 'a collective "body armor" of our culture, a pathological effort to distance us from close contact with the natural continuum from which we evolve' (Roszak 2002, p. 220). The built environment is thus nothing less than a pathological symptom, of what he calls 'city pox', a disease of our ego: delusions of grandeur, omnipotence and megalomania (ibid., pp. 216, 217).

With the birth of the city we can see the marks of human will graven on the face of the planet, a message of mighty structures that seems to declare to the heavens, 'See, we are here. Take notice of us!' (Roszak 2002, p. 216).

The city is, he says, a 'theatrical arena that magnifies the stature of its occupants and multiplies their energy' (ibid.). In contrast to the city, for Roszak and other commentators of so-called 'green discourses', the natural world is the innocent Other that embodies the healing powers that we neglect through our ego's blind desire to appropriate what it can for its own arbitrary ends.

What do they identify as the underlying cause for our monstrous neglect and defensive stance towards nature? It is, we are often told, found within our impoverished and overly reductive Western epistemological outlook, which finds psyche and all that can be considered meaningful enclosed within the boundaries of our human minds. Two thousand years of philosophising with the likes of Plato, Descartes and Kant have persuaded us to locate the source of meaning within our minds and not therefore within the natural, phenomenal world out there. Nature, as something out there, is a means to our ends. More radically, it is nothing more than a thought that *we* have, and not a source of meaning or an end in itself. The building, as an edifice and extension of ego, is therefore a symbol of our self-ordained authority of meaning-making over and above the natural world.

What is the solution for saving nature from neglect? It is to overcome this dualism by acknowledging psyche as also *out there* and giving nature back its rightful position and autonomy. If this can be done, we are told nature will become re-enchanted and numinous once again and regain its capacity to engender meaning and affect beyond our own projections of meaning on to it.

While this is all well and good, I can't forgo the perception that the so-called 'green discourses' are themselves guilty of sustaining dualistic thinking in the face of their very attempts to undermine it. They do this by forging a dichotomy between the denigrated sick city of ego-construction and the (idealised) natural world that is sublime and sacred. In other words, if psyche is to be found *out there*, is it not also to be found in the bricks and mortar of the dirtiest polluted cities? Can we not find the sublime in the tarmac road to the supermarket, or the numinous housed within the 1960s tower-block apartments of the decrepit city? I believe we can.[9]

We find psyche postulated *out there* within the world and beyond our projections in Jung's later writings, for instance in his attempts to delineate the notion of synchronicity where events in the mind correspond to those in physical matter. We also find similar thinking in the works of James Hillman, who calls upon us to embrace soul in *all* things: 'with each thing, God-given things of nature *and man-made things of the street*' (Hillman 1992, p. 101; italics are mine). In Hillman, psychotherapy is not simply a matter between people, but also between people and the environments in which they find themselves. Hillman includes the built environment in his deliberations,[10] but he tends to do so in derogatory or pathological terms, describing, for instance, buildings that are 'anorexic' or 'catatonic' (1982, p. 104), and skyscrapers that simply reflect back to us what we want to see through their mirror-plated glass (ibid., cf. Sardello 1986, p. 72). Although Hillman concedes that soul is present within the built and constructed world, he still privileges the natural world as the site for psyche, with city spaces more often than not regarded as sites of disease and illness. Thus, he notes,

> The 'bad' place I am 'in' may refer not only to a depressed mood or an anxious state of mind; it may refer to a sealed-up office tower where I work, a set-apart suburban subdivision where I sleep, or the jammed freeway on which I commute between the two.
>
> (Hillman 1995, p. xx)

Jung too alludes – albeit often implicitly – to buildings as sites for psyche and psychological healing. I mentioned Jung's dream of the dark dream-city streets of Liverpool that form a radial network of interconnected parts, like an urban mandala, around the central city square, where Jung encounters what he calls 'the healing function of the psyche' (Jung 1961, pp. 223–4). There are other references, including his dream of a house in which he finds himself descending several storeys, which represent progressively older architectural styles, from eighteenth-century Rococo, to Medieval and Roman, and finally arriving at the ground of the psyche itself represented by the cellar of a prehistoric cave dwelling (Jung 1961, pp. 182–5). Jung's self-designed and self-built tower at Bollingen was a building that represented his individuation process in concrete form (Jung 1961, pp. 250–3). Architectural imagery abounds in Jung's writings, and, as I have argued elsewhere (Huskinson 2008), Jung's building motifs appear in his writings more often than not on those occasions where he recounts moments of personal enlightenment, such as the discovery of new aspects of the personality or a decision to enlist a new line of thinking or approach in his theorising. In Jung's buildings, we therefore find more than mere ego; we find the ego in transformation, the psyche very much *out there*.

Citation of Jung's architectural allusions are sufficient to dispel the dichotomy between the built environment that is ego-centred and sick, and the natural environment that is the site for psyche and healing.

The dichotomy between built and natural environment is tenuous at best, and is one that cannot be sustained. Furthermore, when we turn to the traditional philosophical discourses that explicate the meaning of the 'sacred' notions upon which these green discourses depend to claim primacy for the natural world, we find that they themselves acknowledge the built environment as no less a site for the sublime and numinous.

Here I am concerned with three interrelated issues: first, the difference between the sublime and numinous; second, how these terms reflect different psychodynamic concerns and describe different relationships between ego-consciousness and the unconscious; and third, how their difference relates to the built environment, thereby challenging the proposition that nature has exclusive rights as *the* site for experiences of spiritual or psychological transformation.

I will argue that the term 'sublime' refers to the ego's response to an (incomprehensible) object, not to a property of nature itself. Nature is not sublime, we are. An appeal to the sublime is thus an appeal to a subjective response of a psyche and is exclusively within the mind – *in here*. The green thinkers refer to the city as the place of ego-projection, but the sublime natural world is too. The numinous, by contrast, refers to an incomprehensible (religious) object that is beyond projection. It acts on us and calls us into question. It thus opens up the possibilities of meaning *out there*. As Rudolf Otto in his seminal work on the numinous – *The Idea of the Holy* (1917) – makes clear, the built environment is no less a vehicle for numinous experience than nature. Therefore, the numinous, like the sublime, does not discriminate between the natural and the built worlds.

A practical implication of my argument is that if architects can identify those principles of design that evoke the sublime or numinous, they have the potential to build more inspiring, imaginatively rousing, and even 'mentally healthy' buildings – that is to say, they can construct buildings that facilitate the ego's engagement with the unconscious. Architects may thus be able to build dwelling places for the psyche – places that even the most rampant of ecopsychologists would be keen to endorse and inhabit.

What does it mean for something such as a tree or building to be sublime or numinous or uncanny?

As noted earlier, the uncanny connotes the eerily familiar, and both the sublime and numinous denote an elevated, higher state that inspires awe, fascination and terror. Each notion has a complicated history of different meanings and usages, and each has at times overlapped in meaning, so that clear definitions are tricky at best.

The psychological use of the term 'uncanny' is commonly attributed first to Ernst Jentsch's essay, '*Zur Psychologie des Unheimlichen*' ('On the Psychology of the Uncanny') (1906), where it is portrayed as a feeling of intellectual uncertainty. The term was popularised a decade later by Freud in his essay, '*Das Unheimliche*' (The Uncanny') (1919), where it acquired its distinctive characteristic as something not simply mysterious or weird, but strangely familiar.[11] The word 'sublime' entered the English language at the end of the fourteenth century with a specific alchemical meaning pertaining to purification and elevation. We know Jung was keen to align his psychological model with the alchemical process, but Freud also developed from this specifically alchemical meaning of 'sublime' his psychoanalytic term 'sublimation'.[12] By the seventeenth century, 'the sublime' came to denote spiritual and metaphysical qualities. And it was at this time that the notion of the numinous entered the English language to denote the power or presence of the divine,[13] thereby giving rise to the possibility of their confusing overlap, and likewise, for instilling the notion that the sublime might also be a property of an object itself, *out there*, and not simply an experience of the subject. In the following two centuries, the sublime developed in contrast to the numinous, in secular ways, to become the vehicle for aesthetic and philosophical theories on the evocation of awesome experiences, popularised by such figures as Edmund Burke (in *A Philosophical Enquiry into the Origin of our Ideas of the Sublime and the Beautiful*, 1757), and Immanuel Kant (in 'Observations on the Feeling of the Beautiful and Sublime', 1764, and *Critique of the Power of Judgment*, 1790). In 1917, when the notion of the numinous received wide recognition in Rudolf Otto's attempt to redefine religion away from the prevailing Kantian perspective, which had reduced religion to ideals of reason and morality, the sublime became fused with the numinous in Otto's attempt to convey the terrifying yet fascinating non-rational experiences of God.

According to Otto, the uncanny, sublime and numinous are an historical series of different stimuli or ways in which we have come to experience the affects of Otherness. The idea of the numinous is innate within us; it is 'implanted', Otto says, within the human spirit and has the potential to be released. Yet, historically it could not be 'woken' all at once. It has required a series of more primitive and 'natural' experiences that have something in common with the numinous to set it free. In its more primitive form, the human mind has been able to experience first feelings of uncanny dread, and then, as we have evolved to become more rational, we have unlocked the capacity to experience the sublime. Only later, further along in our rational development, have we been able to experience the numinous in its full potential as a religious category, of the holy.[14]

In Otto's account, the numinous is a religious concept that designates the total Otherness of divinity, and as such it can only be talked about in analogous terms – that is to say, by making comparisons within those 'natural moments of consciousness' (Otto 1917, p. 27) that we readily experience and are able to conceptualise. Two terms that he uses to describe certain features of the numinous are the 'sublime' (in the Kantian sense of the term) and the 'uncanny'. When Jung talks about Otto's notion of the numinous, as he did from the mid-1930s to characterise an experience of the unconscious, we can assume that he is also talking about, by way of analogy, the Kantian notion of the sublime.

The murky overlap between the terms is apparent in Otto's own writings on the numinous, on such occasions where he notes, for instance, that the notion of the uncanny encapsulates every aspect of the numinous (Otto 1917, p. 40), and his assertion that the experience of the numinous in developed religions can still evoke the feelings of uncanny dread alongside the sublime, whereby uncanny dread comes to stand for the *tremendum* aspect of the numinous, and the sublime for its *mysterium* characteristic (Otto 1917, pp. 17, 63).[15] The overlap in meaning of the three terms is perhaps best illustrated in Otto's explanation of Gothic architecture, which for him is the 'most numinous' of the arts (Otto 1917, p. 67). Although numinous, Otto asserts, the peculiar impressiveness of Gothic consists in its sublimity *and* sense of 'magic' (Otto 1917, p. 67). This 'magic' he describes as the 'shudder of the uncanny' (cf. Otto 1917, pp. 117–19). Otto claims that we can clearly tell the difference between this uncanny magic and the numinous by looking at what he calls 'the splendid plate', or illustration, of the tower of the Minster of Ulm that Wilhelm Worringer – a German art historian and critic and a contemporary of Otto – includes in his book, *Formprobleme der Gotik* (1911) (*Form Problems of the Gothic*). This tower (Figure 5.1) Otto says, is 'emphatically not' uncanny ('magical'), and, as an example of Gothic architecture, it is 'more' 'than the effect of sublimity'. 'It is', he says, '*numinous*' (Otto 1917, p. 68). However, if we compare this image with, say, the plate of Reims Cathedral (Figure 5.2) that Worringer also includes in his book to explain the powerful effects of Gothic architecture, or with images he doesn't include of other Gothic cathedrals such as that at Cologne (Figure 5.3), which exemplifies for Worringer the purest kind of Gothic architecture (German Gothic), we find the distinction that Otto seeks to convey between the sublime and numinous not at all clear. Or, indeed, if we compare Otto's numinous building with one that Goethe (who influenced Worringer's thinking on this matter[16]) celebrated precisely for its sublime effect – that is, the cathedral at Strasbourg (Figure 5.4), we find the difference between the sublime and numinous far from

Figure 5.1 The tower of the Minster of Ulm (Worringer, *Formprobleme der Gotik*, 1911, p. 40, creative commons attribution)

Figure 5.2 Reims Cathedral (Worringer, *Formprobleme der Gotik*, 1911, p. 35, creative commons attribution)

obvious. Most cryptically, we find Otto on one occasion contradicting his earlier stance, by stating that the relationship between the sublime and numinous is actually much closer than a mere analogy of feeling: the sublime is rather an authentic conceptualisation of the numinous in its fully developed state (which is to say, the 'holy') (Otto 1917, pp. 45–6, 63). Sadly, Otto does not elaborate on this curious comment beyond noting that they are similar in 'structure' in that they both have in them 'something mysterious' and are both 'at once daunting, and yet again singularly attracting'(Otto 1917, p. 42), yet they will always remain, he says, absolutely different in kind (Otto 1917, pp. 44, 24).

Figure 5.3 Cologne Cathedral (Max Hasak, 1911, creative commons attribution)

Figure 5.4 Strasbourg Cathedral (author unknown, *c.*1890, creative commons attribution)

The psychodynamic difference between the numinous, sublime and uncanny

The difficulty in differentiating the meaning of these terms may be resolved by a Jungian reading that sees the difference between the sublime and numinous as pertaining to the ego's encounter with and assimilation of different kinds of unconscious material – that is to say, the sublime best describes the ego's experience of the personal unconscious, while the numinous describes the ego's encounter with the collective unconscious. In such a reading, the ego is involved in similar psychodynamic processes in its encounter with either realm of the unconscious, but the different nuances of each realm initiate a different *kind* of experience in the ego. In the experience of the sublime, the ego integrates material from the personal unconscious, material that is knowable, has been repressed and is uncannily familiar. The ego is thereby confronted with contents from the psyche within, a psyche *in here*. By contrast, experience of the numinous is one in which the ego engages with material from the collective unconscious, material that is archetypal and is not of the subject's individual personality and has not therefore been repressed and subject to projection. The numinous is an experience of that which has come from the autonomous collective realm, *out there*. The division between the two is not phenomenologically apparent, as we have seen in the similar architectural illustrations – which is to say, the ego cannot immediately tell the difference between an affective experience of a personal or collective nature. Both are *fascinating* – a term that Otto uses to describe both the sublime and the numinous.

To clarify further, I shall now briefly outline the three terms – uncanny, sublime and numinous – to elucidate their psychodynamic relevance and differences.

According to Otto, the uncanny describes the first stirrings and primitive awareness of the numinous, or, as we might say, the ego's awareness of the effects of the unconscious. We turn to Freud's essay, 'The Uncanny', for further analysis of a psychodynamic meaning of this term.[17]

For Freud, the uncanny denotes an awareness of a repressed psychic content that has been projected into an object and experienced as something strangely familiar. It describes, in Jungian terms, an encounter with the shadow. Such encounters may prove overwhelming to the ego or may be mildly irritating. They may be, as Otto aptly states, a 'mere fleeting shadow passing across his mood' (Otto 1917, p. 16).

If the uncanny describes the effect of the repressed unconscious on the ego, the sublime, in Otto's Kantian use of the term, describes the process that can follow these stirrings when the ego responds to the demands of the unconscious Other. Kant describes the experience of the sublime in two stages. First, it is a negative experience, when the subject encounters something astonishingly vast, difficult or obscure, and feels powerless to represent or make sense of what appears to the imagination and senses as wholly unrepresentable. This feeling of powerlessness and limitation before something seemingly greater than oneself induces further negative emotional responses – terror, pain and anxiety (Kant 1790, §27). In psychodynamic terms, this is the moment when the ego is confronted with the enormity of the unconscious contents before it. In Jungian terms, the ego is seized and paralysed by the complex. Yet, just as we are forced to acknowledge our limitations and failure to gather the experience into a single conceptual unity, Kant claims we discover 'within us a power of resistance of quite another kind, which gives us courage to be able to measure ourselves against the seeming omnipotence' (Kant 1790, §285: 261). It is at this point that the positive aspect of the sublime is triggered, wherein the mind releases, what Kant refers to as 'stronger outflow of vital powers' (Kant 1790, §23: 245). It is then that the mind's capacity for reason intervenes in the experience and presents 'the idea of totality or infinitude' (Kant 1790, §27: 258). The subject is overwhelmed and feels elation with an 'enlargement of mind' as the capacity for reason empowers consciousness and affirms our significance as moral beings capable of reason and possessing a value that surpasses the terror inspired by the object (Kant 1790, §26: 255). The sublime is a subjective category. '"Sublimity"', Kant writes, 'does not reside in any of the things of nature, but only in our mind [. . .]. Everything that provokes this feeling in us, including the might of nature which challenges our strength, is then, improperly called the sublime' (Kant 1790, §28: 264). The sublime is, for Kant, the experience of the infinite human power of reason that overcomes and surpasses the human capacity of imagination or sensibility. When imagination is confronted with an object that is too vast in its magnitude or too dynamic for it to comprehend, the rational capacity of the mind comes to the rescue to contain and appropriate it. In Jungian terms, the positive moment of the sublime describes the ego's confrontation with the personal unconscious, and the subsequent integration of unconscious material into ego conscious. Thus, the experience, daunting and *uncanny* at first, turns to elation as the ego-personality experiences its expansion and enjoys its new position within a more objective and moral disposition, with the withdrawal of its shadow projections. The ego dissolves the experience without remainder, so to speak, and is able to understand it fully once the projection is withdrawn. Thus the sublime comes to an end in ego integration.

The triumphant assertion of the subject's sense of control over the sublime designates the overcoming of repression and of the once terrifying feelings experienced in the presence of the projection. The numinous, by contrast, sustains the alterity of the Other, making its unapproachability absolute and preserving the uneasy feelings this evokes in the subject. The ego does not dissolve it. While the Kantian sublime marks that all-too-human moment when we recoil back into ourselves in order to negotiate and finally appropriate the repressed and projected as our own, the numinous calls upon us to sustain our gaze at that which continues to exceed our capacity to understand, to explain or to integrate. The numinous and sublime share similar negative moments of ego-powerlessness in the face of the Other, an experience Otto describes as 'creaturely consciousness' (Otto 1917, pp. 8–11, 18–23), wherein we find ourselves 'utterly cowed and cast down', rendering us mute and dumb (Otto 1917, p. 31). Sublime and numinous experiences likewise share similar feelings of elation, and an 'impulse' of fascination that causes us, as Otto says of the numinous 'object', to 'turn to it, nay even to make it somehow our own' (Otto 1917, p. 31). But, unlike the sublime, the numinous 'object' evades our appropriation of it and our understanding. Unlike the sublime, the elation of the numinous is not an effect of our having withdrawn and subsequently integrated our projections into ego-consciousness. The numinous religious 'object' resides beyond our projections. It was never ours to repress or to project. It is the Other outside us, which affects us by calling our ego-personality and experience of ourselves as a cohesive, unified whole into question. The numinous is thus, as Jung asserts, an experience of the archetypal, autonomous, (and non-moral[18]) collective unconscious impinging on our ego-world.

Conclusion

The green discourses would do well to avoid adopting the sublime as a key term in support of their arguments,[19] for the sublime denotes the ego's triumph over nature in its superior capacity for reason. As Kant asserts, 'Nature is not sublime, we are'. To experience nature as sublimely magnificent is – in echo of the ecopsychologists' grievance with the egoistic city-structure – simply to experience the projection of our magnificent minds. Both nature and city as sublime are locations for the triumph of ego. Perhaps it would be more apposite for the green thinkers to regard nature as numinous to avoid such charges of ego-projection. However, to do so would be to characterise nature as essentially 'religious' (thereby charging ecopsychology with pantheism) and, furthermore, the humanly constructed or built environment for Otto is, as we have seen, no less a site for the numinous.[20]

Architectural forms that are described as uncanny, sublime or numinous are describing different capacities to evoke different unconscious experiences. Unfortunately, the very best architects cannot design a building that is numinous rather than sublime. Psyche 'out there' rather than 'in here' designates the numinous site. Yet they can at least design so as to challenge the prevailing presumptions of ego, and thwart the imagination's attempts to order and unify its experiences. I am not referring particularly to those playful attempts of postmodern architecture that seek to amuse or mock our ego-sensibilities, nor to the sublime precepts of vastness and lofty height designated by such classic architects as John Ruskin, but rather to those places that sneak up on us unannounced and enable us to think in a non-directed manner, spaces that encourage us to interact with them, and to play and to think or dream through them.

Although it is unlikely to challenge the green thinkers' opinions about the physical threat of the built world toward nature, the built environment as a site for the sublime challenges their understanding of the symbolic value of buildings and the nature of the ego the building is said to represent. Buildings are not strongholds for the prejudices and lofty ambitions of the ego, as Roszak among others would have us believe, they are rather, more akin to dynamic 'freeholds', so to speak, dynamic sites of the individuating ego that is morally concerned with its own shortcomings.

Notes

1 See, for instance, Clarkson (1997) *On the Sublime in Psychoanalysis, Archetypal Psychology, and Psychotherapy*. There several chapters conflate the terms 'sublime' and 'numinous', assuming them to be identical (e.g. Paris, p. 87; Adler, p. 106).
2 See Bulkeley and Weldon 2011, pp. 249–51.
3 See, for example, the range of self-tanning sprays from L' Oréal, Paris called Sublime Bronze (www.loreal-paris.co.uk/_en/_gb/minisites/solar-expertise/sublime-bronze/index.aspx). This spray-on-sublime purports to enable ladies to 'look natural'. See also the perfume, Iris Nobile Sublime by Acqua Di Parma, described

as 'Timeless elegance' (www.acquadiparma.us/it/home.html). Both websites accessed June 2013.

4 And an English one at that!

5 Elsewhere (Huskinson 2006) I argue that Jung was mistaken in his appropriation of Rudolf Otto's concept of the numinous (a concept Jung himself attributes to Otto) and that he inadvertently refers instead to Otto's concept of the 'holy'. The holy is a different category of experience in which the essentially 'non-rational' experience of the numinous has been rendered purposeful by the consciousness that beholds it. I argued that the essential difference between the 'numinous' and the 'holy' has implications for Jung's thinking about the relationship between ego-consciousness and unconscious. I recommend this paper be read in conjunction with my current discussion.

6 Of the inextricable link between the numinous and mental health, Jung is explicit. In a letter of 20 August 1945 he writes, 'But the fact is that the approach to the numinous is the real therapy and inasmuch as you attain to the numinous experiences you are released from the curse of pathology' (Jung 1945, p. 377). For classic instances of the overt use of 'numinous' as pertaining to the natural world, see Allen Carlson and Arnold Berleant (eds) *The Aesthetics of Natural Environments* (2004), especially those chapters by Berleant, Godlovitch, Hepburn, Saito and Rolston. While Rolston's chapter conflates the sublime and numinous (see p. 192), Godlovitch's chapter alone differentiates between the two. For Godlovitch, the sublime inadequately characterises the natural world as it reveals our human experience of nature and not nature itself. The 'numinous', on the other hand, provides for Godlovitch a more adequate characterisation of nature in its acknowledgement of autonomy and sense of Otherness that are, he maintains, essential to nature.

7 For instance, John Clinebell, in *Ecotherapy: Healing ourselves, healing the earth* (1996) asserts 'the need of city-dwellers to find healing in wilderness'. He argues, 'Entering the wilderness and its microcosms—gardens and parks—gives us an opportunity to reconnect with that instinct and rests our fragile psyches from the exhaustion of trying to stay intact in the civilized world, which is so alien to many of us' (p. 46).

8 As Yi-Fu Tuan asserts in his influential work, *Topophilia: A study of environmental perceptions, attitudes, and values* (1990): 'the virtues of the countryside require their anti-image, the city, for the sharpening of focus, and vice versa' p. 102; 'of city corruption and rural virtue' (p. 108; cf. pp. 103–9).

9 But others think not. For instance, Holmes Rolston III, an environmental philosopher, asserts: 'In the primeval forest humans know the most authentic of wilderness emotions, the sense of the sublime.' But '[b]y contrast, few persons get goose pimples indoors, in art museums, in fashionable shopping centers, or at the city park' (Rolston III 2004, p. 191). Yet, I find it amusing that despite his efforts to deny the built environment its sublimity, he goes on to describe the 'sublime forest' as a building (specifically, a church). He notes in architectural terms that '[t]rees pierce the sky, like cathedral spires. Light filters down, as through stained glass'. He continues, 'In common with churches, forests, like sea and sky, invite transcending the human world and experiencing comprehensive, embracing realm' (Rolston III 2004, p. 193).

10 See, for instance, Hillman 2006. Also note, Hillman 1992, where in contradistinction to Roznak's buildings that announce the power of the human ego in their proclamation, 'See we are here' (2002, p. 216, cited earlier), Hillman acknowledges the power of buildings or 'man made things of the street' to speak to us and thereby announce *themselves* to us through their proclamation, 'Look, here we are', p. 103.

11 There are several historical accounts of the developing meaning and appropriation of the term 'uncanny'. One lucid account is *The Uncanny* (2003) by Nicolas Royle. For particularly good writing on the history of the uncanny and its relationship to architecture, see Anthony Vidler's *The Architectural Uncanny* (1994). For enlightening discussion on the many uses and historical development of the 'sublime', I recommend Philip Shaw's introductory work *The Sublime* (2005).

12 See Cohn and Miles (1977) for a fascinating discussion on the relationship between 'sublime' and 'sublimation'. They note that both terms pertain to the notion of going 'up', while, curiously, the related psychoanalytic term 'subliminal' connotes a going 'down'. The etymological Latin roots of both 'sublime' and 'subliminal' are *sub-* plus *limin*, which, in the case of 'subliminal' means 'below the threshold', and for 'sublime' means 'up to the lintel'; in other words, architectural terms pertaining to the door way. From the etymological roots of 'sublime' and 'subliminal' Cohn and Miles infer 'not only that the Romans had the same term for lintel and threshold, but also that the civilisation which invented the arch had one word to mean both *down* and *up*' (Cohn and Miles 1977, p. 289).

13 The first documented use of the term 'numinous' in English is Reverend Nathaniel Ward's *The Simple Cobler of Aggawam in America*, published in 1647 in London, by 'J. D. & R. I. for STEPHEN BOWTELL, at the signe of the Bible in Popes Head-Alley'. Ward writes, 'The Will of a King is very numinous; it hath a kinde of vast universality in it [. . .]' For the complete work see: www.gutenberg.org/files/34974/34974.txt (accessed June 2013).

14 Jung himself comments on our modern-day positioning within this developmental schema, when he repeatedly laments our over-reliance on reason, which has, he claims, led to our incapacity to experience the numinous (Jung 1962, par. 582; cf. par. 581; 1948, par. 274).

15 With similar ambiguity, Otto speaks metaphorically of the close-knit relationship between 'sublime' and 'numinous' as 'vibrating chords of the numinous along with the note of the sublime' (Otto 1917, p. 69).

16 Worringer cites Goethe talking about the sublime: 'These words of Goethe could stand as motto for our whole study' (Worringer 1911, p. 67).

17 Freud here alludes to the sublime (*Erhaben*) in the Kantian sense.

18 Otto states that the numinous is that 'which can be in itself ethically neutral' (Otto 1917, p. 5); and Jung asserts: 'the unconscious [. . .] as far as moral sense, aesthetic taste, and intellectual judgement go, is completely neutral' (Jung 1934, par. 329)

19 Especially those that dialogue with or appeal to Jungian thought, for Jung, in his allusion to Otto's notion of the numinous, is, as I have asserted, an appeal to a Kantian reading of the sublime.

20 Otto comments rather eloquently on the impartiality of the numinous to natural and built environments alike: 'The semi-darkness that glimmers in vaulted halls, or beneath the branches of a lofty forest glade, strangely quickened and stirred by the mysterious play of half-lights, has always spoken eloquently to the soul, and the builders of temples, mosques, churches have made full use of it' (Otto 1917, p. 68).

References

Adler, Gerhard (1997) 'Reflections on chance, fate and synchronicity', in Petrūska Clarkson (ed.), *On the Sublime: In psychoanalysis, archetypal psychology and psychotherapy*, London: Whurr Publishers, pp. 96–108.

Berleant, Arnold (2004) 'The aesthetics of art and nature', in Carlson, Allen and Berleant (eds) *The Aesthetics of Natural Environments*, New York and Plymouth: Broadview Press, pp. 76–88.

Bulkeley, Kelly and Weldon, Clodagh (eds) (2011) *Teaching Jung*, Oxford: Oxford University Press.

Burke, Edmund (1957) *A Philosophical Enquiry into the Origin of our Ideas of the Sublime and the Beautiful*. See recent edition: Adam Phillips (ed.) Oxford World's Classics, Oxford: Oxford University Press, 2008.

Carlson, Allen and Berleant (eds) (2004) *The Aesthetics of Natural Environments*, New York and Plymouth: Broadview Press.

Clarkson, Petrūska (ed.) (1997) *On the Sublime: In psychoanalysis, archetypal psychology and psychotherapy*, London: Whurr Publishers.

Clinebell, John (1996) *Ecotherapy: Healing ourselves, healing the earth*, Philadelphia, PA: Haworth Press.

Cohn, Jan and Miles, Thomas, H. (1977) 'The Sublime: In alchemy, aesthetics, and psychoanalysis', *Modern Philology*, vol. 74, no.3 (February 1977), pp. 289–304.

Freud, Sigmund (1919) '(Das Unheimliche'/'The uncanny' in *Standard Edition*, vol. 17, pp. 219–56.

Godlovitch, Stan (2004) 'Icebreakers: Environmentalism and natural aesthetics', in Carlson, Allen and Berleant (eds) *The Aesthetics of Natural Environments*, New York and Plymouth: Broadview Press, pp. 108–26.

Hauke, Christopher (1997) 'The phallus, alchemy and Christ: Jungian analysis and the sublime', in Petrūska Clarkson (ed.), *On the Sublime: In psychoanalysis, archetypal psychology and psychotherapy*, London: Whurr Publishers, pp. 123–44.

Hepburn, Ronald (2004) 'Landscape and metaphysical imagination', in Carlson, Allen and Berleant (eds) *The Aesthetics of Natural Environments*, New York and Plymouth: Broadview Press, pp. 127–40.

Hillman, James (1992) '*Anima Mundi*: Return of the soul to the world', in *The Thought of the Heart and the Soul of the* World, 5th edn, pp. 89–130.

Hillman, James (1995) 'A psyche the size of the earth: A psychological foreword', in Theodore Roszak, Mary E. Gomes and Allen D. Kanner (eds) *Ecopsychology: Restoring the earth, healing the mind,* Berkeley, CA and London: Sierra Club Books, pp. xvii–xxiii.

Hillman, James (1996) 'Interiors in the design of the city: The ceiling', in Robert Sardello and Gail Thomas (eds) *Stirrings of Culture: Essays from the Dallas Institute*, Dallas, TX: Dallas Institute Publications, pp. 78–84.

Hillman, James (2006) *City & Soul*, Robert J. Leaver (ed.), Putnam, CT: Spring Publications.

Huskinson, Lucy (2006) 'Holy, Holy, Holy: the misappropriation of the numinous in Jung, in Ann Casement and David Tacey (eds) *The Idea of the Numinous: Contemporary Jungian and psychoanalytic perspectives*, London and New York: Routledge, pp. 200–12.

Huskinson, Lucy (2008) 'Archetypal dwelling, building individuation', in Susan Rowland (ed.) *Psyche and the Arts: Jungian approaches to music, architecture, literature, painting, and film*, London and New York: Routledge, pp. 35–44.

Jentsch, Ernst (1906) 'Zur Psychologie des Unheimlichen', *Psychiatrisch-Neurologische Wochenschrift,* vol 8, no. 22 (25 August 1906), pp. 195–8; and vol 8, no. 23 (1 September 1906), pp. 203–5.

Jung, Carl (1934) 'The practical use of dream analysis', in *Collected Works*, vol. 16.

Jung, Carl (1945) *Letters*, G. Adler and A. Jaffé (eds), in 2 volumes, Princeton, NJ: Princeton University Press.

Jung, Carl (1948) 'A psychological approach to the dogma of the trinity', *Collected Works*, vol.11, pars. 169–295.

Jung, Carl (1961) *Memories, Dreams, Reflections*, Richard and Clara Winston (trans.) (1995), London: Fontana Press.

Jung, Carl (1962) 'Symbols and the interpretation of dreams', *Collected Works,* vol. 18, pars. 416–607.

Kant, Immanuel (1764) 'Observations on the feeling of the beautiful and sublime'. See recent edition: Patrick Frierson and Paul Guyer (eds and trans.) (2011) *Observations on the Feeling of the Beautiful and Sublime and Other Writings*, Cambridge Texts in the History of Philosophy, Cambridge: Cambridge University Press, pp. 11–64. See also Kant's annotations on his essay 'Remarks in the *Observations on the Feeling of the Beautiful and Sublime* (1964–5), pp. 65–204.

Kant, Immanuel (1790) *Critique of the Power of Judgment*. See recent edition: Paul Guyer (ed. and trans.) (2011) *Critique of the Power of Judgment*, The Cambridge Edition of the Works of Immanuel Kant, Cambridge: Cambridge University Press. Citations are to section and paragraph number.

L'Oréal, Paris, Sublime Bronze, www.loreal-paris.co.uk/_en/_gb/minisites/solar-expertise/sublime-bronze/index.aspx, accessed August 2012.

Nietzsche, Friedrich (1883) *Thus Spoke Zarathustra*, trans. R.J. Hollingdale (1974), Middlesex: Penguin Classics.

Otto, Rudolf (1917) *The Idea of the Holy: An inquiry into the non-rational factor in the idea of the divine and its relation to the rational*, J.W. Harvey (trans.) (1968), Oxford: Oxford University Press.

Paris, Ginette (1997) 'Everyday epiphanies', in Petrūska Clarkson (ed.), *On the Sublime: In psychoanalysis, archetypal psychology and psychotherapy*, London: Whurr Publishers, pp. 85–95.

Rolston III, Holmes (2004) 'The aesthetic experience of forests', Carlson, Allen and Berleant (eds) *The Aesthetics of Natural Environments*, New York and Plymouth: Broadview Press, pp. 182–96.

Roszak, Theodore (2002) *The Voice of the Earth: An exploration of ecopsychology* (new edn). Grand Rapids, MI: Phanes Press.

Royle, Nicholas (2003) *The Uncanny*, Manchester: Manchester University Press.

Saito, Yuriko (2004) 'Appreciating nature on its own terms', in Allen Carlson and Arnold Berleant (eds) *The Aesthetics of Natural Environments*, New York and Plymouth: Broadview Press, pp. 141–55.

Sardello, Robert (1986) 'A note on new and old buildings', in *Stirrings of Culture: Essays from the Dallas Institute*, Dallas, TX: Dallas Institute Publications, pp. 71–4.

Shaw, Philip (2005) *The Sublime*, London and New York: Routledge.

The Times (2012) 'England's 3–2 victory over Sweden', Sports section, Saturday 16 June.

Tuan, Yi-Fu (1990) *Topophilia: A study of environmental perceptions, attitudes, and values*, New York: Columbia University Press.

Vidler, Anthony (1994) *The Architectural Uncanny: Essays in the modern unhomely* (new edn), Cambridge, MA: MIT Press.

Worringer, Wilhelm (1911) *Formprobleme der Gotik*, Form Problems of the Gothic, authorised American edition (1918), New York: G.E. Stechert & Co.

6

JUNGIAN CONVERSATIONS WITH FEMINISM AND SOCIETY IN JAPAN

Konoyu Nakamura

Introduction

Hayao Kawai was the first Japanese Jungian analyst. Thanks to him, analytical psychology came to influence in Japan not only psychotherapy but also clinical psychology and other academic fields, for example, mythology, education and sociology. Kawai and his followers published numerous books on Jungian and analytical psychology, and the trend even became a 'cultural fashion' in the 1980s (Igeta 1998, p. 351).

Many Jungian analysts and Jungian-oriented psychotherapists, including myself, obtained their qualifications at graduate schools, and became involved in training as counsellors or psychotherapists (referred to as 'certificated clinical psychologists'), using Jungian training techniques in part. There are now 23,400 of us, the largest such clinical group in Japan (Otsuka 2012, p. 7), so we can say that Japan is a place where Jungian psychology has bloomed.

However, recently, the trend has started to decline and Japan is no longer a haven for Jungians. Since the 1990s, evidence-based psychologists have been pre-eminent. For example, Haruhiko Shimoyama says:

> In Japan, since the psychodynamic schools of the 80s, analytical psychology has greatly influenced clinical psychology, and psychotherapy has dominated Japanese clinical psychology. Psychotherapy, of course, needs strict training grounded on its own theory, and there are only a few authentic psychotherapists among 'certificated clinical psychologists.' Actually, most of them are involved in general supportive activities as counsellors. [. . .] Consequently, the model for clinical psychology in Japan is counselling. There are few clinical psychologists who relate to experimental psychology or who work as cognitive behavioural psychotherapists. [. . .] This distorted situation disturbs the sound development of Japanese psychology.
>
> (2004, p. 297)

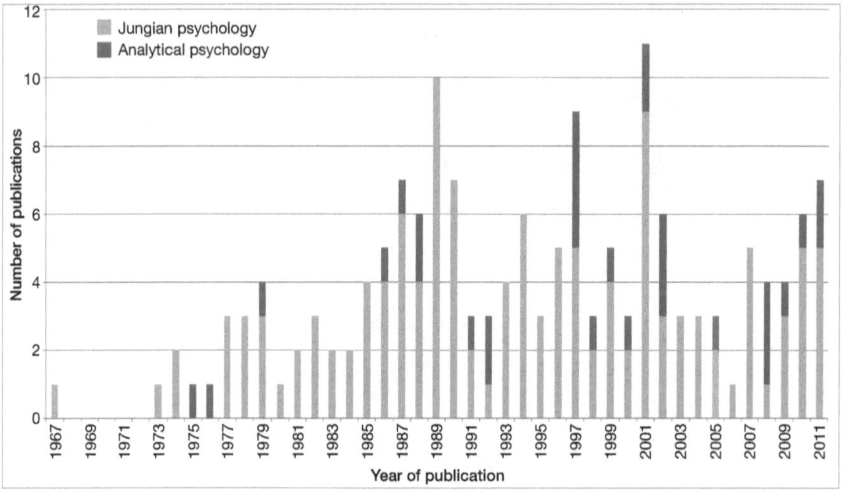

Figure 6.1 The number of annual publications listed under 'Jungian psychology' or 'analytical psychology' on the website of the National Diet Library of Japan

As Figures 6.1 and 6.2 show, academic interest in Jungian psychology has been decreasing among Japanese clinical psychologists. Yet it seems to me that in this crisis, Jungian psychology can survive as a clinical theory. As a Jungian-oriented psychotherapist, I am concerned about the future of Jungian psychology in Japan as an effective clinical theory. Although I know there are many ways to develop Jungian psychology in future (for example, through conversations with cognitive behaviour therapy or narrative therapy), I would like to clarify some problems it faces from a feminist viewpoint, and to try to search for a new therapeutic approach that can adapt to a rapidly changing society.

Jung and feminism

Jung said, 'There is no problem of "woman in Europe" without man and his world. If she is married, she usually has to depend economically on her husband; if she is unmarried and earning a living, she is working in some profession designed by a man' (1982, p. 58). Susan Rowland has responded to this warily:

> A defining feature of Jung's treatment of gender is his placing of the feminine at the centre of his psychology while at the same time displacing women as social, material and historical beings. As a theorist of the feminine in culture, Jung provides a useful starting

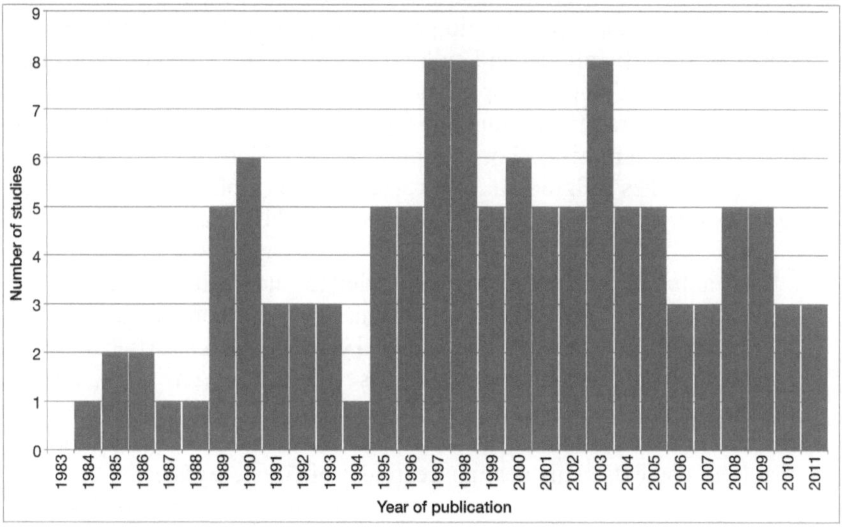

Figure 6.2 The number of annual studies related to analytical psychology published in the *Journal of Japanese Clinical Psychology*

> point, as long as the gender politics and the historical location of his authoritative texts are scrutinized.
>
> (2002, p. 44)

She clarifies the sexism of Jungian theories in her book *Jung, a Feminist Revision*. There she focuses on three Jungian schools – classical, archetypal and developmental. According to Rowland, the classical school tries to follow Jung faithfully, and any feminism generated by it falls into the tradition (ibid., pp. 74–5). Rowland addresses traditional Jungian feminism as goddess feminism, and says:

> These ideas include the exploration of 'the feminine' in symbols and myths, proclaiming the presence of the feminine and masculine in each gender, protesting at the harm done to psyche and culture through repression of the feminine, and an insistence on full individuation for women in analytic practice.
>
> (Rowland 2002, p. 67)

Although Rowland greatly respects these works, she thinks that what they have yet to appreciate is a postmodern, poststructuralist and wider feminist theoretical context (ibid., p. 70). 'Feminist studies gathered momentum as women began to realize that male-authored systems of knowledge of all kinds, in medicine, history, religion, literature, philosophy, psychology, had either omitted or distorted the representation of women' (ibid., p. 73). Furthermore, 'feminism as a wider political and cultural movement became conscious that it could not sustain a single, simple category of "woman"' (ibid., p. 74).

Other critics of traditional Jungian feminism or goddess feminism also question goddess feminism. For example, Kazuo Matsumura, a Japanese scientist who studies religion, takes up Jean Shinoda Bolen's work *Goddess in Everywoman: A New Psychology of Women* (1984), to assert:

> I have a lot of hesitation to acknowledge such attempts at the application of Greek myths to the present age as a scientist, because their scientific neutrality is suspicious. Typology such as Athena as a career woman, Hera as a suffering housewife, Demeter as a devoted mother and Aphrodite as a loving woman, does not consider the original roles of these myths, local differences, cultural diversity, or historical contexts. This is a maltreatment of Greek myths.
>
> (Matsumura 1998, p. 204)

Similarly, Demaris Wehr quotes Edward Whitmont's work *The Symbolic Quest* (1969) to claim 'The squalid life of a prostitute can, for example, take on quasi-romantic overtones and a sacred legitimation when understood in such archetypal terms' (Wehr 1987, p. 116).

Rowland also discusses Jungian feminism in the archetypal and developmental schools, and refers to them as 'Jungian feminisms', and thereby introduces post-Jungian works by such scholars as Andrew Samuels, James Hillman and other disciples of these schools, such as Demaris Wehr and Naomi Goldenberg, who propose ideas far from Jung's grand theory of 'personal myth'.

Of course, Hillman's epoch-making studies revised essential Jungian concepts of the anima and archetype. Hillman says:

> The syndromes (conversion hysteria or raving mania, for example), are relative to the dominance of the culture and the *Zeitgeist*. Syndromes current when Freud began psychoanalysis are less current today; the anima as a syndrome of excessive or inferior feminine traits is less evident as the culture moves toward incorporation of 'typically anima' attitudes into its collective values. We should therefore not identify a *description* of the anima in a rigidly patriarchal, puritanically defensive, extravertedly wilful and unsoulful period of history with her *definition*.
>
> (Hillman 1985, p. 13)

Hillman thus seems to free us from the gender bias in old-fashioned Jungian psychology, and he releases the anima concept from Jung's contra-sexuality, placing it in the psyche of both women and men against their ego. Yet it is apparent that 'archetypal psychology's Jungian feminism does have limitations', and that 'the desire to dissolve the masterful claims of the ego cannot always be received with unalloyed enthusiasm by feminism' (Rowland 2002, p. 78).

Apart from this, Toshio Kawai says, 'there is a possibility that archetypal psychology may be dangerous or impossible in real psychotherapy' (1993, p. 179), and Samuels more clearly notes, 'the archetypal school has been either integrated or eliminated as a clinical entity' (1998, p. 21). As a clinician, I am sorry about that. Yet as Rowland notes, Samuels's work 'contributes to radical analysis of the father-relation in feminist-friendly ways' (2002, pp. 88–9). I want to explore this line of thinking.

Jungian psychology in Japan and feminism

As we have seen, varied feminist revisions of Jungian psychology are going on. Unfortunately, however, it seems to me that discourses on such matters have not yet developed among Japanese Jungians. When Jungian psychology was introduced into Japan in the 1960s and 1970s, its elitism and sexism were obvious. Kawai published one of his most famous books, *Boseisyakai Nihon no Byori* (The Pathology of the Maternal Society of Japan), in 1976. In this book, he mentions night consciousness in a strikingly misogynistic way:

> We adult men see a lot of 'lovely women' and some times even experiences 'romantic love' at a bar we drop in on our way home from work. Under dark light, women are pretty, young, and their talk is so sweet. But if we see the same women with day consciousness with whom we have experienced [sweet love] in night consciousness, how do they look? They are probably around 35, living together with a bartender. Also, they may not be so pretty.
>
> (Kawai 1976, p. 186)

Reading this, we cannot think that he embraced even Jung's limited feminism. In the same book, Kawai asserts that Japan is a maternal society, unlike Western countries:

> Working with clients with school phobia or with *Taijin kyofusho symptoms* found only in Japan, I have recently started to believe that maternal cultural background exists in Japan behind its psychological problems. I think that it is important to establish the ego in these cases, which stem from Japanese maternal culture.
>
> (ibid., p. 8)

He also explains Japanese psychological problems in negative ways related to the maternal or great mother archetype, saying 'Since children are overwhelmed with the strong power of the great mother, they should not go to school' (ibid., p. 41). Regarding such 'mother blaming', Polly Young-Eisendrath critically says:

> Images of the overwhelming and engulfing mother dominate the psychotherapy literature from psychoanalysis to family therapy, and infuse our popular psychology with a 'fear of mother' and a 'wish for mother' which is archetypal, impersonal and extremely troubling for individual women.
>
> (Young-Eisendrath 1984, p. 70)

According to her, 'Mother blaming continues to be one of the most harmful by-products of psychoanalysis' (1993, p. 20), and she concludes: 'the combination of excluding men from mothering roles and attributing inferior human qualities to the female gender constitutes a social problem resulting in a negative mother complex' (1984, p. 72). Unfortunately, we cannot find such a discussion among Japanese Jungians.

However, let's now carefully examine some of Kawai's other thoughts. Following Erich Neumann, Kawai argues that symbolically killing the mother is absolutely necessary as an initiation to establish one's ego, and that most Japanese (men) cannot do it and become *puer eternus.* As a result, he claims, 'Japan is a country with a strong maternal principle. Strictly speaking, Japan is a society of "*puer eternus*" grounded on the maternal principle' (Kawai 1976, p. 24). Kawai and his colleagues made 'the transformation of *Sosa no wo no Mikoto*' their central issue, as seen in the title of their book *Nihonshinwa no Siso Susano-ron* (Thoughts on Japanese Myth: The Theory of *Sosa no wo*) (Kawai *et al.*, 1983). Regarding this work, Midori Igeta, a Japanese sociologist, takes a feminist viewpoint: 'Yoshida mentions that their interest in *Sosa no wo no Mikoto* is related to the "structure of the Japanese psyche". Yet we cannot ignore the fact that what they mean by "Japanese" does not include women, and that they focus on "Japanese men" alone' (1998, p. 341).

On the other hand, compared with Western societies, Kawai asserts the uniqueness of the Japanese ego and society. He maintained that 'Japanese myths create a subtle balance of femininity and masculinity' (1976, p. 32), which he offers as proof that the 'Japanese ego stands on a subtle balance of femininity and masculinity' (ibid., p. 30). We can see such views echoed in the work of Hiroshi Yokoyama, another Japanese Jungian. He also refers to the goddess *Amaterasu-oh-kami* as a symbol of this 'subtle balance':

> We can see a beautiful example of the integration of the upper and lower parts of the psyche in the transformation of *Amaterasu-oh-kami,* in which consciousness maintains a good balance of femininity and masculinity while adapting to circumstance and one's role. In sum,

> the image of *Amaterasu-oh-kami* survived the formative process of Japanese patriarchal society because femininity harmonized with the patriarchal system in Japan, unlike in the West.
>
> (Kawai 1976, pp. 130–1)

Igeta criticizes these ideas, noting how they 'fail to account for the way men severely control women' (1998, pp. 353–4). Shinichi Ankei, another Jungian analyst, also notes how

> Many well-known Japanese authors have insisted that Japanese society is strongly tinged with a matriarchal atmosphere and principles. This assertion leads readers to conclude that the authority and influence of the father is weaker than that of the mother.
>
> (Ankei 1985, p. 38)

Yet he counters that 'Japanese society is extremely male-oriented. One can agree without difficulty to the statement that this country is virtually ruled one-sidedly by men' (1985, p. 41). And 'In spite of the "dominance of the maternal principle," femininity seems to have been strictly repressed and disregarded in Japanese society' (ibid., p. 42). He connects this to the tradition called *Bushi-do* (the way of the warrior): '*Bushi-do* is a specific mixture of Zen-Buddhism and Confucianism, in which the feminine nature is strongly rejected' (ibid., p. 10), and in which 'the collective conscious attitude is one-sidedly masculine' (ibid., p. 43). Regarding the Japanese ego, Shoji Yabuki says, 'they often say that Japanese do not have a firm ego, but people have a very strong ego in Japan. However, it is hard to find their egos due to their collectivity and similarity' (Ankei and Yabuki 1989, p. 206).

Hiroyuki Takao, another Japanese Jungian, deals with the Japanese ego by focusing directly on Japanese collective consciousness:

> Since persona is very important in Japanese society and culture, Japanese collective consciousness has a superior position, directly influencing individual consciousness. Traditionally, even now, blood, the occupations of one's parents, academic achievements, career, appointments, and social status are greatly respected. (omission) Since persona strongly exists in people's psyches, they endeavor to adapt to social needs and they are not interested in the 'formation of their own ego' in western terms.
>
> (Takao 2001, p. 24)

These claims seem to me much more reasonable than Kawai's. Nevertheless, the notions that a negative mother complex causes psychological problems in Japan and that Japan is a matriarchal society or a unique nation in which femininity harmonises with the patriarchal system, unlike in the West, have been popular for a long time and are still alive among Japanese psychologists. As Shimoyama says, in practical terms, analytical psychology has been the mainstream for training 'clinical psychologists'. So many 'clinical psychologists' are more or less influenced by the traditional goddess feminism of Jungian psychology. We can see some evidence of this even in the research of developmental psychologists and family therapists who are more gender sensitive than Jungian ones.

Kiyoko Muto, a developmental psychologist, has explored 102 case studies from 1983 to 1994 in Japanese psychology journals, and found clients in recovery classified in the literature by gender. She points out that while Japanese therapists describe recovery of male clients in diverse ways, they stress femininity and maternity in relation to female clients' recovery. Also, she reports covert pressure in the clinical arena, forcing women to develop their maternity and fostering a tendency to discuss motherhood as separate from other aspects of their lives (1995, p. 207). Similarly, Yoko Nakagama, a family therapist, has surveyed 126 case studies in the *Journal of Japanese Clinical Psychology* (arguably, the most important journal for clinical psychology in Japan), from 1997 to 2002, and she concludes that many Japanese therapists tend to stress maternity development in psychotherapy for those children who are without fathers (2003, p. 188). These research projects show that Japanese psychotherapists tend to focus on the femininity and maternity of women when dealing with their psychological problems. And when they discuss children's problems, they often ignore social contexts, focusing instead on the way that only women have to take responsibility for raising children. According to Nakagama, female therapists exhibit this tendency more than male therapists (2007, p. 16). In short, Japanese therapists, in particular female therapists, are never free from gender bias, which means they covertly encourage or reproduce gender bias in clinical practice. This is a big problem.

Why is it so difficult to have a conversation between Jungian psychology and feminism in Japan?

Andrew Samuels divides the classical school into two subgroups, calling one of them extreme Jungian fundamentalism (1998, p. 21) and says, 'Like all fundamentalism, Jungian fundamentalism desires to control who and what is in or out . . . . Or typology is used to settle complex interpersonal, cultural or social situations in altogether unproductive, oracular ways' (ibid., p. 21). Ever since Kawai's heyday, however, almost all Japanese Jungian analysts obtain their diplomas at the Jungian Institute in Zurich and they belong to the classical school. Most of them accept Kawai's notions of Japan as a maternal society that respects femininity and maternity. Therefore, theoretically, traditional Jungian feminism, goddess feminism and archetypal psychology are welcomed in Japan, but other Jungian feminisms are not.

Samuels also says, 'There is sometimes excessive deference shown in Jungian groups to analysts in general, and senior analysts in particular, deference which it is quite often hard to justify in terms of the productivity and output of those individuals' (ibid., p. 17). In fact, Japan is a very patriarchal society, *not* a maternal one (Nakamura 2010, 2011). Yet the first Jungian generation, including Kawai, was so influential that it appears to me there is a solid hierarchy among Japanese Jungians, and an atmosphere among following generations that makes it difficult to suggest opinions that differ from those of that generation. Shoji Yabuki, a Jungian-oriented psychotherapist says:

> He [Ankei] questions the notion that Japanese society is maternal. He presented his diploma thesis about this theme to the Jung Institute in Zurich. This was a great gateway to obtain a diploma for a Jungian analyst, but he had to take up his courage, because his thesis in a part revised essential theories of Jung and Neumann. Moreover, it radically upset the beliefs of Japanese Jungians or fans of Jungian psychology.
>
> (Ankei and Yabuki 1989, p. 224)

Shoji Muramoto and I have posited four fundamental obstructions to conversations between clinical psychologists, including Jungians, and feminists:

1. Andro-centralism is dominant in Western and Eastern societies and is so commonplace that psychologists also internalise this viewpoint as 'natural'.
2. Since feminist movements have functioned more or less politically, psychologists who respect their academic 'neutrality' have a lot of hesitation to engage with them. Also, clinicians trained in traditional psychodynamic theories are encouraged to be therapeutically 'neutral'.
3. The *a priori* concept of the archetype is presupposed in analytical psychology, and thus gender issues are overlooked in social contexts.
4. Psychological studies and practice as well as all other social activities are grounded on theories founded by men who are not free from andro-centralism. And men almost always play authoritative and leading roles in every arena.

Under such circumstances, there are many difficulties for female psychologists and clinicians to raise their voices and to develop new theories based on their own private and clinical experiences. As a result, although there are substantially more female than male mental health professionals, these women are resigned to accepting misogynistic descriptions by authoritative men (2002, pp. 190–1). In the past, feminist theologians have asked, 'Does religion enforce and perpetuate sex-role stereotypes and the power of men over women?' (Christ and Plaskow 1979, p. 3). We Jungians are now asking the same question. As Samuels has said:

> My enquiry here concerns whether or not we have dealt as well as we should with the well-known problems of Jung's elitism, sexism, racism and anti-Semitism – not in terms of Jung the man, but in terms of us, the Jungian analysts, with our own responsibilities. Not *his* problem, but *our* problem.
>
> (Samuels 1998, p. 25)

In short, if we would like analytical psychology to be helpful and effective for all people, we should never ignore our own gender bias, because no one is free from patriarchal norms.

Jungian psychology for whom?

There is another important problem. The fees for Jungian analysis in Japan are very high, from 10,000 to 20,000 yen (about \$125–\$250) for one session, so the number of people who can work with Jungian analysts possessing diplomas is very limited. Robert Stein has said:

> The Feminine in both men and women is suffering. The liberation of the Feminine, rather than of women, is really what is needed. While the economic, educational, and social advantages that men have had over women are obvious and need to be corrected, I don't believe this is the main issue.
>
> (Stein 1990, p. 4)

I agree completely with him, but the difference in economic power between women and men is so great in Japan that we cannot ignore the imbalance. Indeed, most single mothers are suffering from poverty. According to annual reports from the Japanese Ministry of Health, Labour and Welfare in 2012, the average annual income of single mothers is about 2,626,000 yen (about \$33,200), but 4,210,000 yen for single fathers (about \$50,632). For such women, it is out of the question to ask a Jungian analyst's help. Midori Igeta points out: 'Kawai's idea regarding the Japanese is supported by women who did not want to lose their gains in the contemporary social system' (1998, p. 354). In short, supporters of Jungian psychology are comparatively wealthy and well educated. However, Japanese economic, social and family systems are quickly changing. The middle class, with a modern family system that has supported Jungian psychology as a 'cultural fashion', is rapidly shrinking, while the number of single parents, single seniors and unmarried young people outside of the modern family system is increasing.

Of course, a related problem is the high training costs for Jungian analysts, which lie behind their high fees. Samuels comments on this cogently:

> The fees in the United States had got too high, and hence the incomes of some of the analysts had become too large. This was not just a Jungian problem, it is also a psychoanalytic one. It has to do with the professional self-image of the psychotherapists being aligned with the professional self-image and hence income expectations of gynaecologists, ophthalmologists, surgeons and the like [. . .] I think if fees are cut, people in the United States will continue to seek out Jungian and indeed other forms of other depth therapy [. . .] We need to think in terms of affirmative action for Jungian analysis because of the enormous costs of training and the Eurocentrism of Jungian analysis for the patients.
>
> (Samuels 1998, p. 30)

Directly related to this is a general shortage of Jungians. The Association of Jungian Analysts, Japan (AJAJ) was established in 2002, but there are now only thirty members, and most of them are in urban areas, with a ratio per population far lower than in the United States. Accordingly, their fees never come down, due to their rarity value. And, according to the guidelines of their training programme (AJAJ, 2012), only those candidates who finish the early programme and pass the mid-term examination at the Jungian Institute in Zurich are accepted, which obviously raises the cost of becoming a Jungian analyst, leading many to give up their careers. In short, in Japan, to be a Jungian analyst or to work with them, people have to be rich. It is easy to see the elitism and Eurocentrism in this that Samuels describes. Fortunately, the AJAJ founded the Japan Association of Jungian Psychology this year, and they provide another way to become a Jungian analyst without studying abroad, which may help improve the situation.

Another alternative

As we have seen, the average person is unlikely to work with a Jungian analyst. The consequences, for women in particular, are obvious. They have to wrestle with their psychological problems by themselves. One positive note in this situation is the rise of spontaneous activities by non-professionals – self-help groups for eating disorders, for example. In this sense the consciousness-raising movement of the 1960s has made a fruitful contribution to feminist therapy. As Samuels (2001) notes regarding *Women's Growth in Connection* by Judith Jordan *et al.*, this reflects 'a morality of care based on relational values' and these values 'are further indications of a tradition very different from an individualistic version of humanity'. Janet Surrey says:

> The notion of the self-in-relation involves an important shift in emphasis from separation to relationship as the basis for self-experience and development. Further, relationship is seen as the basic goal development: that is, deepening capacity for relationship and relational competence. The self-in-relation model assumes that other aspects of self (e.g., creativity, autonomy, assertion) develop within this primary context.
>
> (Surrey 1991, p. 53)

Of course, the concept of self-in-relation is helpful for men, too, as Jean Baker Miller mentions:

> Much recent writing deploring men's inability to engage in intimacy has come from the women's movement. But men, too, have been making the same point. Almost all modern literature, philosophy, and commentary in older forms portrays men's lack of a sense of community – indeed, it denies even the possibility of communicating with others.
>
> (Miller 1991, p. 12)

My own recent work has been focused precisely on the sense of community. I have started to work with a self-help group for eating disorders, including women and men, as a coordinator. What I have noticed in the members' raw voices and within their network is that they have a lot of clinical wisdom and flexible methods for obtaining it, such as using the Internet, and therefore the potential for generating a new approach. On the other hand, I, as a Jungian-oriented psychotherapist, may lead them to deeper insights, because I take heed to avoid a common shortcoming that Young-Eisendrath has noted – that is to say:

> While clinicians may exclude *gender* from the discussion of eating disorders, feminist scholars and researchers frequently exclude the *unconscious* or unintended aspects of gender, such as projection and projective identification, as they affect women's concerns about body image and sexuality.
>
> (Young-Eisendrath 1993, pp. 9–10)

Renos Papadopoulos, a Jungian analyst and a systematic family therapist, has given some useful suggestions about dealing with such a challenge. He writes from his experience working with survivors of violence and disasters: 'In this way, I understood my main role as providing what could be called a "therapeutic presence" where my main function was "therapeutic witnessing" of their predicament, rather than imposing formal psychotherapy' (1998, p. 178). Although I cannot yet say a lot about my activities with the self-help group that I coordinate, like Papadopoulos, I do not directly attend its meetings, because I do not want to disturb the emergence of the spontaneous recovery power of the members. Instead, I restrict myself to giving lectures or offering suggestions to facilitators (so-called 'recovery friends') when they ask me.

Jung said:

> A system of healing that fails to account for the epoch-making *representation collectives,* political, economic, philosophical, or religious, hardly deserves the name of therapy. It is more a deviation into a pathologically exaggerated attitude of protest which is the very reverse of adapted. Adaptedness as a criterion for cure is absolutely necessary, though of course it is not the only one.
>
> (Jung 1935, para. 549)

The world is rapidly changing. I think it is important for Jungians to search for new therapeutic approaches to adapt to our changing society. If Japanese Jungians get more involved in conversations with feminism and society, including such non-professional activities as self-help groups, with open minds, leaving behind their elitism, authoritarianism and fundamentalism, we may be able to develop an alternative Jungian psychology better suited to this new century.

References

Ankei, S. (1985) *Father, Dead or Alive.* Unpublished diploma thesis. Zurich: C.G.Jung Institute.

Ankei, S. and Yabuki, S. (1989) *Nihonteki Fusei no Hakken: Bosei-shakai- ron wo Koete* (Discovery of the Japanese Paternal: Beyond the Theory of Maternal Society). Tokyo: Yuhikaku.

Association of Jungian Analysts, Japan. Available online at: www.ajaj.info/menber.html.pdf (accessed 22 August 2012).

Christ, C.P. and Plaskow, J. (1979) 'Introduction', in C.P. Christ and J. Plaskow (eds) *Womanspirit Rising: A Feminst Reader in Religion*, San Francisco, CA: Harper & Row.

Hillman, J. (1985) *Anima: An Anatomy of a Personified Notion*, Dallas, TX: Spring Publications.

Igeta, M. (1998) 'Daimegami no Musukotachi-Boseigenri to iu Shiza' (Sons of great goddesses from the viewpoint of the 'maternal principle'), in K. Tanaka (ed.) *Megami Sei to Sei no Jinruigaku* (Goddess Anthropology, the Sacred and the Sexual), Tokyo: Heibonsya.

The Japan Association of Jungian Psychology. Available online at: www.jajp-jung.info/setsuritsu/?page_id=7.pdf (accessed 22 August 2012).

Jung, C.G. (1935) 'Editorial, for *Zentralblatt,* viii: 1', in *Collected Works,* Vol. 10.

Jung, C.G. (1982) *Aspects of the Feminine*, Princeton, NJ: Princeton University Press, and London: Routledge.

Kawai, H. (1976) *Boseisyakai Nihon no Byori* (The Pathology of the Maternal Society of Japan), Tokyo: Chuo-koron-sha.

Kawai, H., Yuasa, Y. and Yoshida, A. (1983) *Nihonshinwa no Siso* Susanoo-ron (Thoughts on Japanese Myth: The Theory of Susa-no-o), Kyoto: Minerva Sohobo.

Kawai, T. (1993) 'Jung/Hillman no Genkeishinrigaku' (The archetypal psychology of Jung/Hillman), in J. Hillman and T. Kawai (trans.) *Genkeishinrigaku* (Archetypal Psychology), Tokyo: Seidosha.

Matsumura, K. (1998) 'Megami to Polis – Athena to Athēnai' (Goddess and Polis-Athena and Athēnai), in K. Tanaka (ed.) *Megami Sei to Sei no Jinruigaku* (Goddess Anthropology, the Sacred and the Sexual), Tokyo: Heibonsya.

Miller, J.B. (1991) 'The development of women's sense of self', in J.V. Jordan, A.G. Kaplan, J.B. Miller, I.P. Stiver and J.L. Surrey (eds) *Women's Growth in Connection*, New York, London: The Guilford Press.

Ministry of Health, Labour and Welfare (2012) 'Hitorioya Katei no Shien ni Tuite' (Supports for single-parents families). Retrieved from the Ministry of Health, Labour and Welfare. Available online at: www.mhlw.go.jp/seisakunitsuite/bunka/kodomo/kodomo_kosodate/boshi-katei/index.html.pdf (accessed 22 August 2012).

Muramoto, S. and Nakamura, K. (2002) 'Translator's epilog', in D. Wehr, S. Muramoto and K. Nakamura (trans.) *Jung to Feminism* (Jung and Feminism: Liberating Archetypes), Kyoto: Minerva Shobo.

Muto, K. (1995) 'Shinririnnsho ni okeru gender no mondai' (Gender problems in clinical practice), in K. Kashiwagi and K. Takahashi (eds) *Hattatsushinnrigaku to Feminism* (Developmental Psychology and Feminism), Kyoto: Minerva Shobo.

Nakagama, Y. (2003) 'Kodomo no Shinri-Chiryo ni Tojosuru Chichiova to Hahaoya (Fathers and Mothers Appearing in Psychotherapy for Children)' in K. Kashiwagi and K. Takahashi (eds) *Shinrigaku to Gender* (Psychology and Gender), Tokyo: Yuhikaku.

Nakagama, Y. (2007) 'Gender Sensitivity wo Takameru tamenni' (For Raising Gender Sensitivity), *Japanese Journal of Family Therapy*, 24(2): 16–19.

Nakamura, K. (2010) 'Struggles, commercialism, "ideal" feminine image and internal oppression: Eating disorders and the pursuit of thinness in Japan', in R. Jones (ed.) *Body, Mind, and Healing After Jung: A Space of Questions,* London: Routledge.

Nakamura, K. (2011) 'The masculine and the feminine in Japanese women: Expression in sandplay and myth', in R. Jones and M. Morioka (eds) *Jungian and Dialogical Self Perspectives*, New York: Palgrave Macmillan.

Otsuka, Y. (2012) 'Annual reports on projects and activities', *Bulletin of the Foundation of the Japanese Certification Board for Clinical Psychologists*, 23(2): 4–9.

Papadopoulos, R. (1998) 'Jungian perspective in new contexts', in A. Casement (ed.) *Post-Jungians Today: Key Papers in Contemporary Analytical Psychology*, London: Routledge.

Rowland, S. (2002) *Jung: A Feminist Revision*, Cambridge: Polity Press.

Samuels, A. (1998) 'Will the post-Jungian survive?', in A. Casement (ed.) *Post Jungians Today: Key Papers in Contemporary Analytical Psychology*, London: Routledge.

Samuels, A. (2001) *Politics on the Couch: Citizenship and the Internal Life*. London: Karnac Books.

Shimoyama, H. (2004) 'Rinshoshinrigaku no Kadai to Tenbo' (The Problems and Future of Clinical Psychology [in Japan]), in Y. Otsuka (ed.) *Rinshoshinrigaku Genron* (The Principal of Clinical Psychology),Tokyo: Seishin-Shobo.

Stein, R.M. (1990) 'From the liberation of women to the feminine', in C. Zweig (ed.) *To Be a Woman: The Birth of the Conscious Feminine*, Los Angeles, CA: Tarcher.

Surrey, J.L. (1991) 'The self-in-relation: A theory of women's development', in J. V. Jordan, A.G. Kaplan, J.B. Miller, I.P. Stiver and J.L. Surrey (eds) *Women's Growth In Connection*, New York, London: The Guilford Press.

Takao, H. (2001) *Nihonteki Ishiki no Kigen: Jung Shinrigaku de Yomu Kojiki* (Origins of Japanese Consciousness: Reading *Kojiki* in terms of Jungian Psychology), Tokyo: Shinyosya.

Wehr, D. (1987) *Jung and Feminism: Liberating Archetypes*, Boston, MA: Beacon Press.

Whitmont, E. (1969) *The Symbolic Quest: Basic Concepts of Analytical Psychology*, Princeton, NJ: Princeton University Press.

Young-Eisendrath, P. (1984) *Hags and Heroes: A Feminist Approach to Jungian Psychotherapy with Couples*, Toronto: Inner City Books.

Young-Eisendrtah, P. (1993) 'Entanglement: Food, sex and aggression in female development', *Feminine Life Cycle*, Annual Report of the Feminine Life Cycle Insititute, Vol. 3: 9–22.

7

TRANSFORMING CONSCIOUSNESS AS THE PATH TO END SUFFERING

Mahayana Buddhism and analytical psychology as complementary traditions

William E. Kotsch

Introduction

Analytical psychology is an applied psychology that seeks to reduce suffering by transforming consciousness through an extensive search for meaning. In this, it shares a mission with Buddhism, which holds the reduction of human suffering as a primary aim. An eighth-century Buddhist text, Shantarakshita's Madhyamakalankara (*The Adornment of the Middle Way*), and an accompanying commentary (2005) by Jamgon Mipham, a nineteenth-century Tibetan monk and scholar, provide valuable insights into ways that practices of mind or psyche can be harnessed to reduce and potentially end suffering through the transformation of consciousness into wisdom. This chapter will explore how these synthetic texts, spanning more than 2,500 years of Buddhist teaching, may inform the understanding and practice of depth psychology.

The discussion is organized as follows. First, I provide some historical context regarding the role Shantarakshita played in the development of Buddhist thought. Next, I summarize key ideas from his 97-verse text. A special focus of this summary will be on four major themes that, in my view, have relevance for the study and practice of psychology. I then make the case that Buddhism – as articulated by Shantarakshita and Mipham – can contribute to psychology. Specifically, I describe his view of the inner world and write of the process of transformation from dual consciousness to non-conceptual wisdom that is embedded in Shantarakshita's text. I argue that his process is distinctly psychological and, as such, provides a model to guide our academic and therapeutic endeavors. I then, briefly, discuss what might be called a transformational "method." This method, simply put, involves processes often associated with sound psychological study and practice: observation, inference, reason, and the like. Finally, I assert that Buddhist teachings, as articulated by Shantarakshita and Mipham (2005), may be helpful to analysts as they seek to create a therapeutic space for souls' healing and the emergence of new beginnings. I conclude with a call for a dialogue between Mahayana Buddhism and analytical psychology, arguing that the two traditions share common ground, and can inform and enrich one another.

Shantarakshita and *The Adornment of the Middle Way*: historical context

After enlightenment, Buddha began teaching. His first major lesson, known as the first turning of the wheel of *dharma*, presented the Four Noble Truths concerning suffering and causality. At the second turning of the wheel, as recorded in the prajnaparamita sutras, he taught the emptiness of all phenomena (*dharma*). At the third turning of the wheel, Buddha directed his teaching toward mind, as exemplified by the Lankavatara Sutra (Red Pine 2012).[1] Thus, in the course of turning the wheel of *dharma* three times, Buddha presented everything necessary to follow and to complete the path to end suffering. This is known as the Mahayana or Great Vehicle.

Over the next thousand years, two scholar practitioners who were great doctrinal system builders or "charioteers" appeared in India. In the second century, Nagarjuna developed the Middle Way School, which systematized the Buddhist philosophy of emptiness and provided a rigorous critique of metaphysical categories.[2] In the fourth century, Asanga developed the Yogic Practice or Mind Only School, which emphasized the centrality of mind/consciousness and provided a detailed account of experience and the path transforming dual consciousness into wisdom realizing emptiness.[3] A third figure of importance emerged in the seventh century. Dharmakirti (Dunne 2004)[4] outlined the major tenets of Buddhist logic and epistemology. Among other things, he taught that cognition, in the form of direct perception and inference, can provide valid knowledge both about emptiness (the ultimate nature of all entities) and about our conventional experience of objects and their causal relationships.

Adopting the logico-eptistemological framework of Dharmakirti, Shantarakshita, in the eighth century, founded a system synthesizing the analytic approach of the Middle Way School with the experiential approach of the Yogic Practice (Mind Only) School. Called the third charioteer by commentator Jamgon Mipham (2005), Shantarakshita not only systematized the entire Mahayana tradition, but personally carried his philosophy to Tibet where, with the assistance of Guru Padmasambhava, it flourished for hundreds of years, and today is identified as the Nyingma, or Old School tradition and with the meditative practice of Dzogchen.[5] Central to Shantarakshita's teaching is the notion that our individual experience of objects and their causal relations is relative truth, which is best understood from the Yogic Practice (Mind Only) perspective, while our analytical inquiry into the way things actually exist in the final analysis (the ultimate truth of the emptiness of all phenomena) is best understood through the Middle Way. Thus, two viewpoints, the experiential Yogic Practice view and the analytic Middle Way view, provide understanding of two truths:[6] the truth of conventional reality experienced as impermanent objects, and their relations and the truth of the ultimate nature of things that is their emptiness or lack of inherent existence.

Further, Shantarakshita makes a unique presentation of ultimate truth. He distinguishes between a categorized, conceptual ultimate that results from valid reasoning and a true ultimate, free from all conceptual categories. Understood separately, the two truths, relative and ultimate, constitute two opposite conceptual poles. Together, these two opposing views create a bipolar construction in which the pole designated "emptiness" approximates ultimate truth. Since the true ultimate is entirely beyond extremes imposed by conceptual categories and constructs, it cannot be named but only experienced directly as a unity, the inseparable union of relative appearance and the conceptual ultimate or emptiness.

To summarize, Shantarakshita maintains that all entities are empty of inherent independent existence and asserts that persons may become certain of this by studying and analyzing entities and relations as they appear to the uncritical, conventional consciousness. Thus, by following a path of reason and employing valid perception and inference, we can realize the (approximate) truth of emptiness. By continuing along this path or through the more immediate tantric path, individuals can finally realize the ultimate truth beyond duality and conceptualization that is the unity of appearance and emptiness.

Exegesis of Shantarakshita's *Adornment of the Middle Way*: major themes

Shantarakshita's 97 concise verses bring together the Yogic Practice (Mind Only) view of relative appearance and the Middle Way view of emptiness, presenting them as interdependent and non-contradictory, yet conceptually distinguishable. His text is built around four key themes discussed in the following sections.

Theme I: The ultimate – the non-existence of all entities

In the early verses of the text, Shantarakshita establishes a perspective that is unique to Buddhism and is foundational to its understanding of mind. Things that appear to us as real and independent entities, when examined with valid instruments of cognition, are found to be empty – that is, they are found to be lacking substance, essence, or inherent existence. These "objects" are merely appearances, like reflections or dreams, and are inextricably linked to the subject perceiving them. This view is presented in the text's opening verse:

The entities that our and other schools affirm,
Since they exist inherently in neither singular nor plural
In ultimate reality are without intrinsic being:
They are like reflections.

(v.1)

In subsequent verses (v.2–v.15), using inference and logic, Shantarakshita extends the point made in the first verse and provides specific examples of things that cannot inherently exist as independent, external objects, such as persons, a creator, partless particles, and individual moments of time.

In verse 16, Shantarakshita considers what remains if one rejects the notion of independently existing, external objects (matter). He concludes that the answer is consciousness understood as mind and its contents or aspects.

Consciousness arises as the contrary
Of matter, gross, inanimate.
By nature, mind is immaterial.
And it is self-aware.

(v. 16)

This verse establishes two properties of mind or consciousness: it is immaterial and it is self-aware. This self-awareness is not reflective in the sense of a subject's apprehending an object; rather, it is reflexive.[7] Consciousness is simply aware of itself. And through a series of logical, inferential arguments, Shantarakshita establishes that "non-mental . . . external objects" (v. 21) "do not exist" (v. 40), apart from or independent of the mind that perceives them. Neither mind nor its object is singular; therefore, both are empty of inherent existence. They exist in a state of interdependence and, thus, are called "other powered" or "dependent nature[s]" (v. 58 and v. 60) – that is, they co-emerge.

Theme 2: Relative existence – appearances and their relations

Even as he makes the case for the ultimate emptiness of all things, Shantarakshita acknowledges that humans experience mind and its objects as if they were distinct independent entities. Indeed, in conventional time and space, objects appear as distant and separate from the mind that perceives them. Thus he asks:

If these aspects [and objects] are without [inherent] existence,
How do we experience them so clearly?

(v. 53a)

For Shantarakshita, the answer to this question lies within mind – within consciousness itself. He presents a pragmatic theory of mind as found in the

Yogic Practice (Mind Only) view as a way to explain how consciousness engages with objects. The Mind Only theory or view holds that extra-mental objects, objects we experience as existing independently "out there," are merely projections of mind. The authentic nature of appearances is obscured through a natural process that bifurcates subject and object, and reifies self and other. This natural process is innate and, thus, the work of overcoming this mistaken conceptualization is a work *contra naturum*. Shantarakshita describes this view thus:

> Within the mental stream without beginning
> Through the maturation of habitual tendencies,
> Things manifest, yet these [dual] appearances
> Are mirage-like and due to the delusion of the mind.
>
> (v. 44)

In this view, a ground or repository consciousness that legitimately may be called the Buddhist unconscious (Waldron 2003) projects stored habitual tendencies as perceptions. When the perception is not realized as a projection of mind, it is mistakenly taken to be external and independent of consciousness. In Shantarakshita's system, the Mind Only view is concerned with relative truth and operates within conventional constructs of space and time. It is a pragmatic theory that is an aid in overcoming mistaken cognitions about the independent existence of things.

In Shantarakshita's theory of mind, objects that do not exist independently and intrinsically nevertheless exist in interdependent relationships with the minds that perceive them – that is, things exist only in relationship to other things.

> Therefore, all these things possess
> Defining features only in the relative.
>
> (v. 63a)

The realm of the relative, the dependent arising or the co-emergence of mind and world, for Shantarakshita, is the realm in which karma is operative. Karma, defined simply, is the idea that our actions (which include intentions, speech, and affect) have effects, that present experience is the result of past actions, and that present actions determine future experience. Shantarakshita describes karma using metaphors from nature, "shoots from seeds" (v. 82) and "cause and fruit" (v. 84) as he underscores the interdependence between effects and causes. Yet in spite of his use of these natural metaphors, Shantarakshita clearly states that karma is a relative truth understood within the Mind Only view:

> Things arise as though they were the causes' subsequent effects.
>
> (v. 65b)

> Thus, it is incorrect to say that in the absence of a (true existing)
> cause, the relative could not appear.
>
> (v.66a)

and

> All cause and effect are consciousness alone.
>
> (v. 91a)

Theme 3: Valid cognition – approximating the ultimate nature of things

After establishing the emptiness of all things as ultimate truth and the experience of appearances and their causal relations as relative truth, Shantarakshita points out that the two truths – the truth of emptiness and the truth of interrelatedness and co-emergence – are derived through valid cognition using the instruments of perception and inference. Through the application of reason, he has identified and dichotomized appearance and emptiness. Because this emptiness is conceptual, it only approximates the ultimate. Ultimately, emptiness is inseparable from appearance; and since emptiness itself lacks intrinsic existence. Emptiness, like any other entity, is itself empty.

> Since with the ultimate this is attuned,
> It is referred to as the ultimate.
> And yet the actual ultimate is free
> From constructs and elaborations.
>
> (v. 70)

Shantarakshita now focuses on the realization of the actual non-conceptual ultimate, noting that it can be achieved either by continuing to follow the path of reason or by direct experience.

> Those who sound the nature of phenomena with reasoning
> That cuts through misconception and brings understanding
> Know this nature. It is known by powerful yogis also,
> Through their direct and clear experience.
>
> (v. 75)

The point here is that reason is not an end in itself. Rather, reason provides a cure for doubt. Metaphorically, reason is the antidote to the poison of misconception. It is needed only when the poison of doubt is present and causing distress. Thus reason is a path to an end. Shantarakshita, in this verse, points to another path, that of direct experience or looking directly at the mind through meditative practices such as mahamudra or dzogchen.[8]

Theme 4: Unity and equality – a path beyond concepts

Realizing the unity of emptiness and appearance establishes the equality of all phenomena as ultimately empty, yet existing relatively. This, in Buddhism, is the correct view. Shantarakshita summarizes this view over several verses. First, he posits reason as a valid instrument for engaging with relative appearances:

> Things as they appear
> I do not negate.
> And therefore, unconfused,
> I may set forth both predicate and evidence.
>
> (v. 78)

He then states that things appear because they lack inherent existence.

> Thus the views of permanence and nothingness
> Are far from the teaching of this text.
> When causes cease, effects will follow,
> As plants derive from shoots and shoots from seeds.
>
> (v. 82)

All actions have effects, and through right understanding or view these effects gain power.

> From the view that things have not such real existence
> Great results proliferate
>
> (v. 90)

Linking relative truth with view of the centrality of mind (Mind Only), Shantarakshita states:

> All causes and effects
> Are consciousness alone.
> And all that this establishes
> Abides in consciousness.
>
> (v. 91)

And once again, Shantarakshita states that his opening premise that all things "in ultimate reality are without intrinsic being" (v. 1) applies to both outer things and to mind or consciousness. First he restates the non-duality of subject and object:

> On the basis of the Mind Alone,
> We should know that outer things do not exist.
>
> (v. 92a)

And he continues:

> On the basis of the method set forth here,
> We should know that mind is utterly devoid of self.
>
> (v. 92b)

The method is the middle-way reasoning that establishes that all entities are empty of inherent existence. The unity of appearance and emptiness is the inexpressible ultimate reality, described by Shantarakshita as "this perfect state, this pure ambrosia" (v. 95). This unity is the non-duality of thing and "no thing."

Adornment of the Middle Way as a soteriological and psychological text

Shantarakshita's *Adornment of the Middle Way* is a sacred text. Not only an argument concerning the appearance and nature of reality, it is also a psychological method for transforming consciousness. In the sections that follow, I describe three key dimensions of Shantarakshita's psychology: his understanding of mind, one useful method for healing or transforming mind, and the value of emptiness in the therapeutic milieu.

Buddhism's map of the soul – a view of the inner world

Shantarakshita, from the opening verse of his text, is unerring in his focus on the interior. Indeed, his demonstration that external objects lack "intrinsic being" is a turn inward, into mind or psyche, for if objects that seem to exist lack intrinsic being, then they must somehow appear within mind. This point, while distinctly psychological in nature, is only the starting point in Shantarakshita's presentation of the inner. His robust psychological and spiritual perspectives guide us beyond mere understanding toward an experience of interiority – of mind or psyche or soul as wisdom realizing and experiencing psychic wholeness – that is, unity and multiplicity.

The central quality of mind, for Shantarakshita, the ultimate truth of the interior, is its emptiness. This emptiness is not, however, nihilism or nothingness. Rather, it is the emptiness of inherent duality (in the Mind Only view) and the emptiness of all entities (in the Middle Way view). Put differently, the truth of the interior is not only the unity of subject and object, but also the unity of thing and no thing, of appearance and mind, or, in terms more familiar to depth psychologists, the unity of consciousness and unconsciousness, glossed here as inseparability of presence and absence. All entities are equal in their emptiness and arise dependently or co-emerge because of their emptiness. When one recognizes such a unity, one begins to approach the experience of wholeness. In moments of consciousness, one begins to see the variety inherent in differences and, at the same time, to see the emptiness of differences in each moment of consciousness. When such seeing becomes automatic or habitual, mind has transformed from dual consciousness to non-conceptual wisdom.

A description of healing through the transformation from dual consciousness to non-conceptual wisdom following the path of reason

As discussed at some length above, Shantarakshita devotes considerable time to describing a path to wisdom that uses reason and its various tools, including observation, inference, and logic. This path of reason, by establishing emptiness and investigating appearances, has both soteriological and psychological value. It provides a "correct" or useful view as the basis for transforming dual consciousness into wisdom that realizes the unity of the subjective and objective within experience as well as the equality of all phenomena by virtue of their shared nature of emptiness. From Shantarakshita's text, Mipham (2005) describes this path of reason in terms of four steps or stages: (1) emptiness; (2) unity; (3) freedom from constructs; and (4) equality.

The first step, called emptiness, involves serious examination of the world as it appears. It should be noted that the process starts with the relative truth: the objects and events of the world , including their relations and changes over time. We come to know this conventional "given" world over time through the application of valid cognition. When we carefully and empirically investigate our world, we recognize that things are not as they seem.[9] When analyzed, solid and vivid appearances are found, ultimately, to be empty. When we realize this, we are confronted with a stark contrast: the relative world of objects and their relations, in which we function quite well vs. the "unfindablity" of a single entity and the logical inference that all entities are empty.

As we consciously move between the realms of appearance and emptiness, their enmity, or incompatibility, seems to diminish. Indeed, eventually we discover that appearance and emptiness are inextricably linked through their mutual dependence. Once we understand the dependence of these two seemingly contradictory realms, we begin to appreciate unity as a characteristic of wisdom. In the words of the Mipham scholar, Douglas Duckworth:

> We come to understand that emptiness and appearance are not in conflict, because dependent arising is the meaning of emptiness. Phenomena are empty simply because they do not exist independently. At this stage we come to understand that being empty does not stop phenomena from appearing; rather, we recognize that being empty is the necessary condition for appearance. So this stage points further to the genuine unity of appearance and emptiness.
>
> (Duckworth 2011, p. 101)

Thus, v. 65b states:

> Things arise as though they were
> The causes' subsequent effects.

To paraphrase v. 66a, the relative appears in the absence of a truly existing cause. The next stage in the transformational process occurs as we reflect upon the reality that all entities are ultimately empty. This reality pushes us to acknowledge that even the concepts or constructs of appearance and emptiness logically must be, in themselves, empty. This recognition enables us to experience liberation in the form of freedom from constructs. To continue in Professor Duckworth's words:

> In the next stage, freedom from constructs, we come to understand that things being empty and things appearing do not have a different meaning. Other than different modes of expression, or different ways of conceiving reality, we now see that there is actually no difference between appearance and emptiness. In this phase, we recognize that an object "being empty"– as a property separate from that appearing object – is only a linguistic or conceptual distinction: there is no such distinction in reality.
>
> (Duckworth 2011, p. 102)

To summarize, although they seem different, appearance and emptiness are simply different ways of describing one reality,[10] a reality that is ultimately empty. Appearance and emptiness are neither the same nor different. The true ultimate is non-dual, non-conceptual, inconceivable, and yet, experienceable.

As we become accustomed to the freedom from language and constructs, we take the step by which all duality is dissolved. This is the state called equality, awareness without conceptual fabrication. We can say that this equality is directly perceived, but no expression can capture non-conceptual wisdom.[11] This state of equality is authentic experience. It is simply "knowing" or gnosis, without error, a wisdom that neither negates nor affirms but sees reality as it is.

The analytic attitude and the value of emptiness

Shantarakshita's path of reason requires commitment and discipline. This path of reason and processes of psychic transformation (or mind training) that it promotes may be of great benefit for the analyst in developing what is called the analytic attitude – the attitude of the analyst that shapes and structures the therapeutic process.

The analyst who lives the reality of psyche remains open to the communication between conscious and unconscious processes, between what is present and what is not (yet) present. In this process, the analyst develops an intuitive appreciation for the equality of self and other and, valuing both, expresses acceptance, compassion, and empathy for each patient. This "attitude" is the basis for the "holding environment" experienced by the patient. Bounded by the analytic frame (or structure of the therapy), this holding environment becomes a contained therapeutic field that alchemists called the sacred vessel. It is both the place and the process of transformation – the psychic (internal) process described by both Shantarakshita and Jung.

Shantarakshita's contribution to the understanding of the therapeutic process is that the therapeutic field contains nothing at all. And this aspect of the field, its emptiness, is its secret active ingredient – the essential factor in a psychotherapy that aims toward psychic transformation. From therapeutic frame, to holding environment, to sacred vessel, to emptiness of both the therapeutic field and its contents, this continuum of images of container and containment forms and informs the practice of psychotherapy. From the emptiness of the therapeutic field emerges the "new thing," a new dawn, the renewal of life. The old boundaries disintegrate; the bounded suffering soul is freed to move, to flow; and, thus, it heals itself.

The importance of silence and waiting, the witnessing of the emergence of new attitudes, and the coming together of the inner and outer aspects of psyche experienced as synchronicities repeatedly appear in the clinical writings of analytical psychologists. One beautiful example of this emphasis can be found in Stein's chapter, "Spiritual and Religious Aspects of Modern Analysis." Stein describes what he calls the negative religious attitude as a defining quality of analytical psychotherapy. He writes, "In analysis, one practices the discipline of emptiness . . . which sets up a 'free and sheltered space'. . . for the analysand's psyche to enter and reveal itself as fully as possible" (2004, p. 215). Stein further notes, "the 'analytical space' therefore is ideally empty" (2004, p. 216). In sum, emptiness is the necessary condition for emergence or becoming.

Toward a dialogue between yogachara/madyamikda's view of Shantarakshita and analytical psychology

My purpose in this chapter is to encourage a dialogue between Mahayana Buddhism, as articulated by Shantarakshita and explicated by those who comment on his work such as Mipham (2005) and depth psychology. My hope is that such a dialogue will highlight the psychological value of Shantarakshita's Great Mahayana view and will infuse depth psychology with key Buddhist teachings that provide a firm and time-tested basis for understanding experience and alleviating suffering. The common ground of both perspectives is the reality of mind or soul. The common aim is to unify the dual mind through the transformation of consciousness. In the closing sections of this chapter, I suggest ways that analytical psychology affirms and aligns with Buddhism as expressed by Shantarakshita, and call for continued dialogue with the belief that these two intellectual and healing traditions can inform and enrich one another.

Jung as a physician of mind and healer of soul

Considering himself a metaphysician of the mind, Henri Corbin uses the phrase "physician of the mind" to describe Jung. Jung's abiding interest was the human mind, not the brain or behavior. Jung took seriously the reality of psyche, or *esse in anima*, and devoted himself primarily to its healing. Pragmatic and practical, Jung sought to describe psychic reality as a precondition for the treatment of the soul. For Jung, mind is human experience: "the psyche is indistinguishable from its manifestations" (Jung 1942/1954, par. 87). And the realm of psyche is all experienceable objects and events. Emphasis on experience "interiorizes" objects and events by never failing to take into account the experiencer or subject. Living with a culture that valued the exterior, extraverted view, Jung continually "made the case" for recognizing and honoring the introverted perspective. As a physician of mind, Jung's descriptions of mind also were meant to be curative. Thus in his writings, he tried hard not to lose sight of his patient. Because, psyche as soul, by nature, is mercurial, Jung's writings about the inner world are not always consistent. They do, though, reflect his deep commitment to the centrality of mind in the healing process and, therefore, to the importance of understanding mind and its contents and processes.

Jung called the healing process individuation. It may be envisioned as a personal journey that is both a natural process and an individual effort. Jung also describes individuation in alchemical images such as the transformation of impure metals into gold (the treasure hard to attain), death and rebirth, and the union of the male and female. In psychological terms, he describes the process as overcoming or joining the opposites through the transcendent function. While Jungian terms such as "extravert" and "complex" have become part of our common psychological vocabulary, "individuation" and "transcendent function" are less well known and understood. I believe the reason for this is that the former terms are descriptive, whereas the latter reflect Jung's soteriological concerns – the transformation of mind not only for the purpose of healing but also as an act of salvation. This involves overcoming the opposition between the secular and the spiritual, the mundane and transcendent.

Situated in Europe in the early 1900s, Jung was one of the pioneers of what Ellenberger called the "discovery of the unconscious" (1970). This discovery of the unconscious led Jung to a rediscovery of psychic reality, the long obscured "reality" of the early Christian Gnostics and then the alchemists. As a physician of mind and curer of souls, Jung appreciated the centrality of psychic reality, understanding that suffering or dis-ease emanated from within. Indeed, for Jung, pathogens were conceptual, or rather, mis-conceptional, arising when we mistake our concepts of reality for the "thing in itself" (to borrow from Kant). The process of healing, as envisioned by Jung, is one that requires engagement with and within mind/psyche, using an array of tools, including those provided by direct observation of mind and its contents through dreams and active imagination, and by the use of reasoned inferences to aid in interpretation, understanding, and integration.

Working within the intellectual Western culture of science, philosophy, and religion, Jung fought a bruising and lonely fight against not only academia, but also conventional opinion (the "common sense" of his era). He was forced to pick his battles wisely. As a result, while Jung's writings are rich and insightful, they sometimes have a defensive or provincial quality that can hide their meaning. It has been the task of analytical psychologists such as Lopez-Pedraza (1977), Hillman (1985), and Giegerich (2012) not just to defend a view of psychic reality but to "go on the offensive" and aggressively elaborate the psyche's movement and self-expression as well as the "logical life of the soul."

In a previous work (Kotsch 2000), I discussed the efforts of contemporary philosophers (Bernstein 1991; Putnam 1981) and cognitive scientists (Lakoff 1987; Varela *et al.* 1992) who move beyond the conceptual dichotomy of objectivism/relativism toward a study of lived experience. More recently, the writings of other analytical psychologists (e.g. Cambray 2009; Hogenson 2004) point in the same direction. Contemporary ideas of embodiment, enaction, emergence, structural coupling, and synchronicity reflect our contemporary awareness of the importance of mind/psyche as the proper subject for our study and practice.

Buddhism and analytical psychology: implications and next steps in a dialogue

Jung intuitively grasped the importance of the "Eastern" or "Oriental" view of mind and had a keen interest in understanding the relationships between Western and Eastern concepts. However, Jung, like many other Western thinkers contemplating "Eastern" thought, failed to understand and appreciate its variety, breadth, and depth. Jung's limited perspective is evident in his often-used phrase, "the Oriental" (e.g. Jung 1963, pp. 275–6). He seemed to assume that the East, unlike the West, produced thinkers with a singular way of engaging with many issues. While Jung valued Eastern thought because he believed the culture of the East appreciated psychic reality, in contrast to the extraverted materialistic perspective of the West, he also offered a superficial and stereotypical opinion that, in "the Eastern mind" (Wilhelm and Jung 1962, pp. 86, 111, 136) psychic reality is a given (a psychological or temperamental fact) rather than the result of (philosophical) reasoning. Building on this notion, he stated that the "East" has produced no psychology, only metaphysics. This he contrasted with his emerging analytical psychology, which does not consider the mind to be a metaphysical entity (Jung 1942/1954, par. 759).

I suspect that there are many reasons why Jung undervalued the psychological contributions of the East and, especially, of Buddhism. Nevertheless, I believe his assertion that the East has produced no psychology is mistaken. I further believe that the Shantarakshita's text highlights at least three dimensions of Buddhist thought worthy of further exploration. The first is the theory of mind or soul held by analytical psychology and Buddhism; the second is the use of reason or "valid cognition" in establishing the correct view of the healing process as the transformation of consciousness into wisdom; and the third is the value of realizing emptiness within the therapeutic frame.

As noted above, Shantarakshita's theory of mind, like Jung's psychic reality, presumes the interdependence of mind and its contents, and recognizes that both illness and healing emanate from mind. Shantarakshita further offers a clear methodology for healing the soul through transforming mind. Healing is accomplished in the relative realm as we use reason or valid cognition to understand projections as perceptions of mind and as we act upon the causal import of this understanding. Healing or the overcoming of mistaken thought (or ignorance) is ultimately accomplished through the realization of the ultimate emptiness of all things (including mind and its contents) and the liberation, wisdom, and compassion that such realization affords. Finally, Buddhism's understanding of emptiness, beautifully articulated by Shantarakshita and amplified by Mipham and others in their commentaries, both describes ultimate reality and provides a powerful way to image an analytic attitude that creates a therapeutic and open space for healing and transformation.

Notes

1 The *Lankavatara Sutra* is the seminal text for Zen Buddhism as well as for the Yogic Practice school, as discussed. This sutra is cited frequently in Mipham's overview of Shantarakshita's text.

2 A key verse from Nagarjuna's *The Fundamental Wisdom of the Middle Way* states: "Whatever is dependently co-arisen/ That is explained as emptiness. That, being a dependent designation/ Is itself the middle way." Jay Garfield , the translator and interpreter of the text, explains, "Here Nagarjuna asserts the fundamental identity of (1) emptiness, or ultimate truth; (2) the dependently originated, that is, all phenomena; and (3) verbal convention. Moreover, he asserts that understanding this relation is itself the middle-way philosophical view" (2004, p. 93).

3 "After the awareness there is nothing other than mind / Comes the understanding that mind, too, is nothing itself./ The intelligent know that these two understandings are not things./ And then, not holding on to even this knowledge, they come to rest in the realm of totality" (McLeod 2005, p. 76, n. 58).

4 Dunne (2004) discusses Dharmakirti in the context of Indian thought. For a thorough discussion of the influence of Dharmakirti's philosophy on Tibetan thought, see Dreyfus (1977).

5 See Reynolds (2010) for a translation of Padmasambava's text on the view of Dzogchen.
6 The Sanskrit word translated as "truth" may also be translated as "real" or "existent" depending on the context. Thus the word "truth" may be applied to a statement or an object (Newland 1992, pp. 39–50).
7 See Williams (1998) for a discussion of reflexive vs. reflective awareness.
8 In addition to the paths of reason and direct experience, Buddhist practice acknowledges a third path, the path of method (tantra). Although a tantric practitioner, Shantarakshita does not dwell on this path in this text which is devoted to the view, rather than to the practice. It is, however, compatible with his teaching and with Western psychology. Western tantric-like methods could include dream analysis, active imagination, and the therapeutic use of narrative as found in myth, parable, and story.
9 What is often called "common sense" is far from simple. Indeed, it is based on a myriad of unconscious, metaphysical assumptions. For example, the assumption that phenomena exist in clear and distinct categories is pervasive, influential, and, ultimately, based on an inaccurate understanding of the nature of things and the social construction of categories (Lakoff and Johnson 1999).
10 As an example to reflect on, one might consider figure ground reversal (i.e. the experience of a glass of water as half full or half empty; the experience of music as rests and notes; the experience of a painting as background and figure, etc.).
11 For example, it cannot be asserted that things are the same or that they are different. Things are not the same in that there are clear differences between objects in their appearances and function, but all objects are also the same in that they share the same essential nature of emptiness.

References

Bernstein, R.J. (1991) *Beyond Objectivism and Relativism: Science, Hermeneutics, and Praxis,* Philadelphia, PA: University of Pennsylvania Press.

Cambray, J. (2009) *Synchronicity: Nature and Psyche in an Interconnected Universe,* College Station, TX: A & M Press.

Dreyfus, G.B.J. (1977*) Recognizing Reality: Dharmakirti's Philosophy and its Tibetan Interpretations*, Albany, NY: State University of New York Press.

Duckworth, D. (2011) *Jamgon Mipham: His Life and Teaching,* Boston, MA: Shambhala.

Dunne, J. D. (2004) *Foundations of Dharmakiriti's Philosophy*, Boston, MA: Wisdom Publications.

Ellenberger, H.F. (1970) *The Discovery of the Unconscious: The History and Evolution of Dynamic Psychology,* New York: Basic.

Garfield, J. (trans.) (2004) *The Fundamental Wisdom of the Middle Way: Nagarjuna's Mlamadhyamakakrik,* New York: Oxford University Press.

Giegerich, W. (2012) *What Is Soul?*, New Orleans: Spring Publications.

Hillman, J. (1985) *Archetypal Psychology: A Brief Course*, Dallas, TX: Spring Publications.

Hogenson, G. B. (2004) "Archetypes: emergence and the psyche's deep structure". In J. Cambray and L. Carter (eds.) *Analytical Psychology: Contemporary Perspectives in Jungian Analysis,* New York: Brunner-Routledge.

Jung, C.G. (1942/1954) *Psychology and Religion: West and East.* In *The Collected Works of C.G. Jung* (Vol. 11). Princeton, NJ: Princeton University Press.

—— (1963) *Memories, Dreams, Reflections*, New York: Random House.

Kotsch, W.E. (2000) "Jung's mediatory science as a psychology beyond objectivism", *Journal of Analytical Psychology*, 45(2), pp. 217–44.

Lakoff, G. (1987) *Women, Fire, and Dangerous Things: What Categories Reveal about the Mind*, Chicago: University of Chicago Press.

Lakoff, G. and Johnson, M. (1999) *Philosophy in the Flesh: The Embodied Mind and Its Challenge to Western Thought,* New York: Basic Books.

Lopez-Pedraza, R. (1997) *Hermes and His Children*. Dallas, TX: Spring Publications.

McLeod, K. (trans.) (2005) *The Great Path of Awakening: The Classic Guide to Jojong, a Tibetan Buddhist Practice for Cultivating the Heart of Compassion*, Boston, MA: Shambhala.

Mipham, J. (comm.) (2005) *The Adornment of the Middle Way: Shantarakshita's Madhyamakalankara* (trans.the Padmakara Translation Group), Boston, MA: Shambhala.

Newland, G. (1992) *The Two Truths in the Madhyamika Philosphy of the Ge-luk-ba Order of Tibetan Buddhism,* Ithaca, NY: Snow Lion Publications.

Putnam, H. (1981) *Reason, Truth, and History*, Cambridge: Cambridge University Press.

Red Pine (2012) *The Lankavatara Sutra*, Berkeley, CA: Counterpoint.

Reynolds, J.M. (trans.) (2010) *Self-Liberation Through Seeing With Naked Awareness,* Ithaca, NY: Snow Lion Publications.

Shantarakshita (2005) *The Adornment of the Middle Way: Shantarakshita's Madhyamakalankara with commentary by Jamgön Mipham,* Boston, MA: Shambhala Publications.

Stein, M. (2004) "Spiritual and religious aspects of modern analysis", in J. Cambray and L. Carter (eds.), *Analytical Psychology: Contemporary Perspectives in Jungian Analysis*, New York: Brunner-Routledge.

Varela, F. J., Thompson, E. and Rosch, E. (1992) *The Embodied Mind*, Cambridge, MA: The MIT Press.

Waldron, W. (2003) *The Buddhist Unconscious: The Alaya-Vinjñaña in the Context of Indian Buddhist Thought*, New York: Routledge Curzon.

Wilhelm, R. and Jung, C.G. (1962) *The Secret of the Golden Glower: A Chinese Book of Life* (trans. into C.F. Bayne), New York: Harcourt, Brace & Company.

Williams, P. (1998) *The Reflexive Nature of Awareness: A Tibetan Madhyaana Defence,* Delhi: Motilal Banarsidass Publishers.

8

JUNG'S ATHEISM AND THE GOD ABOVE THE GOD OF THEISM

John Dourley

The universality of anxiety

The phrase in the title, '. . . the God above the God of theism . . .' is taken from Paul Tillich's work, *The Courage to Be* (Tillich 1952, pp. 186–190). In this work Tillich argues that to be human is to be finite and to be finite is to be anxious. 'Anxiety is finitude experienced as one's own finitude' (ibid., p. 35). Such existential anxiety is unavoidable in the face of life's three greatest negations: fate and its extremity, death; guilt and its extremity, condemnation; and emptiness, and its extremity, meaninglessness (ibid., pp. 40–56). All three of these negations are always present in each epoch of Western history though, for Tillich, one predominates in each discernible period (ibid., pp. 47–63). The anxiety of fate and death characterized humanity's tribal origins. The anxiety of guilt and condemnation were to the fore in the medieval West. The anxiety of emptiness and meaninglessness pervaded twentieth-century culture and arguably our own.

In his characterization of the anxiety ruling the twentieth century, Tillich approaches Jung's confession made early in *The Red Book*. Here, Jung simply states that severance of the spirit of his time from the spirit of humanity's depths and the resultant pervasive meaninglessness constituted the predominant pathology in his personal life and in his surrounding social environment (Jung 2008, pp. 229, 232, 238). Both Jung and Tillich, from their different perspectives, worked throughout their lives to reconnect the contemporary human spirit with its own life-giving profundity. Tillich would argue that only the recovery of the experience of the ultimate, on which all religion rested, could restore credibility to any specific religion. Jung worked to show that human and religious maturation effectively coincide as God becomes conscious in the history of humanity – that is, in the life of the individual and of the species. The work of reconnecting humanity with its own unfathomable depths became for both the substance of authentic contemporary religion, psychologically and theologically revisioned.

Strategies to defeat anxiety

Tillich thus understands the universality of anxiety to drive individual and society to find the courage to be in the face of life's great negations and so to negate these negations. In doing so he distinguishes two main strategies to defeat anxiety and its identifiable presence in each epoch. The first strategy is to seek the courage to be through membership in collectivities – that is, to be as a part of a larger society as the basis of one's individual security (ibid., pp. 86–112). The second is to seek the courage to be as an individual, and so to live out of one's truest self (ibid., pp. 113–151). Each strategy will usually implicate the other since individual and society are never wholly divested of mutual influence. Yet the emphasis on one or the other, on social membership or individual affirmation, is again evident in the movement of historical epochs and in the ongoing shifting dialectic between the societal and individual search for the courage to be in the face of an always present existential anxiety.

For Tillich the courage to be as a part is predominant in humanity's early tribal history where individuality was almost totally subsumed in the collective. But even at this early stage, individualizing factors played a large role in corroding the collective unconsciousness of tribal membership. The prophetic insistence that the individual is not responsible for the sins of the father contributed to the sense of individual guilt and so individual responsibility. Greek philosophy and its critical questioning asked after the place of the individual in the personal and collective search for truth (ibid., p. 94). Both of these individualizing influences, religious prophecy and classical philosophy, went on to inform what Tillich calls the 'semi-collectivism' of the high Middle Ages, the period of Christendom. However, such semi-tribalism was itself dissolved by powerful currents working within it. Paradoxically, group orthodoxies, in both Roman and Reformed collectivities, were modified by the ecclesially induced sense of universal but personal guilt, by the individualism of Christian mysticism and by the renewed emphasis on the person in Protestant pietism and the experience of the inner light. In fact, Tillich will contend that the sharpening of the sense of personal guilt through ecclesially concocted penitentials led to a sense of guilt the presiding institution could no longer alleviate and so contributed to the Reformation. Nominalism's denial of universals in favour of the particular further contributed to deepening the sense of the individual before an individual and omnipotent God as other (ibid., pp. 95–96). All these forces tended to undermine the defeat of anxiety through the individual's immersion in Christendom.

Closer to the present, these religious forms of individualism were the remote but real precedents to the autonomy or freeing of reason, especially from the collusion of state and ecclesial suppression. Here, Tillich joins other historians of culture in documenting the Reformation's culmination in the Enlightenment. Tillich appreciates Enlightenment reason as promoting a sense of individuality existing in harmony with a universal reason manifest in the individual resonant with a deeper basis of collective accord (ibid., pp. 114–116). However, Tillich understands the Romantic reaction to the Enlightenment to go well beyond the relation of individual reason to a universal rational ground. Romanticism more intensely affirmed the individual as embedded in the totality through the depths of one's personal being and its native connection to all that is (ibid., pp. 120–121).

This position would be particularly evident in Schleiermacher's early work. In his Romantic enthusiasm Schleiermacher solves the tension of individual and community by showing the individual to be potentially related to all that is through the depths of one's personal being, a sensitivity he related closely to the true meaning of piety and so of religion (Schleiermacher 1958, pp. 1–25). In the sense of the internal connectedness of the individual with the totality, Jung had to admit that his own psychology, even in the face of its 'scientific' nature, could not wholly deny its affinity with romanticism (Jung 1935/1976, pars. 1739–1740). This is an important point when discussing Jung's psychology as a 'science'. When Jung concedes to a romantic element in his 'science' his admission removes his psychology from the realm of science as science is widely understood today, based on an empirical 'objectivity' removed from the deeper subjectivity of the scientist. The Romantic element in Jung's psychology aligns it more with gnosis, alchemy and mysticism than strict science responsible only to its empirical basis in the senses or their enhancement. Not that these aspects of mind need be mutually exclusive, although they are widely thought of as being so, beyond Jung's bringing them together in a unified perspective that remains unique to his psychology among the current categorization of the disciplines. The effort to reduce Jung to a 'scientist' and his psychology to a 'science' becomes a truncation demeaning to the full experience and vision of the person and the profundity of his work taken in its totality.

The existentialist fervor

To continue Tillich's narrative, Nietzsche gave to nineteenth-century individualism a decidedly religious and theological hue when he declared God to be dead, and eventually the bourgeois reluctantly had to agree (Tillich 1952, pp. 118–119). But at some point the Romantic nineteenth-century rooting of the courage to be in the individual's subjective connectedness with the all itself turned sour. The prolonged scrutiny of human interiority revealed not only the potential experience of the participation of the individual in all that is, but also the dark and demonic shadow in these depths newly emerging into consciousness. Tillich pays high tribute to the impact of the discovery of the repulsive side of humanity on both existentialism and depth psychology. Not only were there dimensions of humanity beyond reason and order, but they had to be allowed entrance into consciousness and culture. Such respect emerged not only in the form of depth psychology, particularly in Freud's depiction of human atavism, but in the protest against the reduction of the human cognitive potential first to consciousness and then to technology and technological 'productivity' to the neglect or repression of the complete human spirit and cognitive potential (ibid., p. 122; Tillich 1964a, p. 114; Dourley 2009, p. 245).

The nineteenth-century version of the individual as the source of the courage was to be continued into twentieth-century existentialism and its revolt against the theological and scientific reduction of the individual to an object. Theology did this by making humanity an object to an objective supernatural and transcendent voyeur or terrorist invading humanity from beyond humanity. The appropriate spiritual response to such an image of God is for Tillich the legitimate basis of atheism including his own (Tillich 1951, pp. 237, 239). Science, and especially the social sciences, can also reduce the individual subject to an object then to be manipulated by social ideologies (Tillich 1952, pp. 135–9: Dourley 2008a). In short, a leading cause of atheism is theism thus understood. This paradoxical side of Tillich would understand religion and science to join hands in corroding humanity's natural sense of God, the former by placing God in supernatural skies beyond human experience, the latter by an all-encompassing fascination with the visible, the quantifiable and all the senses can yield. Such scientism soon covered the religious instinct as the desert sands can bury the evidence of entire civilizations. Of this human decline Heidegger was to remark that humanity forgot and then forgot it had forgotten.

The impulse toward individual affirmation was magnified and distorted in the radical forms of existential individualism in the wake of the First World War. In the aftermath of the war's carnage, the sense of a shared meaning resting on essential structures of mind and morality was largely lost. The individual, liberated from any objectively shared understanding of essential humanity, was then free, indeed obliged, to create one's essential truth, through the exercise of one's own will (ibid., p. 137). The individual thus became responsible for the creation of one's essence in existence through one's purposeful and willful resolution of life's possibilities free of all influence from pre-existing essential determination human or divine. The question then becomes, 'How to shape the essence that one confers upon oneself in an absolute freedom from any legitimate determinant based on a sense of the essentially human?'

Tillich respects the values of existentialism thus understood and the legitimacy of its revolt against a dehumanizing objectivity. However, his admiration is far from unqualified. He critiques existentialism in that the existentialist turns to values and activity that rest on an essential structure of mind and reality of whose nature the existentialist remains usually unaware and whose influence is evaded or denied (Tillich 1964a, pp. 119–122). Both the distortions of existential life and the proposed response presume a picture of the essential in the existentialist. This essential structure is also the basis of the morality lodged in what Tillich calls the 'essential self' (Tillich 1963,

p. 235). In its primordial form the self is what one can and ought to be. It is the individual's pristine expression in the life of the divine – for Tillich, the Trinity. In existence the self is distorted. The distance between the essential and existential self is the difference between what one ought to be and what one is, a distance never to be wholly overcome in existential life. Such distance is also the basis of existential guilt. There will be no utopian realization of the 'kingdom' in history, time or finitude. Nevertheless, once one says 'ought' or 'should' one is a crypto-essentialist because one is describing the difference between what exists and what should be as grounded in the essential. On the essentialist/existentialist divide Tillich claims to be 'fifty-fifty' (Tillich 1967, p. 245). He remains respectful of the essential structures of the human mind and ethical activity as grounded in divine life but is deeply aware of the distortion of such structures in existence distanced but never severed from their essential reality in the divine.

In this, Tillich is in close affinity with Jung's archetypal essentialism, which also rests mind and ethical activity on the life of the universal potentiality of numinous archetypal structuring ever engaging human consciousness. At the same time both men are keenly aware that the mind may be distant from the awareness of such structures and so lapse into the drift of meaninglessness, or, on the other hand, become possessed by archetypal powers, religiously or politically, and become a victim of fanaticism in either or both realms. Jung's work on Job clearly reveals his understanding of human history to be driven by archetypal energies seeking their full realization in human historical consciousness as the meaning of history itself (Dourley 2008b, pp. 111–126). And, like Tillich, Jung is aware that these energies will never be fully consciously realized in existential history, although such realization remains history's unavoidable goal and deepest impulse. For both, the final *Kairos*, or fullness of time, is beyond history, although its allure is the foundational dynamic of history.

The neo-collectivitist backlash

In spite of its revolt on behalf of human freedom and subjectivity against all forms of reification, the individualism of twentieth-century existentialism and its nineteenth-century predecessors threatened the many who continued to seek an order alleged to be latent in collective humanity. Such a discernible order was then to be imposed on humanity as its essential meaning. For Tillich, the power of the ongoing modern need to find the courage to be as a part created the twentieth-century 'neo-collectivisms' – namely, communism, fascism and democratic conformism best exemplified in American democracy and its faith in a progressive productivity unable to answer the question 'but for what?' (Tillich 1952, pp. 96–112). Jung's political psychology may appear naive when he identifies the archetypal attraction of fascism as that of the benign despot or father, of communism as that of a paradise on earth and of democracy as simply another variant of contemporary state totalitarianism (Jung 1936b/1964, pars. 396–397; 1933/1964, par. 1019; 1936a/1976, pars. 1323–1326). However, Jung's political sociology gains credible substantiation from Tillich's more detailed treatment of the neo-collectivisms of twentieth-century fascism, extreme socialism and American infatuation with progressive productivity empty of deeper meaning. These became the three faces of a questionable collectivist victory over the aspiration of the free individual concerned with the irreducible dignity of the uniqueness of each human spirit.

The triumph of the meaningless and the courage of despair

It is at this point that Tillich's analysis of the spirit of the early and mid twentieth-century West most resonates with Jung's experience of a culture of meaninglessness removed from the spirit of its depths. In *The Red Book*, Jung frankly acknowledges that in the spirit of the times his science and scholarship led him to objectify the soul and in so doing he and his culture had lost theirs (Jung 2008, pp. 220, 232, 233). Only the recovery of their native soul in the depths of their being could resolve such personal and societal tragedy. For, in the end, Tillich concludes that the all-pervasive sense of meaninglessness in his culture invalidated the search for the courage to be as either part of a collectivity on one hand, or, on the other, as an existential individual free to confer on one's life whatever essential meaning it might afford. Further, the permeating sense of meaninglessness surrounding the modern corroded both the individual mystic's immediate sense of identity with God, as well as communal faith in a God before whom individual and community stood (Tillich 1952, pp. 156–160). Individual and social self-assertion shared a joint despair, a despair bravely depicted in the artistic and literary expressions of the meaninglessness of that time and possibly ours (ibid., pp. 142–148). The question then became how one finds the courage to be in the face of the all corrosive despair of modern emptiness and meaninglessness. Put simply, Tillich asks, 'Can faith resist meaninglessness?' (ibid., p. 174).

Tillich's paradoxical and basic answer is not the defeat of such despair but the courage to affirm oneself in its face out of 'the courage of despair' (ibid., p. 175). This faith within despair or faith as despair he calls 'absolute faith'. Its source is the ground of being itself grasping the individual in the depths of his or her being and so sustaining the individual in despair rather than removing it. The symbols of the 'ground of being', and 'depth of reason' are for Tillich symbols of the divine in whose being all that is participates and whose power is immediately evident to reason in its own depths. This ground is the divine ground of both individual and society. As such, it engenders a courage to be as both an individual and a social participant. Because of the depth at which it grasps the individual, this ground shares in both the immediacy of the mystic and the reality of the divine as institutionally mediated. In the face of current despair over attainable meaning, however, such courage could and would manifest beyond the need for all confessional or political expression in creeds, dogma, ritual and collective alignment, religious or political. In short, one affirms oneself in one's despair of meaning in a faith without traditional form or content, and certainly without the solace of God as saving object or person toward the despairing individual. Such faith without religious or political trappings Tillich will occasionally relate to the 'essential self', one's eternal truth, primordially expressed in the Logos within the life of the Trinity toward whose recovery one is naturally driven in existential removal therefrom (Tillich 1963, p. 235). In this, Tillich's understanding of the 'essential self' closely approximates Jung's understanding of the 'immortal self' existing in time and eternity and as the ultimate support and goal of the individual in existential life (Jung 1942/1967, par. 210).

Jungian scholarship has recently discovered Jung's affinity with nineteenth-century German idealism and in particular with F.W.J. Schelling's work. Tillich wrote two theses on Schelling in his student days. One was his philosophical doctoral dissertation at the University of Breslau in 1910. Its subject was Schelling's work on the history of religion (Tillich 1974a). The other was his theological dissertation at the University of Halle in 1912 (Tillich 1974b). It was on Schelling's conception of mysticism and guilt consciousness. Both works evidence Tillich's early adoption of what he was to term the 'principle of identity' – that is, that humanity and divinity share a point of identity in their being as the basis of humanity's inescapable and native sense of God's reality, a point in considerable continuity with Schleiermacher's romanticism. This point of identity is located in the essential, in turn lodged in the Trinity's expression of its potential manifest in the Logos within and beyond the Trinity. As such, it is the basis of what Tillich comes to term 'participation' – that is, the participation of human being in divine being as the ontological basis of humanity's unmediated epistemic experience of the divine. For Tillich and Jung this understanding of participation runs throughout their theology and psychology as its very life. Without the experiential basis of humanity's natural sense of the divine both systems remain unintelligible, then are reduced to mere mental pursuits through their emasculation and trivialization.

The God beyond the God of theism

In the context of absolute faith and the courage of despair, Tillich introduces his understanding of 'the God beyond the God of theism' (Tillich 1952, pp. 186–188). His critique of theism would extend by implication to all three monotheisms and dissolves three of the foundational features common to each. First, he speaks of theism as generating a vague but shallow sense of the divine, the kind that can be exploited for votes by politicians at election time. Such activity is an obvious but unfortunately ongoing exploitation of the numinosity native to religion for purposes far removed from the religious realm (ibid.,

p. 182). Second, he speaks of theism as informing the biblical imagination of the individual before a foreign God, a God one meets as total stranger rather than as a power from which one is currently estranged (ibid., p. 183; 1964b, p. 10). Such divinity he describes elsewhere as heteronomous, invading humanity from beyond humanity and demeaning human and divine dignity in doing so (ibid., p. 183; 1951, p. 84). The legitimate response to heteronomy is atheism in the service of divine and human honor. Third, Tillich identifies the worst feature of theism. In some continuity with the second, he simply terms this position as 'bad theology'. 'Bad theology' reduces the divine/human relation to a subject/object relation between, 'two persons who may or may not meet but who have a reality independent of each other' (Tillich 1952, p. 264). This theology depicts divinity as a divine subject over against a human object whose subjective reaction is to objectify God in the completion of mutual reification. Tillich's response to such imagination is to call for its corrosion by an atheism functioning as a form of spiritual purification (Tillich 1951, pp. 237, 245).

In his work on courage and in his *Systematic Theology* such cleansing atheism drives to the search for the God beyond the God of theism. One would assume that this would take him to a dimension of the divine, which precedes all form as the basis of the subject/object split and yet from whom all form derives. It would drive him to the innermost reaches of divinity understood as a creative nothingness endowed with a pleromatic fullness. Tillich never goes there at length or explicitly. The closest he comes to such a concept is in his Trinitarian theology where he refers to a maternal dimension of the divine preceding all form. Such divine maternity would resonate with Jung's understanding of the maternal nature of the seat and container of the archetypal unconscious as herself without form but the matrix of all form. In this respect Tillich toys with the idea of a quaternity insinuating a maternal power birthing the Trinity itself, but comes to this insight too late in life to give it further elaboration (Tillich 1963, pp. 293, 294). Moreover, his motif in this late exploration was the search for the feminine in Western Reformed theology spurred by the rise of feminism in the early sixties (Dourley 2001, pp. 79–96). The yield of this late enquiry remained peripheral and without systematic elaboration, no doubt due in part to Tillich's age.

Jung and the immanent – religious and political implications

Jung is also aware of the basis of a universal faith and courage afforded by the deepening co-inherence of ego and that ground from which all consciousness derives. He describes this ground as the 'eternal Ground of all empirical being' (Jung 1955/1970, par. 760; Dourley 2011, pp. 514–531). The conscious experience of this ground marks the culmination of that individuation Dorn describes in his alchemy. As the soul and body are purified and reunited, there emerges the sense of the *unus mundus*, the one world. Jung attaches a truly marvelous consciousness to this experience. For in itself it unites significant psychic opposites. Jung describes it as working toward the enhanced integration of the individual's psychic multiplicity, the complexes in the service of the ego, even as it leads the integrated individual toward a greater empathy with the multiple beyond the individual (Jung 1954b, pars. 440, 445). In this sense Jung's understanding of divine immanence is as strong as Tillich's and bears many of the same consequences. Both identify a religious dimension native to humanity and indistinguishable from the substance of human maturation, but both can see this agency as creating and operating through recognizable religious symbols and their institutionalization as well as doing quite well without them. Jung in particular would characterize the sequence of dreams in an individual's life as the equivalent of an ongoing personal revelation. The individual is then charged with the sometimes suffering vocation of relating one's developing revelation and personal myth to the collective myths into which one is born. In this conflict Jung would stand on the side of the individual's emerging myth as the greatest contribution the individual can make to society.

Jung's sense of this radical immanence underlies his thinking on quaternity. The move from trinitarian to quaternitarian imagination negates the monotheistic notion of a wholly other and eternally self-sufficient God. Such a traditional image of God cannot embrace all that God allegedly creates. It excludes from the divine the reality of the feminine, the demonic and embodied matter. The myth endemic to Jung's psychology works to restore the natural divinity of these realities and, indeed, the latent divinity of all that is. The quaternity thus moves to a unity of opposites in a Holy Spirit of a far more inclusive embrace than is possible in the trinitarian and patriarchal starkness of a Spirit worked unity between Father and Son stripped of the feminine, the body and the dark demonic (Jung 1948, par. 158).

Of even greater importance in Jung's post-Trinitarian imagination is his precise delineation of the divine approach to consciousness in the extension of the sacred to all that is. Jung is clear in writing that the myth of quaternity owes its energy to 'the fact that God's action springs from one's own inner being' (Jung 1920, par. 413). In this Jung is formulating a psychology of revelation based on the impact of archetypal forces compensating the culture and individuals addressed by a personal revelation psychologically understood. This position would open the religious canon indefinitely as an infinite divinity sought ever greater expression of its total resource in human consciousness. There could be, in Tillich's terms, no 'final revelation'. This realization would corrode the ever present possibility of another 'final solution'.

Jung's psychology of revelation correlates smoothly with his powerful and credible philosophy of history. It would imply that the meaning of history, personal and societal, is the 'incarnation' or 'penetration' – in a later formulation – of the wealth of the unconscious into human historical consciousness (Jung 1958/1976, pars. 1660–1661). In this historical and psychological dialectic God and humanity do not live separated from each other in natural and supernatural spheres but are 'functions' of each other in the only significant world that exists, the world of the interchange of consciousness with the unconscious in the ongoing embodiment of humanity's divinity (Jung 1971: par. 412). Jung's phrase, 'the relativity of God' refers to a divinity becoming progressively conscious in human consciousness in their mutual maturation in time and the flow of history (ibid., par. 452; Dourley 2010, pp. 46–48). The monotheistic myth and its Gods cannot assimilate the substance of this vision. It assumes a latent point of identity between the divine and the human as preceding their separation and understands their reunion as contributing to the maturation of both as the ground meaning of history. Consequently, Jung's imaging of the divine moves with Tillich to a God beyond the wholly transcendent and self-sufficient Gods of theism to the libido native to humanity driving to the mutual maturation of humanity and its origin in one self-contained process intolerant of divine intrusion from beyond the process itself.

Nor can theism assimilate the full thrust of Jung's late *Answer to Job*. This work is a piece of Hegelian mythology resting on the proposition that divinity creates consciousness in order to become conscious in its creature as the fulfillment of both creator and creature. In his work on Job Jung is unequivocal in equating the unconscious with the polarized origin of consciousness, Yaweh, reluctantly seeking and eventually demanding that consciousness unite the opposites of its origin in human consciousness itself (Jung 1954a/1969, pars. 595, 631, 642, 734, 749). Effectively, this process unifies a divine polarity in time that could not be united in eternity as the basic implication of the symbol of Trinity would have it. Rather, the divine self-contradiction can only be united in historical humanity at the divine insistence and with the power of the divine, now revisioned as the power of the self. For Jung, cooperation with these energies is something, in his words, that now depends on man – that is, on humanity aligning with the emergence of a myth that appreciates even as it surpasses all forms of foundational monotheistic imagination of a divinity even potentially discontinuous from humanity (ibid., par. 745). For Jung the alternative to such a surpassing myth is 'universal genocide' as fragmentary communities of collective unconsciousness strive for the supremacy of conflicting and provincial versions of their one and only Gods (Jung 1958/1976, par. 1661).

The surfacing of a mythic consciousness as an alternative to the genocidal potential endemic to the theistic myth entails for Jung a vision of divinity even more radically destructive of subject/object categories than is the case with Tillich. It may come as a surprise that Jung spells out this going beyond the subject/object structure most dramatically in his treatment of the mystics and especially of Meister Eckhart. He signals it in his Gnostic poem, *Septem Sermones ad Mortuos*, where he traces the origin of all definition, distinction and so otherness to a nothingness at once empty and full, and so as the *Pleroma* from which all modes of otherness proceed (Jung 1965, p. 379). In his work on Job he describes the need for the ego to undergo baptism in the pleromatic fullness of the nothing as an initiatory and ongoing moment in the process of individuation itself (Jung 1954a/1969: par. 677). However, he makes the implication of such baptism into the nothing most explicit in his treatment of Eckhart. Such baptism is there explicitly described as a process of the regression of the anima, and with her the ego, into an abyss beyond all differentiation. He writes: 'As a result of this retrograde process the original state of identity with God is re-established and a new potential is produced' (Jung 1971, par. 431).

In terms of Jung's wider psychology such regression would indicate an ingression into the depths of the unconscious somehow deeper than the archetypal urgency to express itself in individuals but, more importantly, in the creation of the diverse theistic Gods whose conflicting adherents now threaten the future of the species. A moment's respite in the creative nothingness beyond any distinction between the divine and human, and free of any will to expression would effectively moderate the divisive effect of archetypally based passion to become conscious, especially in the lethal religious/political forum. Momentary rest in the pre-archetypal would attain the common basis of all theisms henceforth perceived as varying concretions of this creative nothingness. A pause, however transient, in these depths would forbid claims to a final, exclusive and exhaustive truth now made by each member of the family of theistic Gods. A consciousness returned from its identity with its origins would foster a mutual appreciation by theistic communities in their self-understanding as three versions of the same archetypal expression now seeking their joint supersession in a myth of more universal sympathy for all that is. At this point the atheism implied in the God beyond the God of theism is no longer a religious, philosophical or political luxury. It becomes a major resource in humanity's strategy for survival, especially from the threat of monotheistic faiths in religious or secular guise. On the innovative consciousness evident in the Book of Job, Jung writes: 'An unusual scandal was blowing up in the realm of metaphysics, with supposedly devastating consequences, and nobody was ready with a saving formula which could rescue the monotheistic conception of God from disaster' (Jung 1954a/1969, par. 607). In the spirit of Jung and Tillich the winds of the scandal continues to blow. Both offer kindred but effective strategies to parry the disaster the monotheistic mind still presents to human survival.

References

Dourley, J. (2001) 'The Goddess Mother of the Trinity: Tillich's late suggestion', in R. Bulman, F. Parrella (eds.) *Religion in the New Millennium*: *Theology in the Spirit of Paul Tillich*, Macon, GA: Mercer University Press.

—— (2008a) 'Tillich, Jung and the wisdom and morality of doing science and technology', in *Paul Tillich, Carl Jung and the Recovery of Religion*, Hove: Routledge.

—— (2008b) 'Bringing up father: Jung on Job and the education of God in history', in *Paul Tillich, Carl Jung and the recovery of Religion*, Hove: Routledge.
—— (2009) 'Tillich in dialogue with psychology', in R.R. Manning (ed.), *The Cambridge Companion to Paul Tillich*, Cambridge: Cambridge University Press.
—— (2010) 'Taking back divinity: Jung on the relativity of God', in *On Behalf of the Mystical Fool: Jung on the Religious Situation*, Hove: Routledge.
—— (2011), 'Jung's equation of the ground of being with the ground of psyche', *The Journal of Analytical Psychology*, Vol. 56, No. 4, September.
Jung, C.G. (1920/1971) *Psychological Types*, *Collected Works*, Vol. 6, Princeton, NJ: Princeton University Press.
—— (1933/1964) 'Rejoinder to Dr. Bally', in *Civilization in Transition*, *Collected Works*, Vol. 10, Princeton, NJ: Princeton University Press.
—— (1935/1976) 'Foreword to von Koenig-Fachsenfeld: "Wandlungen des Traumsproblem von der Romantik bis zur Gegenwart"', *The Symbolic Life*: *Miscellaneous Writings*, Vol. 18, Princeton, NJ: Princeton University Press.
—— (1936a/1976), 'Psychology and national problems', in *The Symbolic Life*, *Collected Works,* Vol. 18, Princeton, NJ: Princeton University Press.
—— (1936b/1964) 'Wotan', in *Civilization in Transition*, *Collected Works*, Vol. 10, Princeton, NJ: Princeton University Press.
—— (1942/1967) 'Paracelsus as a spiritual phenomenon', in *Alchemical Studies*, *Collected Works*, Vol. 13, Princeton, NJ: Princeton University Press.
—— (1948/1969) 'A psychological approach to the dogma of the Trinity', in *Psychology and Religion*, *Collected Works,* Vol. 11, Princeton, NJ: Princeton University Press.
—— (1954a/1969) 'Answer to Job', *Psychology and Religion*, *Collected Works,* Vol. 11, Princeton, NJ: Princeton University Press.
—— (1954b/1969) 'Transformation symbolism in the Mass', in *Psychology and Religion*, *Collected Works,* Vol. 11, Princeton, NJ: Princeton University Press.
—— (1955/1970) *Mysterium Coniunctionis*, *Collected Works*, Vol. 14, Princeton, NJ: Princeton University Press.
—— (1958/1976) 'Jung and Religious Belief', *The Symbolic Life*: *Miscellaneous Writings*, *Collected Works,* Vol. 18, Princeton, NJ: Princeton University Press.
—— (1965) 'Appendix V, Septem Sermones ad Mortuos', in *Memories*, *Dreams*, *Reflections*, A. Jaffe (ed.), New York: Vintage, Random House.
—— (1971) 'The Relativity of the God Concept in Meister Eckhart', *Psychological Types*, *Collected Works*, Vol. 6, Princeton, NJ: Princeton University Press.
—— (2008) *The Red Book*, Sonu Shamdasani, (ed.) London, New York: W.W. Norton & Company.
Schleiermacher, F. (1958) *On Religion*: *Speeches to its Cultured Despisers,* New York: Harper & Row.
Tillich, P. (1951) *Systematic Theology*, *Volume I*, Chicago: Chicago University Press.
—— (1952) *The Courage to Be*, New Haven, CT and London: Yale University Press.
—— (1963) *Systematic Theology*, *Volume III*, Chicago: Chicago University Press.
—— (1964a) 'The theological significance of existentialism and psychoanalysis', in *Theology of Culture*, R.C. Kimball (ed.) New York: Oxford University Press.
—— (1964b) 'Two types of philosophy of religion', in *Theology of Culture*, R.C. Kimball (ed.), New York: Oxford University Press.

—— (1967) *Perspectives on 19th and 20th Century Protestant Theology*, C.E. Braaten (ed.), New York: Harper & Row.

—— (1974a) *The Construction of the History of Religion in Schelling's Positive Philosophy: Its Presuppositions and Principles*, V. Nuovo (trans., Intro.), Cranbury, NJ and London: Associated University Presses.

—— (1974b) *Mysticism and Guilt-Consciousness in Schelling's Philosophical Development*, V. Nuovo (trans., intro.), Cranbury, NJ and London: Associated University Presses.

9

SPEAKING WITH THE DEAD

Remembering James Hillman

Elizabeth Eowyn Nelson

Seven days after James Hillman died, Pacifica Graduate Institute held a private memorial in his honor. Barrett Center, the largest lecture hall on our campus, was transformed into a candlelit sanctuary of great beauty. After opening remarks by Steve Aizenstat, the founding president and chancellor, and Carol Pearson, the current president at the time, anyone in the circle of friends who gathered to remember James was welcome to say a few words: staff, faculty, administration, there was no distinction. For the next ninety minutes I listened to my colleagues speak of James. I thought I might say something—and in the end, did not. As I walked away, I was bewildered and disturbed. Where was my grief?

I devised an excellent rationalization. I knew Hillman primarily through his writing; I didn't have memories of leisurely dinners at his home in Thompson, Connecticut, or personal conversations during his annual visits to Pacifica. Not one of his infamous faxes arrived in my office. So, I said to myself, James isn't really dead, not for me. He is still very much alive and speaking the way he first appeared: on the page, where his commanding and occasionally infuriating intellect vibrated with vigor. With this comforting thought in mind, I spent the next two weeks immersed in his work, rewriting my lectures to honor him. I teach archetypal psychology, but this time I wanted my students to know more clearly how Hillman had profoundly shaped Pacifica and me. As I stood at the lectern, the calm I felt at his memorial simply evaporated. I opened my mouth to speak and could not. Instead, I wept.

It is impossible to calculate the influence of James Hillman on my thinking and on the mission of my *alma mater*. As we all know, Hillman wrote on a great many subjects, and would have written on many more had he another life to devote to psyche. However, his most lasting contribution was his method. Method, from the concatenation of two Greek words *meta* and *hodos*, roughly translates as "the way": a path or route. Even more, method is an attitude or posture, as in the phrase "way of being." I will circle back to the topic of James Hillman's method, but first I want to speak with the dead.

Speaking with the dead

On 23 May, 2012 I dreamt of a tall man, emaciated, skeletal, who was reclining in an effortless pose. His taut skin was chestnut brown, as though he had been buried in the earth. He looked fragile: close to death—already dead? I awakened, thinking that he reminded me a little of James, lanky and loose-limbed. The color of the skin fascinated me, not at all the pale-complected Hillman I recall, and the difference seems important. It is as though this skeletal dream figure had ripened, become ancient, and the earth had claimed him as one of its own. I thought of the peat of Ireland, colorful fall leaves ground into soft mulch, mysterious bog bodies, and cloudy steam rising from mounds of roasted chestnuts in the London dusk. Although the dream appeared to me in late spring it belonged to autumn, the season of James's death. It called to mind one of Keats's great odes, *To Autumn*, written a little over a year before the poet's death, which describes a season of such full and "mellow fruitfulness" that everything is blessed. Even when it seems that no more richness is possible, the figure of Autumn sets "budding more/And still more, later flowers for the bees" (Keats 1990, p. 324). Keats's Autumn is a drowsy steward of the earth's bounty, harvesting and winnowing the grain so that the barrenness of winter can be endured. It seems fitting that James would be winnowed in late October and that this dream figure would emerge for me, months later, as I mused upon how to speak about him, because the dream seemed to say: don't speak about James, speak to him and with him.

As I pondered this dream, I recalled a moment a few years ago, during the world tour of Jung's *Red Book*. The lecture hall at Los Angeles' *Hammer Museum* was packed with a noisy, energetic crowd, and there was not an empty seat anywhere. As James Hillman and Sonu Shamdasani made their way onto the stage, the noise faded but the excitement intensified. They settled into their chairs, looking as though they were about to continue a good conversation rather than begin a lecture, when Hillman spoke. "I was just reading about the Egyptian practice of opening the mouths of the dead," he said. What an entrance! It was an arresting statement, stopping my mind in its tracks and animating it at the same time, a paradox that Patricia Berry describes in her lovely analysis of the birth of Pegasus (1982, p. 161). Perhaps taking her cue from the freezing glance of the Medusa, Berry stopped the narrative motion of the story by deliberately staying with some of its moments (its images or complexes (in order to "see what mode of animation, if any, occur[ed]" (ibid., p. 148) and discovered that "within . . . stasis we find movement" (ibid., p. 161). Hillman's opening statement also alerted us to the direction of his mind. Like Hermes, he was going to guide us into the underworld and remind us that the dead speak; they have stories to tell us, if we would but listen. I heard echoes of Hillman's *The Dream and the Underworld* (1979b), where he says Hades is both *telos* and *finis*, and that the underworld nourishes. When we make this move toward Hades, everything becomes deeper, "moving from the visible connections to the invisible ones, dying out of life" (1979b, p. 30) and, simultaneously, coming alive in a new and potent way. For, as Hillman says, "when we search for the most revelatory meaning in an experience, we get it most starkly by letting it go to Hades, asking what has this to do with 'my' death. Then essence stands out" (ibid.).

Two years after the *Red Book* lectures in Los Angeles, Pacifica Graduate Institute hosted a public tribute to the life and work of James Hillman. One of the keynote speakers, David Miller, spoke of a marvelous story that touches on this theme of speaking with the dead. In 1975, a young Miller was invited to give a lecture at Eranos, and was understandably nervous about presenting his work to the people there. "They're not dead yet. They don't know anything. Speak to Jung, Freud, Plato, Plotinus, Heraclitus. They know something" (Miller 2012, n.p.).[1]

The necessity of journeying to the underworld is a consistent theme in Hillman's work, developed most fully in *The Dream and the Underworld.* Depth psychology, Hillman says, has brought "Death back from its exile," returning it "to its main place in the midst of the psychological life of each individual, which opens into depth at every step. Our footfalls echo on its vaults below. There is an opening downward within each moment, an unconscious reverberation" (Hillman 1979b, p. 67). Hillman speaks of "many modes of descent into Hades's realm" (ibid., p. 49) and many ways of experiencing the underworld, inscribed in the behavior and attitudes of specific gods. I have a particular affection for the stillness of Hekate. She enacts "a perspective that can witness the soul's struggles without the flap of Persephone or the disaster of Demeter," one that "shines in the dark and that witnesses such events because it already is aware of them a priori" (ibid., p. 49).

Yet five years before the publication of *The Dream and the Underworld*, a text devoted to this journey, Hillman had begun reminding us of the necessity of the underworld, a reminder that itself was necessary to a Western culture puffed up with the heroic fantasy of conquering death, if only we were clever enough. As Philip Aries tells us in his historical study, "Death, so omnipresent in the past that it was familiar, would be effaced, would disappear. It would become shameful and forbidden" (Aries 1974, p. 85). Along with the effacement of death went sorrow, grief, and mourning, which no longer inspired pity but repugnance. Mourning "is the sign of mental instability or of bad manners: it is morbid. . . . Solitary and shameful mourning is the only recourse, like a sort of masturbation" (ibid., p. 90). In *Revisioning Psychology* (1975), Hillman challenged this cultural attitude, invoking the Homeric *Hymn to Demeter* to commend abduction into the realm of death, where we gain a new eye:

> Each of us enacts Persephone in soul, a maiden in a field of narcissi or poppies, lulled drowsy with innocence and pretty comforts until we are dragged off and pulled down by Hades, our intact natural

> consciousness violated and opened to the perspective of death. Once this has happened—through a suicidal despair, through a sudden fall from a smooth-rising career, through an invisible depression in whose grip we struggle vainly—then Persephone reigns in the soul and we see life through her darker eye.
>
> (Hillman 1975, p. 208)

Until we are forced to yield our innocence and comfort, we will not have the perspective of psyche, its darkness and its depth. Until we acknowledge death in the midst of life, giving up the illusion "that growth is but an additive process requiring neither sacrifice nor death" (Hillman 1997, p. 68) we will not be true depth psychologists.

The importance of death for depth psychology helps to explain a curious experience of mine, one shared by my graduate students, when we have been asked "What are you studying?" When we reply "depth psychology," the reaction is often momentary shock followed by the question "Did you say *death* psychology?" The first dozen times this occurred I responded by slowly enunciating the word "depth" and felt the person's anxiety begin to dissipate. Eventually, though, I began to find my Hekate, and simply said, "Well, yes, in a manner of speaking, I am studying death psychology."

Since any knowledge worthy of its name comes from persons and places that exist beyond our fragile time-bound egos, we must speak with the dead. If we are to be Greek in our imagination, as Hillman was, our task is to grow down toward Hades, where the riches dwell. If we are to be aesthetic, we must cherish the displays of the world—what is here right now—as the living, sensitive skin of something that has immeasurable interiority. If we are to be scholars, we must have Hillman's "gift of leisure," said his friend Ed Casey, which is the root meaning of the Greek word *scholare*. Hillman's writing, "came from a deeply felt dimension that had its tempo, its own pace . . . . He loved the slow-moving tortoise . . . . He could combine such seeming opposites as bold and reflective" (Casey 2012, n.p.). I think of Hillman's leisurely attitude, the quality of slowness, as the diligent, detail-oriented awareness of the true craftsperson, one who worked with language as a living thing, listening for the footfall of each word on the page as it echoed in the vaults of Hades.

Attention, the cardinal psychological virtue

Under-worldly, aesthetic, leisurely. All three of these aims are captured in the Latin word *notitia*, which is the starting point of Hillman's method, his way of being psychological. He advocates *notitia* in his profound 1982 essay calling for the return of the soul to the world, where he argues that we have used our pet psychological theories as a defense against the *anima mundi* (Hillman 1982, p. 72). By not noticing, indeed by willfully excluding "the public, objective, physical world of things—buildings, and bureaucratic forms, mattresses and road signs, milk-packages and buses" (ibid., p. 74), we contribute to the world's ugliness.

> I am astounded by the life and beauty in the patients vis-à-vis the dead and ugly world they inhabit. The heightened awareness of subjective realities, that soul sophistication resulting from one hundred years of psychoanalysis, has become incommensurable with the retarded state of external reality, which moved during the same one hundred years toward brutal uniformity and degradation of quality.
> (ibid., p. 72)

Although Hillman had described the dangers of interiorizing and personalizing the soul in earlier works (1972, 1975, 1977, 1978, 1979a, 1979b), this landmark essay states the case most passionately. Hillman's outrage fuels every thought and word, the pen clearly mightier than the sword. Yet none of this would have been possible without the practice of *notitia*, in which Hillman noticed where he and other psychologists had unwittingly placed soul, or assumed it to be, and then noticed the dire consequences of witnessing beautiful and vital human souls as separate from, and unaffected by, a dead, ugly, and soulless world. His conclusion: "We cannot inoculate the individual soul, nor isolate it against the illness in the soul of the world" (Hillman 1982, p. 76). It is too much for the personal soul to bear and it shows too little care for the *anima mundi*.

I want to pause now to ponder the theme of the 2012 international conference of Jungian analysts and scholars, the audience for whom I first wrote this chapter. The theme of the conference was "Jung in Conversation with a Changing World." Thirty years ago, when *Spring Journal* published Hillman's essay "*Anima Mundi*: the return of the soul to the world," the world was changing, and rapidly. Hillman was hardly alone in noticing this change. Instead, he recognized how small our conception of soul had become and saw through that smallness to the comforting illusion it supported—that the world's illness, showing up in overpopulation, ecological devastation, and ongoing war, poverty, disease, and famine, in addition to the daily ugliness in which objects were carelessly made and just as carelessly discarded—had nothing to do with the human soul. "The world, because of its breakdown," Hillman said, "is entering a new moment of consciousness: by drawing attention to itself by means of its symptoms, it is becoming aware of itself as a psychic reality" (1982, p. 75).

Hillman's essay articulates a crucial psychological perspective that makes a substantial contribution to an issue that has crossed, and must cross, disciplinary boundaries: the health of our fragile planet. He recalls us to an indigenous sensibility in which the world is not dead, inert matter designed for the thoughtless convenience of human ingenuity. Instead, Hillman invites us to

> imagine the anima mundi as that particular soul-spark, that seminal image, which offers itself through each thing in its visible form. Then *anima mundi* indicates the animated possibilities presented by each event as it is, its sensuous presentation as a face bespeaking its interior image-in short, its availability to imagination, its presence as a psychic reality. Not only animals and plants ensouled as in the Romantic vision, but soul is given with each thing. God-given things of nature and man-made things of the street.
>
> (ibid., p. 77)

It is easier to imagine soul in the God-given things of nature. The sublimity of nature has been celebrated in the European Romantic tradition for centuries, as Keats's ode *To Autumn*, mentioned a few moments ago, exemplifies. Keats and his fellow Romantics easily sweep the listener into imagining an ensouled world, the *anima mundi*, when speaking of sunlight touching "the stubble-plains with rosy hue," a "wailful choir" of small gnats, and the song of the hedge-crickets (Keats 1990, pp. 324–325). Hillman calls upon us to do something far more challenging: to practice *notitia* with the manufactured objects that go unnoticed and to feel their suffering in the knowledge that they were cheaply and carelessly made, intended for a life that is poor, nasty, brutish, and short. He says:

> Things are composed of poisonous and flammable substances, stamped out of uniform molds, internally fastened cheaply, quickly with the least care, untouched by the human hand. They cannot weather or age. Their existence is hurried by the push of obsolescence as one generation succeeds the next within a few months. Sold by barkers on the slave-blocks of the market, competing by price only, and not by pride or inherent beauty, their suffering is written on their faces.
>
> (1982, p. 83)

Can we notice this? Is it possible to see, in the face of a flimsy plastic drinking cup or the body of a shoddily manufactured garden hoe, the suffering of the *anima mundi*? Or will we take the easy way out and simply not notice, use and then discard the object thoughtlessly, placing it forever out of sight, out of mind, and out of soul? As if that were even possible, of course, the repressed always promising their return, whether as a distant island of plastic, miles in diameter, floating in the middle of the Pacific Ocean or, much closer to home, the heaps of detritus that engulf the hoarder. Dare we notice *this* changing world?

As David Tacey points out in his splendid introduction to *The Jung Reader*,

> the ecological emergency has prompted us to value the whole rather than the part, and Jung offers a vision that is large enough to make sense of the connections between a host of elements that are not usually connected. It could be that these elements have always been connected, but our scientific specialisations have held them apart. Jung's insights into the interconnectedness of the world, together with the revisions of his work by Hillman, have made significant contributions to the rising discipline of ecopsychology. One might say that at last Jungian thought has found acknowledgement and respect in a scholarly field.
>
> (Tacey 2012, p. 18)

I believe Tacey is correct, in part because it is dangerous to ignore the *anima mundi* and in part because tending our fragile planet requires the concerted effort of many open-minded specialists. Not noticing is no longer an option. Hillman made this plain thirty years ago.

In other texts Hillman returns to the importance of *notitia*. For instance, one of the statements I always teach my research students is from the 1994 book *Insearch*: "Attention is the cardinal psychological virtue. On it depends perhaps the other cardinal virtues, for there can hardly be faith nor hope nor love for anything unless it first receives attention" (Hillman 1994, p. 119). How can we love if we do not first notice? Indeed, what is loving if it does not include noticing? It should be added that Hillman's attention was a thing to behold, and not a little scary when he turned it toward you. I sometimes wonder whether one's attention is best practiced with closed eyes; certainly this would offer something different. Hillman himself suggests this when he describes the particular qualities of attention, *notitia*, characteristic of each organ. The ear, for instance, "can get nowhere, make nothing, do no one harm. We receive the other as if he were music, listening to the rhythm and cadence of his tale, its thematic repetitions, and the disharmonies" (ibid., p. 22). In privileging the ear, Hillman says, "we become mythologists of the psyche, that is, students of the tales of the soul" (ibid.).

The importance of *notitia* in research emerged in recent years when psychodynamic theory gained an unlikely ally. One of the surprising outcomes of the "decade of the brain" is that a new group of experts, developmental neurobiologists, is noticing faith, hope, love and other emotions—and they are noticing the act of noticing itself. In Allan Schore's outstanding series of books on the subject of affect regulation and the origin, repair, and expression of the self (1994, 2003a, 2003b), he proposes a hypothesis that has now been confirmed by many different researchers: "that emotion is central to a deeper understanding of the human condition, and that unconscious processes lie at the core of the self, throughout the lifespan (Schore 2012, pp. 1–2).

He goes on to assert that "our highest human functions—stress regulation, intersubjectivity, humor, empathy, compassion, morality, and creativity—are all right brain functions" (ibid., p. 7) that are crucially shaped by the first years of *being* noticed. Attention is the cardinal psychological virtue in the caregiver–infant bond and has profound repercussions for the remainder of the child's life. Schore, who speaks as a neurobiologist and a clinician with forty years of experience of both models and insists upon a transdisciplinary approach which, at the time of his first book on affect regulation in 1994, was "a radical prospect" (ibid., p. 1). It is perhaps less radical now, but no less urgent. We must pool our expertise and practice *notitia* together.

Hillman gave his attention, practiced *notitia*, through his "inexhaustible devotion to the here and now," says my colleague and coauthor Joseph Coppin (2012). I recall seeing this devotion, and Hillman's gift for leisure, one day when he conducted a dialogue with my depth psychology students. He began by asking a deceptively simple question: "What is depth?" The silence in the room may have been three parts fear to one part perplexity—few students felt keen enough to engage Hillman—but curiosity eventually won the day. This question kept us fully occupied for ninety minutes. It was simple, yes, but as Jung pointed out, simplicity is "the most difficult of all things" (1929/1967, p. 16). Noticing our ideas is very difficult indeed, but for a thinker like Hillman, it was crucial. "The soul reveals itself in its ideas, which are not 'just ideas'" he says, "since they are the very modes through which we are envisioning and enacting our lives. We embody them as we speak and move" (Hillman 1975, p. 121). The dearth of ideas in contemporary psychology is one of his great laments. The dearth of ideas in contemporary culture was more painful, a syndrome that Hillman called "inertia of the spirit, a passivity that feels no vocation and shies from imaginative vision, adventurous thinking and intellectual clarification" (Hillman 1995, p. 18).

Notitia is crucially linked to psychological ideas through the medium of language. Speaking the language of the soul requires careful attention and precise articulation. If we are to honor Psyche, who also visited the dead, we must take the time to go down, to notice anew, and question what we mean. Here is an example: At the 2010 Pacifica *Senex and Puer* conference, Hillman says, "one of the words I'd like to lose now is body." That jolted me. Lose the body? When it has been such a long and difficult struggle to reunite body and mind in our philosophies and our psychologies? But then he clarified. Let us return to the precise and the peculiar. Lose body—but keep livers and knees and elbows—because "once we start using that word *body* I have no idea what we're talking about. Where does *body* begin and *me* stop?" Hillman asks. "Let us see how this term 'body' separates us from the thing itself." That question haunts the practice of psychology and the ideas it proposes: how does our language separate us from the thing itself? When and where have we become complacent, unreflective, and dumb? For "without attention to words," says Hillman, "we are dumb—speechless and stupid both" (1995, p. 12).

Hillman was a craftsman in his use of language, and returned to the theme of how language can evoke and honor soul, again and again. We see this in his 1976 essay "Peaks and Vales," where he contrasts spirited language with soulful language. Even earlier, though, in his 1972 text *The Myth of Analysis*, he waxes poetic on this theme:

> Psychological remembrance is given by the kind of speech that carries remembrance within it. This language is both of culture and uncultured, is both of art and artless. It is a mythic metaphoric language a speech of ambiguities that is evocative and detailed, yet not definitive, not productive of dictionaries, textbooks, or even abstract descriptions. Rather it is a speech that leads to participation, in the Platonic sense, in and with the thing spoken of, of stories and insights which would evoke, in the other who listens, new stories and new insights . . . It calls forth, and creates psyche as it speaks . . . It will have . . . body images, speaking from and reaching to the imaginal body in order to provoke the soul's movements. It must be speech that works as an imaginative agent stirring fantasy. Such speech has impact because it carries body in it; it is speech alive, the word itself alive, not a description about a psychic state by a psychologist, not carefully defined, but freely imagined.
>
> (Hillman 1972, p. 206)

He continues:

> Although not fashioned in schools this language will be fashioned and schooled, it will be rich and full of speech, a tongue of metaphor, of poetry and myths, for it is obliged to reflect Psyche's beauty, pregnant with voluptuousness. Its aim will always be soul making.
>
> (ibid., p. 207)

Perhaps it was Hillman's practice of *notitia* that fed his mind with a bounty of ideas. Perhaps it was his emphasis on the aesthetic, a theme he returns to frequently (1975, 1976, 1977, 1978, 1979a, 1982). Hillman vastly preferred the "vale of soul-making" (Keats 1990, p. 473) to the peaks, where the world was less pure but more rich, complex, and troubling. I think his bounty of ideas also exemplified his preference for transgression, much like Jung's, in which no intellectual silo could stand inviolate. Both Jung and Hillman live up to the obligation of the psychologist that Jung describes in his essay *Psychology and Literature*, who must "abandon his thickly-walled specialist fortress . . . and make himself familiar with a wide range of subjects" (1950/1966, p. 85 (para. 133)). Glen Slater, one of my Pacifica colleagues and an editor of Hillman's work, says this:

> Throughout James' work what we find is the unmistakable imprint of many ideas, a large number of which came from outside of psychology. The movement—the dexterity of mind, the spark, the different angles and careful differentiations that enlivened his thought—resulted from forging several different intellectual alliances. In other words, he moved well because he had places to move to and from and between.
>
> (2012, n.p.)

The key word here is movement. As a thinker and writer Hillman moved well, with dexterity, grace, liveliness. It is this movement that leads me from *notitia* to psychologizing.

From *notitia* to psychologizing

Of the four natural moves of the psyche Hillman describes in *Revisioning Psychology*, my favorite is psychologizing, which honors psyche's "flair for the dramatic" (Nelson 2001, p. 1). When speaking of the theatrical psyche, Hillman is elaborating a point Jung makes in *Mysterium Coniunctionis* that psychodynamics is psychodramatics (Jung 1963/1989, p. 496). Psychologizing, or seeing through, transforms "any literal action at all . . . into a metaphorical enactment. I see the act and the scene and stance I am in" (Hillman 1975, p. 127). With this word *enactment* we know we are in the domain of Dionysus and that our ground is the serious play of theater. Here psychologizing can be embodied through "changes of physical position and attitude" to shift our relationship with "events, scenes, persons" (ibid., p. 142). New ideas are not produced through mental gymnastics in a torpid body. It is vital to commit ourselves physically, through actual movement. "The psyche presupposes the living body in order that its images may live," says Jung (1926/1981, p. 326). He adds: "the piece that is being played does not want merely to be watched impartially, it wants to compel participation" (ibid., p. 496).

Participation with psyche's images and psyche's ideas can take many forms, but it is not indifferent or lazy. In fact, it can be combative, underscoring a key metaphor used by Lakoff and Johnson who begin their landmark work, *Metaphors We Live By*, with the example that argument is war (1980, p. 4). This is not a mere figure of speech, they point out. The metaphor of war structures how we think about argumentation and inscribes the rules of participation. "Metaphor is as much a part of our functioning as our sense of touch, and as precious" (ibid., p. 239). If we practice *notitia* with our customary metaphors, we can more clearly see their influence on our thoughts, beliefs, and actions. Lakoff and Johnson offer a different metaphor, something close to the metaphor I will use shortly. "Imagine a culture where an argument is viewed as a dance," they suggest, "the participants seen as performers, and the goal is to perform in a balanced and aesthetically pleasing way" (ibid., p. 5). I think there are few colleagues who did not experience Hillman as occasionally combative, or perhaps perennially combative. He irritated some people, enlivened others, and frightened a good many. One always felt his presence.

I found James enlivening, and recognized the combative stance as a form of devotion. He fought with psychology all of his life because he loved it. At any point, he could have simply left the field, decided it was an unworthy opponent or that the struggle was pointless. In one of his most poignant questions, Hillman (1972, p. 82) asks, "can anyone live authentically unless he believes and trusts in the basic meaningfulness and rightness of the movements of his love?" Again, we note the emphasis on movement, underscoring psyche's theatrical flair, but we also hear the lament of someone who is wholeheartedly committed to what he loves, no matter how much suffering it entails. Hillman knew precisely what the soul endures on behalf of love. "The intimate one opens the deepest wounds," says Perera, "and lovers, thus, become enemies. And they are also beloved enemies, since the woundings create separations across which fresh passions leap" (Perera 1981, p. 80).

Psychologizing and stage combat

The phrase "beloved enemies" along with its milder form "worthy opponent" have captivated me for quite a while, for many reasons. They are reminiscent of one of my hobbies, stage combat, because of the paradox central to this activity: the opponents in stage combat are partners. All else crucially depends upon this one fact. The actors are " 'dancing a fight' together while the audience sit and watch two characters battling away" (Howell 2008, p. 11). My task is to make my partner look good, just as his task is to make me look good. The most satisfying fights are between two highly skilled people, both of whom are trustworthy and committed. Creating the illusion of violence requires the actor-combatants to be in complete control *of their movements together*, such that "the characters are in danger, never the performers" (Ducklin and Waller 2001, p. 19).

The legendary fight choreographer William Hobbs speaks about the contradictions inherent in the best theatrical combat. "Acted aggression" requires the appearance of "highly charged" emotions while the actors work "on a conscious level of coolness, with complete body relaxation and control" (1995, p. 119). Hobbs underscores the necessity of true partnership by speaking about dangerous fighters. "The problem lies in the actor's desire to 'look good' – the kind of person . . . who cares little for anything or anybody outside his own performance. Come what may, he is going to be 'wonderful' " (ibid., p. 119). I imagine that many of us have participated in enough brutal theoretical battles to begin to understand how combat is an apt metaphor for the scholarly life. Most of us have encountered colleagues so zealously preoccupied with looking good that they are not safe or trustworthy. In fact, the aggression is no longer acted, it is real, and the result is more destructive than creative, more tyrannical than collaborative. So the metaphor of theatrical combat can extend from thoughts about Hillman's work to our own style.

The truth of this paradox impressed me the first time I performed a fight with Tim, one of my instructors, who was far and away the more skilled actor–combatant. We were working with single rapiers at performance speed—not the slower practice pace that allows beginners to fight safely. The moment we began, I felt the heightened intensity, astonished that I was moving better than I ever had. That was Tim's skill: my very worthy partner–opponent raised the bar.

What if we were to imagine Hillman as a skilled partner–opponent? What if we were to join him in the theater of psyche, and commit ourselves to serious play, where our ideas could live and breathe and flex their muscles? Our values would shift: our task would no longer be to humiliate our opponent, but instead use all our skills to raise the bar and make us both look good—as Tim did for me in a rapier duel.

As I reread Hillman's work in the last nine months, I began imagining it through the metaphor of theatrical combat. It helped me understand his precise observations and pointed language. He even gives his adversary the stage, for instance, in his 1977 inquiry into image, where he introduces The Protestor. His commitment to the agon of idea-making is even more pronounced when Hillman does battle with Hillman. *I cannot think of another depth psychologist who quotes himself to disagree with himself.* He models for any scholar the partial nature of knowledge and the need to continually question our own thinking. We may discover, as we grow down, that our earlier ideas were wrong or inadequate. Do we have the courage to say so? Perhaps—if we can imagine disagreement as an expression of loyalty and conflict as a form of relating.

Perhaps the best example of Hillman's criticism of Hillman is found in the 1994 edition of his book *Insearch: Psychology and Religion*, first published in 1967. The second revised edition includes a fourteen-page critical postscript by the author, in which Hillman identifies and questions the two big assumptions that are the starting premise for the entire text: one, that the soul is interior and two, that it is lost (1994, p. 128). He goes on to say that

> Maybe the soul is right here at hand, not abandoned, not lost at all. We just haven't noticed. We've been looking in the wrong place. How curious this paranoid tendency of the mind: when we don't see something we are looking for, we at once imagine it to be stolen, hidden, or lost. Why not instead imagine that the fault exists in our eyesight, that the thick glasses we are wearing are too far-sighted to see what's close at hand.
>
> (ibid., p. 129)

This is, of course, the idea that Hillman develops in his pivotal 1982 essay, published in *Spring*, entitled "*Anima mundi*: The return of the soul to the world," mentioned earlier.

In fact, disagreement with other keen and committed thinkers dramatizes the liveliness of thinking, the autonomy of ideas, and the continuously creative psyche. Ideas don't just drop into consciousness whole, complete, and solitary. They require the companionship of other ideas, an active participation much like the graceful moves of the actor–combatant. To repeat: we know we are engaged in psychodramatics, the theater of psyche, even in the individuation of our ideas, or perhaps most especially there. "As we cannot go it alone, we cannot know it alone," Hillman says, because "consciousness itself has an erotic, Dionysian component which points to participation . . . We are conscious only in some form of related sharing" (1972, pp. 295–296).

If consciousness is produced through related sharing, then what better way to imagine this for a martial person by birth, as Hillman was, than theatrical combat? I believe he tested himself and his notions through the serious play of acted aggression. Such a partnership requires precision, coordination, and trust. Out of these grow the moving grace of psychological ideas at play with one another in the world.

The next move is yours.

Note

1 I am grateful to David Miller for giving me permission to tell this story (personal communication, August 2012).

References

Aries, P. (1974) *Western attitudes toward death*. Baltimore, MD: Johns Hopkins University Press.

Berry, P. (1982) *Echo's subtle body*. Dallas, TX: Spring Publications.

Casey, E. (2012) "Remembering Hillman," in *A Tribute to James Hillman*. Symposium conducted at Pacifica Graduate Institute, Carpinteria, CA.

Coppin, J. (2012) "The image of the living fence," in *A Tribute to James Hillman*. Symposium conducted at Pacifica Graduate Institute, Carpinteria, CA.

Ducklin, K. and Waller, J. (2001) *Sword fighting: A manual for actors and directors*. New York: Applause Theatre Books.

Hillman, J. (1972) *The myth of analysis: Three essays in archetypal psychology*. Evanston, IL: Northwestern University Press.

Hillman, J. (1975) *Revisioning psychology*. New York: Harper Colophon Books.

Hillman, J. (1976) "Peaks and vales." *Spring*. Dallas, TX: Spring Publications, pp. 66–79.

Hillman, J. (1977) "An inquiry into image." *Spring*. Dallas, TX: Spring Publications, pp. 62–88.

Hillman, J. (1978) "Further notes on images." *Spring*. Dallas, TX: Spring Publications, pp. 171–185.

Hillman, J. (1979a) "Image sense." *Spring*. Dallas, TX: Spring Publications, pp. 152–182.
Hillman, J. (1979b) *The dream and the underworld*. New York: Harper & Row.
Hillman, J. (1982) "*Anima mundi*: The return of the soul to the world." *Spring*. Dallas, TX: Spring Publications, pp. 71–93.
Hillman, J. (1994) *Insearch* (2nd revised ed.). Woodstock, CT: Spring Publications.
Hillman, J. (1995) *Kinds of power*. New York: Doubleday.
Hillman, J. (1997) *Suicide and the soul* (2nd ed.). Woodstock, CT: Spring Publications.
Hobbs, W. (1995) *Fight direction for stage and screen*. Portsmouth, NH: Heinemann.
Howell, J. (2008) *Stage fighting, a practical guide*. Wiltshire, UK: The Crowood Press.
Jung, C. G. (1966 [1950]) "Psychology and literature," in *The spirit in man, art and literature*. In R. F. C. Hull (trans.), *The collected works of C. G. Jung* (2nd ed., Vol. 15, pp. 84–105). Princeton, NJ: Princeton University Press.
Jung, C. G. (1967 [1929]) "Commentary on 'The secret of the golden flower,'" in R. F. C. Hull (trans.). *The collected works of C. G. Jung* (2nd ed., Vol 13, pp. 1–55). Princeton, NJ: Princeton University Press.
Jung, C. G. (1981 [1926]) "Spirit and life," in R. F. C. Hull (trans.), *The Collected Works of C. G. Jung* (2nd ed., Vol. 8, pp. 319–337). Princeton, NJ: Princeton University Press.
Jung, C. (1989 [1963]) *Mysterium Coniunctionis*. In R. F. C. Hull (trans.), *The collected works of C. G. Jung* (2nd ed., Vol. 14). Princeton, NJ: Princeton University Press.
Keats, J. (1990) *John Keats* (E. Cook (ed.)) Oxford: Oxford University Press.
Lakoff, G. and Johnson, M. (1980) *Metaphors we live by*. Chicago: University of Chicago Press.
Miller, D. (2012) "Devar 'Aher': On the other handle," in *A Tribute to James Hillman*. Symposium conducted at Pacifica Graduate Institute, Carpinteria, CA.
Nelson, E. (2001) "Psyche's knife." Carpinteria, CA: Pacifica Graduate Institute. Unpublished dissertation.
Perera, S. (1981) *Descent to the goddess*. Toronto: Inner City Books.
Schore, A. (1994) *Affect regulation and the origin of the self*. Mahwah, NJ: Erlbaum.
Schore, A. (2003a) *Affect regulation and the repair of the self*. New York: Norton.
Schore, A. (2003b) *Affect dysregulation and disorders of the self*. New York: Norton.
Schore, A. (2012) *The science of the art of psychotherapy*. New York: Norton.
Slater, G. (2012) "Befriending ideas," in *A Tribute to James Hillman*. Symposium conducted at Pacifica Graduate Institute, Carpinteria, CA.
Tacey, D. (ed.) (2012) *The Jung reader*. Hove, East Sussex: Routledge.

10

PRACTICING IMAGES

Clinical implications of James Hillman's theory in a multicultural and changing world

Marta Tibaldi

This chapter has a practical focus, as it attempts to highlight some clinical implications of James Hillman's theories (Hillman 1977, 1979, 1981, 1996) in order to establish new responses to common requests from patients in light of a multicultural reality and a changing world. Something that always surprised me – and keeps on surprising me – is how much, at least in Italy, Hillman's works are considered solely on the theoretical level, and how in various ways they disregard the important practical effects of his ideas. The purpose of my chapter is to honor James Hillman's memory, recalling some of his pivotal statements, and presenting three clinical proposals that are each inspired by his invitation for us 'to see-through' and 'to become an image among images'.

On October 27, 2011, James Hillman died at 86 years of age in his house in Thompson, Connecticut. The news of his death immediately reached Italy, and on the same day, and the days that followed, several articles appeared in the newspapers and on the Internet, either with stressed admiration for James Hillman's courage and lucidity in his experience of dying, or with narratives about his personality and work, and some critique of his thought (Galimberti 2011; Sica 2011; Gioriello 2011). Two newspapers, including *L'Unità* e *Il Fatto quotidiano* published articles by Romano Màdera, entitled, 'Hillman, lo sciamano dell'anima' ['Hillman, the soul's shaman'] (Màdera 2011), and that of Franca D'Agostini, entitled, 'Hillman, il profeta dell'anima' [Hillman, the soul prophet] (D'Agostini 2011). The first stresses Hillman's will 'to heal cultures', and, the second, Hillman's anti-positivism, and his 'abstract cultural therapeutic approach'. I cite these two articles because, as I said before, one of the ways in which the practical application of James Hillman's thoughts in Italy has been ignored is to ignore the theoretical claims of archetypal psychology at the expense of its clinical value. To this regard, it is worth remembering that archetypal psychology arose as a reply to a way of theorizing and practicing deep analysis, which, according to Hillman, had been too focused on conscious and unconscious subjectivity, and imprisoned within Western cultural imagery.

One of the most moving articles that was published in Italy shortly after Hillman's death, and one that was far different from the others, was by Silvia Ronchey, entitled 'Addio a Hillman, così si muore da filosofo antico' [Farewell to Hillman, this is an old philosopher's way of dying] (Ronchey 2011). Ronchey's paper includes an interview with Hillman, and quotes the following words he said just before his death: 'Stay thinking till the last threshold of being (and leave your thoughts to the descendants)'; 'Dying is the essence of life'; 'Finding the right words is fantastic. It is so important [. . .] Words are like pillows: if put correctly they ease the pain'.

I will go back to these statements in the second part of my chapter, where I shall approach them metaphorically, in order to transform them into three practical proposals to apply therapeutically.

Considering that for archetypal psychology the psyche expresses itself through images – a fact well established by neuroscientific research (Damasio 2012) – the aim of archetypal psychotherapy, according to Hillman, is 'the development of a sense of the soul' (Hillman 1981, p. 28) – that is to say, to build a conscious relationship with what he defines as 'the poetic basis of mind' (Hillman 1981, p. 21; see also Hillman 1975, p. xi): that function of mind that produces images naturally. When Hillman speaks of 'soul' he refers to the way we perceive and represent personal and impersonal reality in an imaginal way; that is a metaphorical way that observes and is in relationship with whatever life expresses: 'By soul I mean, first of all, a perspective rather than a substance, a viewpoint toward things rather than a thing itself' (Hillman 1975, p. x). In this sense, archetypal psychology lays in the gaze of the observer and in the relationship they build with the world, with others, and with themselves.

In 'Archetypal Psychology' (1981), by quoting Edward Casey's essay 'Towards an archetypal imagination' (1974), Hillman notices again that 'an image is not what one sees but the way in which one sees'. He continues:

> An image is given by the imagining perspective and can only be perceived by an act of imagining. [. . .] Images come and go (as in dreams) at their own will, with their own rhythm, within their own fields of relations, undetermined by personal psychodynamics. [. . .] It is not we who imagine but we who are imagined.
>
> (Hillman 1981, pp. 18–19)

It is a position that Hillman states again in 'An Inquiry into Image' (1977) when he writes about the method of archetypal psychology:

> I want to be operational. I want to talk about *what we do and not what we think we do*. This is to distinguish between Jungian method

> and methodology. [. . .] Methods are the way we go about things and methodologies are the 'ologies' we invoke to justify our methods. The first is actual tactics, the second the headquarters' strategy, the theoretical definitions and plans for carrying them out.
>
> (Hillman 1977, p. 67)

In order to develop an imaginal approach – 'to look through' – it is necessary to achieve that psychic attitude that recognizes the imaginal nature of the mind and get in touch with it dynamically. Developing an imaginal approach means also becoming aware that the way in which our mind represents itself happens through images and that the mind expresses itself metaphorically. This imaginal activity is 'mine', because it happens to me and I recognize it as such, but it is also 'not-mine', because it is autonomous to my subjectivity. This is the impersonal perspective to which Hillman refers in his works, and on which he focuses his attention. Of course, these statements do not mean that the psychic personal and subjective dimension has to disappear from our horizon or doesn't have to exist any more; it means more simply that archetypal psychology turns its gaze mainly in the direction of the impersonal psychic aspects and of those it speaks.

I would like to describe this 'position' of archetypal psychology as it relates to depth psychology generally, by using the image of a sailing boat sailing upwind. When we are sailing in a boat at this pace and the wind blows strongly on one side to tilt the boat, at a certain point it is necessary to lean to the other side, in order not to capsize. It is necessary then, to rebalance yourself strongly in the opposite direction in respect of where you were before, in order to prevent the boat from turning upside down.

It could be said that the wind of deep analysis has been blowing for a long time in the direction of conscious and unconscious subjectivity, the side on which psychoanalysts put themselves and set out to sail from. Over time, this position reached the limit point of imbalance, risking a fall into the water, unless the analysts moved quickly onto the opposite side. In this sense D'Agostini's words about the decline of a certain position of psychoanalysis finds some justification:

> The death of James Hillman pushes us to reflect on the great anti-theoretical, anti-logic, anti-conceptual vague, that has gone through the European and North American culture since the Eighties of last century, of which Hillman was a distinguish and refined exponent. [. . .] To understand Hillman's operation, I think it is necessary to place it in two well-defined contexts: the decline of psychoanalysis, and the cultural inaction of philosophy. Psychoanalysis in its various forms begins its clear and conspicuous decline in Europe back in the Seventies of last century, alternative and anti-Oedipal psychiatry indicates clearly that the Freudian paradigm, even in the Lacanian

> version, supports badly the new conditions of the imaginary and of the shared language, whereas the Jungian fades more and more in an abstract cultural therapeutics.
>
> (D'Agostini 2011, p. 1)

It could be said that Hillman himself moved to the other side, from the personal and subjective side of the sailboat to that of the impersonal and objective, and made the voyage, formulating his theory from this different viewpoint. But we must not forget that Hillman was also the one who invited his readers 'to see through [. . .] theoretical paradigms' (see Hillman 1997), stating that archetypal psychology represents a dynamic moment of the psychoanalytic voyage as well, and, as such, its position will request changes and settlements over time (see Nelson's chapter within this volume). As with every psychic manifestation, archetypal psychology too is a metaphorical and dynamic narrative of that deeper and common truth of human being: that as we live we produce images.

Focusing on the limits and the opacity of a mainly subjectivistic vision of the psyche, in 'An Approach to the Dream', Patricia Berry, in full tune with Hillman's statements, invites us as her readers to reflect on our way of practicing analysis, starting from our awareness of the unconscious aspects of our theories: an unconsciousness that affects our therapeutic practice, and becomes evident, for example, in the way we process dreams (Berry 1982). In her text Berry proposes seven different interpretations of the same dream by seven hypothetical analysts, showing how each of them emphasizes a different theory. In the same paper, Berry describes what she means by dream analysis, with the patients in the analytical room (hence in clinical practice):

> Because theory so determines practice – after all what we practice is theory – in order to be aware of what we are doing with dreams, we have to become aware of what we are thinking about dreams. We have to examine not only how we put our theory into practice but also what we are putting into practice. This means turning to our assumptions and becoming aware of our unconsciousness in this realm too.
>
> (Berry 1982, p. 56)

Impressing further upon Hillman's position, Berry reaffirms also, in a very clear way, the importance of understanding dream images metaphorically (and ourselves as dreaming those dreams), of 'discovering what the image wants and from that determine our therapy' (Berry 1982, p. 78):

> Analytical training teaches us primarily how to suppose about dreams and how to work out their implications. We learn by imitating the

suppositions of our analysts about our own dreams. What we do not learn is a psychology of the image, comparable to what students or archeology, iconography, aesthetics, or textual criticism would learn about the image in their fields. But we cannot even begin to discover what would be a psychology of the image so long as we in psychology are exploiting the image for what we take to be our therapeutic aims. Perhaps the other way round would be more appropriate: discover what the image wants and from that determine our therapy.

(Berry 1982, p. 78)

In addition to highlighting both the need to consider the objective dimension of psychic experience in the face of a one-sided stress on the subjective dimension, and the need to develop a gaze that looks through, and remembers to stick to 'what we are doing and not what we think we are doing' (Hillman 1977, p. 67), Hillman, in *The Dream and the Underworld*, indicates that there is another aim of archetypal psychology that is, in fact, a practical and clinical challenge. This aim is to develop an imaginal ego, one that enables us to experience ourselves as 'an image among images' (see Hillman 1979).

For archetypal psychology, it is not enough to become aware of the objective and impersonal dimensions of the psyche; it is important also to 'empty out' the ego, according to the perception that we are images as well, and that it is in this way we express ourselves. Our ego identity, our existence – and our death as well, as Hillman testified in the first person in his last interview – if considered from the viewpoint of the mythopoetic functioning of the mind, are also images in movement or metaphorical expressions of that natural psychic creativity, which expresses itself through an endless flux of images. When we gain the perception of our subjective identity as 'an image among images', suddenly we discover – as Prospero says in the most famous monologue of Shakespeare's *The Tempest* – that we are really made of 'the same stuff of dreams/and our little life is rounded with a sleep' (Shakespeare 1611). This is the experience of emptying out our subjectivity that Hillman himself testified to with his own death. In this regard, I want to recall something he said in his last interview to Ronchey.

RONCHEY: What is it like to die?

HILLMAN: An empty out . . . The first thing to do is a complete empty out. But we might ask, what or where is the void? The void is in the loss. And what is lost? I have not 'lost' the common sense of 'to lose'. No, there is no loss in that meaning. It is the end of ambition. The end of what we demand of ourselves. And it is very important. We do not demand anything more from ourselves. We started emptying out our obligations, our links, what we believed were our important needs. And when it all starts to fade, there is an enormous amount of time. And then also the time starts

> to slip away and so we live without the time as well. What time is it? It is half past nine . . . Morning or night? I do not know.
>
> RONCHEY: This is the condition pursued by mystics.
>
> HILLMAN: Yes by Hinduism, for example, Hindus write about it. But in this case everything is *unwillkürlich*. It is accidental.
>
> RONCHEY: Anyhow, I do not think that you have no more ambition.
>
> HILLMAN: Really? [He suddenly opens his half-closed eyes with a blue lamp of challenge].
>
> RONCHEY: It remains the ambition of the ancient Romans: to leave your thoughts to the descendants.
>
> HILLMAN: It is true. It is very important for me that my thoughts remain. But the word descendants brings me to *postea*, to an afterward, to a future, in which I do not want to be transported.
>
> (Ronchey 2011)

Following this, I would like to describe Hillman's last testimony, some clinical developments inspired by archetypal psychology. As I mentioned earlier, these comprise three proposals that exemplify what it could mean 'to look through' and become 'an image among images' within a multicultural reality and changing world.

As I said before, often in Italy we consider Hillman's work above all from a theoretical viewpoint without serious engagement with the meaning of its practical effects in the analytic consulting room. I am convinced that today we have to ask ourselves what Hillman's theoretical reflections can add to our clinical practice, in terms of 'new' answers to be offered to 'new' patients, who bring 'new' requests from out of the changes of a multicultural world, in order that we can then respond seriously and effectively to them.

I would like to approach the topic of 'emptying out' the ego and the Hillmanian invitation to become 'an image among images', by recounting a famous Eastern dream of the Chinese philosopher Zhuangzi, who dreamt he was a butterfly (as recorded in 'Zhuangzi dreams of being a butterfly', the second chapter of the book, *Zhuangzi*; see Watson 1968). I quote from it as follows.

> Once the Chinese philosopher Zhuangzi dreamt he was a butterfly, a butterfly flitting and fluttering around, happy with himself and doing as he pleased. He didn't know he was Zhuangzi. Suddenly he woke up and there he was, solid and unmistakably Zhuangzi. But he didn't know if he was Zhuangzi who had dreamt he was a butterfly, or a butterfly dreaming he was Zhuangzi. Between Zhuangzi and a butterfly there must be some distinction! And this is called the transformation of things.
>
> (Watson 1968, p. 46)

Let's now try to read Zhuangzi's dream in the Hillmanian perspective and 'look through' and 'become an image among images'. As I have said already, in Shakespeare's monologue of *The Tempest*, the magician Prospero affirms that 'we are made of the same stuff of dreams/and our little life is rounded by a sleep' (Shakespeare 1611). This statement, when read metaphorically, is not too far from Zhuangzi's reflection about his dream and from Hillman's words about the imaginal ego. So, what can Zhuangzi's story teach us? Perhaps, that we can experience ourselves either as Zhuangzi (that is, as our ego complex), or as butterflies (that is, as personal and impersonal images), or finally as those who can tell the story of being 'the transformation of things' (reflective attitude)?

Let's recall now once more Hillman's last words, and let's put it all together with Zhuangzi's story in which he dreamt he was a butterfly, with the magician Prospero's statement that 'we are of the same stuff of dreams', and with Hillman's remark that the ego become 'an image among images'. What if, by 'stay thinking', Hillman meant the possibility to perceive ourselves either as our ego complex, or as images among images (for example, Zhuangzi and the butterfly)? And if by 'dying is the essence of life', he meant the possibility to differentiate our reflective attitude from the ego complex (such as Zhuangzi asking himself whether he is Zhuangzi or the butterfly)? And, further, if by 'finding the right words' he could allude to the possibility of telling the stories of our being, 'the transformation of things'?

Bearing in mind these metaphorical cross-references, I would like now to present three practical proposals, arising from my reflections on Hillman's heritage. These are three clinical proposals, which represent both my personal commitment towards Hillman's invitation 'to look through' and 'to become an image among images', and my tribute to Hillman's memory, and also comprise a multicultural reflection in a changing world. They are as follows: (1) 'stay thinking' or 'The technique of Double Objectivation'; (2)'dying is the essence of life', or 'Trauma Imaginal Treatment'; (3)'finding the right words', or 'The Right Words Therapy'.

The technique of Double Objectivation is a clinical modality, which I developed over time through dream-work and the practice of active imagination (Tibaldi 2004a, 2011). The technique of Double Objectivation is aimed at offering the patient the possibility to differentiate their reflective attitude from the conscious and unconscious contents of their ego complex, to enable them to develop the ability to observe themselves from a detached position.[1]

How does this technique work in practice? It is quite easy to explain. The analyst invites the patient who has had a dream, an active imagination, or a spontaneous image, to write their experience down, transcribing it in the first person, and again in direct form, using the personal pronoun 'I'. Once they have transcribed it in this way, the analyst invites them to write it down a second time, now in indirect form, using the third singular person 'he/she'.

This process of double objectivation aims both to objectify the arisen images and their unconscious contents – it is well known that writing is one of the expressive forms suggested by Jung to give objective form to the unconscious images and one of Hillman's clinical most favorite modalities (see Tibaldi 1995) – but also to look at them from a distance, as if they belong to another person. This double detachment puts the patient in the position to observe their ego complex functioning and their ego style from an optimum emotional and cognitive distance.

In order to understand how the technique of Double Objectivation works in practice, and the kind of psychic experience it offers, I refer to the short example below. It is a written transcription, in direct and indirect form, of a dream that a female patient brought into a session with me.[2]

Direct form

> I am in a car with an unknown man who is driving; this man makes me feel calm and secure. The man takes me in a house where there are a lot of people, a vivacious and pleasant *milieu.* There is also another man; I speak with him with great serenity. Awakening, I notice that my feelings in the dream are very different from what I experience normally in my every day-life towards men.

Indirect form

> The lady is in a car with an unknown man who is driving; with this man she feels calm and secure. The man takes her in a house where there are a lot of people, a vivacious and pleasant *milieu.* There is also another man, with whom she speaks with serenity. The lady notices that her feelings in the dream are very different from what she experiences normally in her every day-life towards men.

As you can notice, the indirect form makes visible the difference between the gaze of the observer and what is happening objectively, showing the style and the functioning of the ego complex in that moment. In my analytic practice I use this technique either with patients who have difficulties in reflecting on their subjective identity from a detached position, or with Eastern patients – I am referring to the Chinese, in particular – who for cultural reasons are often reluctant to approach their psychic experiences in a direct form (see Hazel Rose and Shinobu 1991).

With regard to the relationship with Eastern cultures, I would like to tell a story, which happened immediately after I presented the technique of Double Objectivation in the University of Taipei, to Taiwanese students. It is an anecdote that confirms, in an indirect way, the multicultural utility of such a clinical approach (in particular with Asiatic patients).

A young Taiwanese student, who took part in the seminar, informed me that a Chinese professor uses a similar technique, to which he gave the name, 'Psychological Displacement Paradigm of Diary-writing' (PDPD). This is a modality of expressive writing, conceived by Professor Jin Shuh-Ren of the Macau University (China), aimed to depower negative emotions. This method, administered under the instruction of a counselor or a therapist, is rather simple.

The patient is asked to write a diary at home first using 'I' as a pronoun describing whatever the client wants to express, as people do in diary writing. Second, when there is nothing more to write, they are asked to take a few seconds to breathe deeply, to change the 'I' to 'you', concentrating on what's flowing in their mind immediately after the pronoun has been changed, and then to write it down. Third, they are asked to transform the 'you' to 'she/he', following the same procedure in the previous step. After finishing the three steps of writing, clients are asked to become aware of the feelings inside them, from moment to moment. Clients are encouraged to do the PDPD three to five times a week. Shuh-Ren notes that,

> Resulting from empirical studies in the past five years, subjects in different research projects—varying from junior high students, college students, adults to group counseling leaders—the PDPD has shown a reliable short term effect of reducing negative emotions and a long term effect of promoting psychological well-being. The method is simple yet the mechanism of its effectiveness is rather complicated and can be interpreted from the wisdom of Zen and Buddhism.
>
> (Jin Shuh-Ren, personal communication)

It is easy to notice that the Psychological Displacement Paradigm in Diary-writing (PDPD) is a technique in part similar to the technique of Double Objectivation. The main difference is that in Double Objectivation the patient is invited to use only the first and third person. I do not foresee the possibility of using the form 'you' in order to avoid the risk of constellating in the patients possible mechanisms of negative projection onto others ('it is you, not me, who did this and that, you who said this and that, you who felt this or that', etc.). It is about avoiding the risk of paranoid cues in the patients – cues that, as Luigi Zoja pointed out in his book *Paranoia: La follia che fa la storia* characterize, in different ways, our Western cultural belonging (Zoja 2011; see also Quintaes 2011). The main aim of Double Objectivation is to deidentify the patient's reflective attitude from their ego complex and from deep images, consequently increasing their ability 'to look through' the psychic subjective and objective, personal and impersonal contents. Although different in this regard, the technique of Double Objectivation and the Psychological Displacement Paradigm in Diary-writing (PDPD) represents an interesting multicultural confluence in the present time.

Trauma Imaginal Treatment is aimed at approaching traumatic experiences and unconscious traumatic complexes, considering them as a doorway to enter the images from the objective psyche, from the impersonal dimension of the existence. I use this modality in particular with oncologic patients, with whom it is of the greatest practical utility. As I have stated elsewhere (Tibaldi 2010a, 2010b), oncologic trauma brings about first the breakdown of the ego and of its usual references. This situation of traumatic 'emptying out' of the ego – which is quite different from the conscious and voluntary 'empty out' described by Hillman – puts the patient, also unwillingly, face to face with the objective psyche and its images. Although presently, the time that cancer patients live and suffer their disease above all as a private pathology, confined in the space of subjectivity, their experiences actually comprise much wider horizons. When the experience of the breakdown of the ego is approached in the imaginal way, the experience of cancer can completely turn around. In fact, at that point of change it can offer the patient the opportunity to be initiated into the objective dimensions of the psyche, which express themselves in the natural cycle of life, death and renewal through the constellation of autonomous images (Tibaldi 2010a).

As Hillman – who was a cancer patient as well – taught us with his last words, in a severe illness such as cancer, it is not so much a question about how we can avoid our physical mortality – a task anyhow impossible – but how we can live from the imaginal perspective in illness and the prospect of our death (see Tibaldi 2010a, p. 16).

With regard to the proposal of the Trauma Imaginal Treatment, I will present a short clinical flash, which refers to a patient in chemotherapy. This patient asks for sessions in order to face the experience she is living and her consequent anxiety. The first dream she brought to our sessions is the following.

> I dreamt I was in a house and in a town which are not where I am living now, but in the dream I am with people that I know. In the house there is a big fire. I am very anxious, I would like to put it out but I do not know how to do it. I start behaving in an irrational and ineffective way. While I am acting like this, the image of an old wise man comes to my mind. It is the image that I visualized some years ago in a seminar on meditation. The old wise man tells me that if I want to achieve the goal of putting out the fire, I have to concentrate and adopt a focused strategy.

In the second session, she brings another dream:

> I dreamt about a water-hose that could put out the fire I saw in the previous dream. I notice that this water-hose is linked to the analyst's office, it comes from her analytic room.

It is not necessary to comment on these images, which gave shape metaphorically, and neither to the personal and impersonal emotions of the patient, nor the initial relational dynamics with the analyst. Instead, what is important to note is the creative weaving of all these dimensions, which is a challenge to the analyst to recognize and to differentiate what belongs to the patient's personal history and to her journey as a human being who is confronted with a pivotal event of an illness. The question arises, how can these aspects be differentiated in practice? The answers, I contend, are, for example, learning to analyze dreams, spontaneous images and bodily symptoms, in order to allow individual and archetypal layers of her psychological experience emerge and integrate within a metaphorical narrative.

The Right Words Therapy is about a clinical proposal that I am still developing, and which I find very useful above all in clinical practice with patients who belong to different cultures and with whom it is not possible to offer a stable and continuous analytical experience. The Right Words Therapy is an analytical approach aimed at making each single session a complete session in itself. By 'sticking to' the dreams or to deep images that the client brings into the session – as James Hillman used to say – the analyst finds with the patients 'the right words' that bring together the experience of the session and expresses it metaphorically.

The Right Words Therapy helps the client to reflect clearly on the problem they worked out in that single session with the analyst, and it helps to express the essence of the session itself, and provides the therapist and patient with an easy and clear link with which and through which they can reconnect to their previous session in the sessions that follow, irrespective of the distance in space and time between the sessions. I use it above all in the treatment of patients belonging to other cultures – I am referring to Chinese clients, in particular – who often do not have the possibility to have regular and continuous analysis with me.

I provide another clinical example to show this proposal in practice. This is a single session I had with a Chinese patient. I saw the patient for the first time and will probably meet her again in six months. The girl asked for a session because she wants to improve her femininity and her relationships with the opposite sex. She would like to have a boyfriend but she is reluctant to date. She told me that she dreamt of her father, dead for many years, who was a practical man and always played an important role in her life. In the dream her father appears as a complex presence, which offers us the starting point to reflect on different themes related to her femininity and the relationships between men and women. Together she and I reflect on various elements, and the patient begins 'to see through' them. Before closing the session, I ask the patient to imagine what her father would have said to her today regarding her problems and her difficulty to date. Without hesitation, the patient says: 'Just do it!' referring to the need to put herself to the test. In that moment the words 'Just do it!' seem to express at best what emerged during the session. We dwell on these words, which become 'the right words' of our session: the sentence 'Just do it!' will give the patient the possibility to remember what we did together and to both of us to tune ourselves immediately into what we processed in session.

We both know that, when we meet again, we could start from those words to check either what happened meanwhile, or to focus on the present again, bringing forward her confrontation with the conscious and unconscious requests and with the personal and impersonal aspects of her psychic experience.

Conclusion

In this chapter, which arose from my desire to honor James Hillman's memory, I tried to highlight some clinical implications of archetypal psychology, above all in terms of contemporary responses to patients' requests in our changing multicultural world. Being inspired by some of Hillman's writings and by the words he said in his last interview just before he died, I have proposed three possible clinical applications – the technique of Double Objectivation, the Trauma Imaginal Treatment, and the Right Words Therapy – all of which follow Hillman's invitation to develop a gaze of 'looking through' and 'to become an image among images'.

James Hillman in his writings invited readers to release therapy and psychology itself 'from the inevitable narrowing into personalism' and 'the exclusivity of the consulting room' in order to open ourselves up to the impersonal psychic dimension and to the world, imagining them again metaphorically. In fact, 'the aim of working life-events as dreams is to bring reflection to declarative and unreflective discourse, so that words no longer refer to objective referents; instead, speech becomes imagistic, self-referent, descriptive of a psychic condition as its very expression' (Hillman 1981, p. 57).

This invitation by James Hillman meant, for me, to go in search, through the practice of images (Tibaldi 2011), of that common denominator to human beings, whatever culture they belong to – that is, 'the poetic basis of mind'. However, Hillman also wrote that 'the experience is never raw or brute; it is always constructed by images that are revealed in the patient's narrations' and that

> an essential work of therapy is to become conscious of the fictions in which the patient is cast and to re-write or ghost-write collaboratively, the story by re-telling it in a more profound and authentic style. In this re-told version, in which imaginative art becomes the model, the personal failure and sufferings of the patient are essential to the story as they are to art.
>
> (Hillman 1981, p. 56)

Whatever our story is, James Hillman testified the importance of 'staying thinking', keeping alive our reflective attitude, to 'empty out' our ego, in order to discover the essence of life, to find 'the right words', in order to consciously live our being 'images among images'.

The clinical proposals I presented in this chapter arose from this net of cross-references: from personal experience and reflection, from the professional practice, from the analytic sessions in other cultures, from the imaginal treatment of oncologic patients. In this chapter I have tried to interpret, according to my style and my fiction, Hillman's invitation to live in an imaginal way, testifying our experience through 'soul words' (see Tibaldi 2004b). This was my way to celebrate James Hillman's memory, bearing in mind what he used to say: nothing can be changed before we have fresh ideas, until we are able to look at things differently.

Notes

1 I described this technique, among others, in the paper 'Doppia oggettivazione e formazione dell'Io immaginale' [Double objectivation and building of the imagistic ego], published in the edited volume, *Alchimie della formazione analitica* [Alchemy of analytic training] (Tibaldi 2004a), and I presented its ideas within two international seminars, the first, 'The technique of double objectivation', in Hong Kong in May 2012; and the second, in Taipei (Taiwan) in June of the same year, within the experiential workshop 'Masculine and feminine in dreams, men and women in awake life'.

2 I already used this dream to exemplify the method of Double Objectivation, either in the Hong Kong and Taipei seminars or in Italy in the seminar 'Maschile e femminile nei sogni: uomini e donne nella vita da svegli' [Masculine and Femininein Dreams, Men and Women in awake Life], in Milan in 2012, in the cycle of conference 'Ho fatto un sogno strano' [I had a strange dream].

References

Berry, P. (1982), *Echo's Subtle Body: Contribution to an Archetypal Psychology*, New York: Spring Publications.

Casey, E.S. (1974), 'Toward an Archetypal Imagination', Spring, New York: Spring Publications, pp. 32–41.

D'Agostini, F. (2011), 'Hillman, il profeta dell'anima', *Il Fatto quotidiano*, October, 29.

Damasio, A.R. (2012), *The Self Comes to Mind: Constructing the Conscious Brain*, New York: Vintage Books.

Galimberti, U. (2011), 'Dall'analisi di Jung ai miti greci, addio al poeta dell'anima', *La Repubblica*, October, 28.

Gioriello, G. (2011), 'Hillman, detective delle tenebre', *Corriere della sera*, October, 28.

Hazel Rose, M. and Shinobu, K. (1991), 'Culture and the Self: Implications for Cognition, Emotion and Motivation', *Psychological Review*, vol. 98, no. 2, New York: Cambridge University Press, pp. 224–253.

Hillman, J. (1975), *Re-visioning Psychology*, New York: Harper & Row.
Hillman, J. (1977), 'An Inquiry into Image', Spring, pp. 62–88, New York: Spring Publications.
Hillman, J. (1979), *The Dream and the Underworld* , New York: Harper & Row.
Hillman, J. (1981), *Sources of Archetypal Psychology: A Brief Account*, New York: Spring Publications.
Hillman, J. (1996), *The Soul's Code: In Search of Character and Calling*. London: Random House.
Màdera, R. (2011), 'Hillman, lo sciamano dell'anima', *L'Unità*, October, 29.
Nelson, E. (2012), 'Speaking with the Dead: Remembering James Hillman', see Chapter 9 within this volume.
Quintaes, M. (2011), 'When it All Makes Sense: the Failure of Himma and the Victory of the Sign in Paranoia', in Green, C., Stoupas, L., Partridge, R. and Asher Sund, S. (eds.), 'Breaking the Plates: Fracturing Fictions and Archetypal Imaginings' (Kindle edition), *Journal of Archetypal Studies*.
Ronchey, S. (2011), 'Addio a Hillman così si muore da filosofo antico', *Tuttolibri*, *La Stampa*, October, 28.
Shakespeare, W. (1611), *La Tempesta*, Milan: Mondadori.
Sica, L. (2011), 'James Hillman, un pensatore originale e solitario', *La Repubblica*, October, 28.
Tibaldi, M. (1995), 'Psicologia analitica, esperienza della scrittura e conoscenza di sé', *Rivista di Psicologia Analitica*, no. 52, pp. 19–31.
Tibaldi, M. (2004a), 'Doppia oggettivazione e formazione dell'Io immaginale', in AA.VV. *Alchimie della formazione analitica* (G.M. Cerbo, D. Palliccia, A.M. Sassone (eds.)), Milan: Vivarium, pp. 329–338.
Tibaldi, M. (2004b), 'Le parole che curano: il potere archetipico del linguaggio', in Caro Hillman . . . venticinque scambi epistolari con James Hillman (R. Mondo and L. Turinese (eds.)), Turin: Bollati Boringhieri, pp. 141–148.
Tibaldi, M. (2010a), *Oltre il cancro: Trasformare creativamente la malattia che temiamo di più*, Bergamo: Moretti & Vitali.
Tibaldi, M. (2010b), 'Clouds in the Sky, Still Allows a Glimpse of the Moon: Cancer Resilience and Creativity', in Montreal 2010 – Facing Multiplicity: Psyche, Nature, Culture, Proceeding of the XVIIIth Congress of the International Associaton for Analytical Psychology (P. Bennet (ed.)), Einsiedeln, Switzerland: Daimon Verlag.
Tibaldi, M. (2011), *Pratica dell'immaginazione attiva: Dialogare con l'inconscio e vivere meglio*, Rome: La Lepre.
Watson, B. (1968), *The Complete Works of Chuang Tzu*, New York: Columbia University Press.
Zoja, L. (2011), *Paranoia: La follia che fa la storia*, Turin: Bollati Boringhieri.

11

THE RED BOOK AND *PSYCHOLOGICAL TYPES*

A qualitative change of Jung's typology

Yuka Ogiso

Introduction

In 2009 Jung's *The Red Book* was published for the first time, and we can now see the details of his overwhelming visions and images, which we had previously been able only to glimpse in some of his other texts.

His first vision was experienced in October 1913, on a train journey to Schaffhausen. He saw a waking vision of Europe being devastated by a catastrophic flood.[1] With this as a starting point, his 'inner pressure' reached the limit, and he experienced an overflow of visions.

The year 1913 was very important in Jung's life, because at the beginning of the year he had terminated his relations with Sigmund Freud,[2] with whom he had been an intimate associate since February 1907. Although his *The Transformation and the Symbols of the Libido* (1911–12) had already revealed the conflict of views between them and their parting had therefore been expected, it gave Jung a tremendous shock. In later years, he looked back over those days and described them as follows.

> After the parting of the ways with Freud, a period of inner uncertainty began for me. It would be no exaggeration to call it a state of disorientation. I felt totally suspended in mid-air, for I had not yet found my own footing.
>
> (Jung/Jaffé 1962, p. 170)

In this way, without his own certain 'footing,' Jung engaged with images arising inward. He wrote them down in his notebooks called the 'Black Books,' and referred to the first volume of them as the 'book of my most difficult experiment' (Shamdasani 2009, p. 200). Then he transcribed them into the manuscript of *The Red Book*, adding interpretations and illustrations for several years, in a struggle with his own inner world.[3] It is said to have been around 1918 that he finally began to emerge from the darkness. In retrospect, he considered that all of his subsequent works derived from these days, and described those years as 'the *prima materia* for a lifetime's work' (Jung/Jaffé 1962, p. 199).

In 1921, announcing the break of dawn, one of Jung's greatest works, *Psychological Types*, was published. This could be represented as the first work of Jung's own psychology, and is often regarded as the key to his system of thoughts. Peter Homans describes this dramatically: 'Surprisingly, as he left this period [of his spiritual crisis], new thought—Jungian thoughts—came to occupy a central place. And the key to the new system was the theory of types' (Homans 1979, p. 73).

From the period of establishment of his typology, we could guess that the process of Jung's making his own theory and that of engaging himself in *The Red Book* had been deepened in parallel. If he found his own 'footing' in the research of typology, why did he choose it above all? And how did the experience of *The Red Book* ferment *Psychological Types*, the key to Jungian psychology? This chapter will explore these questions, taking its cue from a transition of Jung's attitude to the American philosopher, William James.

This chapter focuses on the impact of James's work, *Pragmatism*, on the development of Jung's *Psychological Types*. Through consideration of a change in his attitude to James's theory, the development of Jung's typology will be clarified.

The establishment of typology and William James

Reconsidering Jung's 'Confrontation with the Unconscious', as quoted above, Jung stated that his parting of the ways with Freud caused his state of disorientation. Actually, in Jung's autobiography, *Memories, Dreams, Reflections* (1962), the section of 'Confrontation with the Unconscious' corresponding to the period of *The Red Book* directly follows the section, 'Sigmund Freud,' which leaves the impression that Jung confronted this loss heroically and bravely, and had overcome the difficulties all by himself. This Freudocentric legend of Jung's life seems clear and dramatic, and has been regarded as a self-evident premise for understanding Jung's own theories. However, recent research suggests the need to approach this matter from a different angle.

According to the research by Sonu Shamdasani (1995, 2003, 2005), the Editor of *The Red Book*, there were some omissions of important passages in the process of editing *Memories, Dreams, Reflections*. They included the section, 'Théodore Flournoy and William James,' which should have appeared between the sections 'Sigmund Freud' and 'Confrontation with the Unconscious.' According to Shamdasani, in this unpublished section on Flournoy and James, Jung revealed a high opinion of the two psychologists, and credited 'their significance in helping him to formulate his criticisms of Freud, and furnish the methodological presuppositions for his formulation of a post-Freudian psychology' (Shamdasani 2005, p. 32). Concerning James especially, Jung attempted to spell out his intellectual debt to him, his recollection of meeting James in 1909, and his esteem for James as a role-model for him.

By taking the proposed location of this unpublished chapter into account, 'Confrontation with the Unconscious' takes on a different meaning—that is to say, Jung might not have gone on his night-sea journey by himself after all, but, as with William James, as a kind of pilot to help guide him through it. Furthermore, it is possible to surmise that Jung's own theory did not happen suddenly, but was composed with some 'methodological presuppositions' with James in mind.[4]

To witness the scene of the formation of his theory, we have to trace back to 1913 again.

Jung's typology preceding The Red Book

Just before his disorientation, a lecture by Jung prepared the formation of his typology. In September 1913, several months after he wrote his letter of parting to Freud, Jung gave a lecture entitled 'A Contribution to the Study of Psychological Types' (hereafter called 'Contribution'), in which he presented some important ideas that could be said to be the germ of his later work, *Psychological Types*. In this lecture, he defined 'extraversion' and 'introversion' as two contrasting flows of libido found in patients exhibiting hysteria and schizophrenia, and also discussed various common problems that afflict normal, healthy people. As to the reason why he developed his interests more directly with regard to the issue of typology and psychological types, Jung himself stated later that:

> This work sprang originally from my need to define the ways in which my outlook differed from Freud's and Adler's. In attempting to answer this question, I came across the problem of types; for it is one's psychological type which from the outset determines and limits a person's judgment.
>
> (Jung/Jaffé 1962, p. 207)

For Jung, the crucial task was thus how to position himself between Freud and Adler—the latter of whom had himself broken away from Freud at around the same time.[5]

In his lecture 'Contribution,' Jung discusses various theoretical disciplines to authenticate his own ideas, such as philosophy, aesthetics, linguistics, and psychiatry, and to various thinkers, including Ostwald, Worringer, Bergson, Schiller, Nietzsche, and Finck (who would all appear later in itemized discussions in *Psychological Types*). But it was James's typology that Jung took up ahead of these prominent philosophers. He said: 'so far as my limited knowledge goes, we have to thank William James for the best observations in this respect' (Jung 1913, par. 864). Following this, he introduced James's argument that James had developed in detail in his *Pragmatism* (1907).

A year prior to his lecture 'Contribution,' Jung had referred to James's *Pragmatism*, in his essay 'The Theory of Psychoanalysis,' and to James's pragmatic rule as his own 'guiding principle' (Jung 1912, p. 110).

According to Peter Homans, 'Jung achieved his first modicum of distance from Freud' by likening his own ideas to those of James. It was therefore Jung's affinity with James that enabled Jung to put Freud in his place (Homans 1979, p. 72). But what kind of theory was presented in James's *Pragmatism*, which Jung immediately after parting with Freud based his ideas on and thought so highly of? The rest of the chapter will explore this.

James's Pragmatism

The theory of pragmatism was advocated for the first time in 1878 by the logician Charles Sanders Peirce. Following this, it flourished in the twentieth century, mainly in the United States, becoming a major philosophical movement. To this day, while having gone out of vogue among the present generation, it is said to remain influential as a basis for modern philosophy, phenomenology, philosophy of language, and so on. Various ideas derived from this movement are referred to as 'pragmatic,' and they have often been collectively understood in terms of emphasizing a perspective of 'utility.' However, the ideas of philosophers have differed in their understanding of this from the outset, and Jung himself distinguished James's theory from those of the other philosophers.[6] So, we should take notice that it was none other than James's theory that Jung valued so highly. James was present in the pioneering days of pragmatism, and he himself introduced it to public awareness in America, and developed it within his own context.

Pragmatism originated in the small town of Cambridge, Massachusetts, in the early 1870s. Six young scholars, including James and Peirce, came together every two weeks and exchanged views about philosophical ideas, ranging from Greek philosophy to British empiricism and Darwinism, which was the latest theory at that time. They then gradually polished their own ideas. Their common way of thinking, despite their different backgrounds and standpoints, was the thesis that the 'thinking' of man is essentially related to his 'actions.'

In 1878, Peirce worked up their ideas into the paper, 'How to Make our Ideas Clear.' Although it was an epoch-making declaration for the academic world at that time, it remained unknown for a long time, because Peirce was not so famous and his expression was obfuscatory. However, just twenty years later, the name of pragmatism attracted much attention. It was no less than William James who drew attention to it. In August 1898, at an address at University of California, James introduced pragmatism as a theory that had been developed by his friend, Peirce. The words of James—who had already built a reputation through his work, *The Principles of Psychology* (1891), and who was in a position of authority as chairperson of the Department of Philosophy of Harvard University—startled people all at once.[7] After systematizing it much more, he later gave a series of lectures at Columbia University in 1906–1907, and published them as *Pragmatism* in 1907.

At the beginning of the lecture, James said: 'I know that you, ladies and gentleman, have a philosophy, each and all of you, and that the most interesting and important thing about you is the way in which it determines the perspective in your several worlds'(James 1907, p. 11).

In the United States of America, where people crowd together with various culture and backgrounds, the most common way of thinking was pluralism, whereby everyone's sense of values were more or less accepted as valuable in their own right. James's pragmatism became the basis of this idea, the monumental achievement that triggered American philosophy making its own development.

According to James's pragmatism, the truth is not singular and absolute, but we should regard as truth those things that are 'useful,' and which give satisfaction to the person believing in them. So we should therefore give up asking what is universally true. James argued as follows: 'The history of philosophy is to a great extent that of a certain clash of human temperaments. [. . .] I shall have to take account of this clash and explain a good many of the divergencies of philosophers by it' (James 1907, p. 12).

He recognized the conflict of views repeated historically by tracing differences in 'temperaments.' According to him, the history of philosophy can be also described as a clash of 'rationalism' and 'empiricism.' He saw the former as 'tender-minded' and the latter as 'tough-minded.' A 'tender-minded' person always believes in abstract and eternal principles: intellectualistic, idealistic, optimistic, religious, free-willist, monistic, and dogmatical. On the other hand, a 'tough-minded' person always loves facts in all their crude variety: sensationalistic, materialistic, pessimistic, irreligious, fatalistic, pluralistic, and skeptical. In these differences of inherent 'temperaments' between various philosophers, James saw an essential cause of conflicting ideas (ibid., pp. 13–14). Now, we may ask, why did this idea become a 'guiding principle' for Jung?

Jung's acceptance of pragmatism

Let's go back to the lecture 'Contribution' by Jung of 1913, specifically to where he refers to James's principle that 'whatever temperament a professional philosopher is, he tries, when philosophizing, to sink the fact of his temperament' (ibid., p. 12) as one that is in accord with the spirit of psychoanalysis. Jung then describes that one can translate James's two types into 'spiritually-minded' and 'materially-minded' respectively, and reinterprets them according to their different localizations of libido. According to Jung's summary, a 'tender-minded' person, as defined by James, is a man of principles and systems. As such they dominate experiences and transcend them by abstract reasoning or logical deductions using purely rational concepts; 'the multiplicity of empirical phenomena hardly bothers or disconcerts them at all' (Jung 1913, par. 865). However, in the domain of pathology, these kinds of philosophers are regarded as paranoiacs, for they impose their delirious conceptions on the universe, ignore every fact that conflicts with them, and make all things dependent on their preconceived system (ibid.). Their characteristics follow logically from premises described by James as 'intellectualistic, idealistic, optimistic, religious, free-willist, monistic, dogmatical,' and these qualities betray the almost exclusive concentration on thinking (par. 866). A 'tough-minded' person, on the contrary, is empirical, and is 'going by facts' (par. 867). As experience is their master, 'principles are always of less value than facts' (ibid.). This is why their theories tend to have inner contradictions, and get overlaid by the accumulation of empirical material. Their characteristics, described by James as 'sensationalistic, materialistic, pessimistic, irreligious, fatalistic, pluralistic, and skeptical,' are based on a tendency to recognize—even what is higher, for instance, the idea of God—as something empirical, as a case of 'nothing but' in a single line with what is lower, and taking much account of all aspects of the phenomenal world and its practical possibilities—that is, a case of 'nothing but . . .'(pars. 867–868). While a 'tender-minded' person directs his or her libido to the inner world of thought, namely 'introversion,' a 'tough-minded' person directs it to material things and objective reality, namely 'extraversion.'

At the end of the lecture, Jung classified the theories of Freud and Adler according to these two types. While the former is 'reductive, pluralistic, causal, and sensualistic,' exhibiting the characteristics of 'extraversion,' the latter is 'intellectualistic, monistic, and finalistic,' manifesting the characteristics of 'introversion' (par. 880). In this way, Jung tried to explain the conflict of theoretical views by their respective psychological types.[8]

In this lecture, Jung consistently accepted the two types that James presented in *Pragmatism* as they were, without changing them, and by immediately connecting them to his own two types of 'extraversion' and 'introversion.' He tried to translate James's idea from the field of philosophy into his own terms of depth-psychology.

A qualitative change of the typology in psychological types

Eight years later, in 1921—written through the period of *The Red Book*—Jung made his typology bear fruit in *Psychological Types*. It is said that he wrote down the text at an incredibly furious pace, completing the first 583 pages in six weeks (Hoeller 1982, p. 6). In a seminar four years later, he talked about this work: 'I drew all my empirical material from my patients, but the solution of the problem I drew from the inside, from my observations of the unconscious processes. I have tried to fuse these two currents of outer and inner experience in the book of Types . . .' (Jung 1925, p. 34).

The 'inner experience' that he mentions here will have included his imaginal experience as reported in *The Red Book*, to no small extent. If his experience had changed something in his theory, the question arises of how had his argument deepened in light of it from the time of the lecture in 1913, 'Contribution', to the writing of *Psychological Types*? The clue to consider here is the change in the way in which Jung accepted James's theory. In *Psychological Types*, Jung valued James's pioneering work, and its basic ideas can be seen to have penetrated those of Jung. At the same time, however, he constructs his own theory by going beyond James's framework. We will now look at this in detail.

In his lecture 'Contribution,' Jung went no further than presenting the classification of two types, 'extraversion' and 'introversion.' But in *Psychological Types* a totally new classification emerged, with four basic psychological functions, 'thinking,' 'feeling,' 'sensation,' and 'intuition,' combined as a subclass of the extraversion and introversion. Accompanying his discussion in Chapter 8, 'The Type Problem in Modern Philosophy,' Jung presents a commentary on typology by James. Due to the difference between his typological accounts,[9] Jung called attention to them by criticizing James's terms on the basis that they were one-sided because they dealt only with the 'thinking' part (Jung 1921, par. 517).[10]

However, Jung valued again James's attempts that 'dug deeper and grasped the conflict as its psychological root, coming up with a pragmatic solution' (par. 540), and expressed that, 'James deserves credit for being the first to draw attention to the extraordinary importance of temperament in coloring philosophical thought' (par. 539). As stated in its introduction of the book, the purpose of *Psychological Types* was to give an account of the conflicts that arise within science and within human personal relations according to a psychological epistemology. For Jung, it was William James who paved the way for this account.

At the end of this chapter, however, there is a notable description. In the last section, titled 'General Criticism of James's Typology,' Jung pointed out the limitations of pragmatic thinking. According to Jung, 'the conflict between the two truths' certainly 'requires a pragmatic attitude if any sort of justice is to be done to the other stand point' (par. 541). Yet, although it cannot be dispensed with, pragmatism presupposes too great a resignation and almost unavoidably leads to a lack of creative formation. Moreover, he wrote as follows:

> The solution of the conflict of opposites cannot come [. . .] from a pragmatic assessment of the practical value of logically irreconcilable views, but only from a positive act of creation which assimilates the opposites as necessary elements of co-ordination [. . .]. Pragmatism

> can be no more than a transitional attitude preparing the way for the creative act by removing prejudices.
>
> (Jung 1921, par. 541)

To appreciate both standpoints, a pragmatic attitude is first of all required, but such an attitude can go no further than making clear their fundamental differences. This is because pragmatism doesn't deal with the problem of how individuals should resolve conflicts. And Jung here was no longer satisfied with this. He thought that the attitude required to deal with the conflict of opposition is one that brought about acts of creation, one that not only recognizes differences, but also integrates them into oneself as necessary elements of oneself. Within this description, the idea of the '*coniunctio* of the opposites' emerges—an idea that would become the central theme of Jung's theory of the individuation processes, and we find here a qualitative change of his typology. While in his 1913 lecture where he directly accepts James's pragmatism, Jung only alludes to the existence of the two opposite principles, in *Psychological Types* he developed the idea, and from out of it established the idea of the *dynamic* formation of the two. Not until Jung went beyond James's ideas, did his own originality come to the fore. And it was through his 'Confrontation with the Unconscious' as it made itself known to him at the same time in his creation of *The Red Book* that he was able to deepen his theory of typology. But, we may ask, what is the nature of this inner experience that prepared the qualitative change of his thought?

The inner experience in *The Red Book*: the opposites presented in images

Various pairs of opposites are prominent throughout *Liber Primus*, *Liber Secundus*, and *Scrutinies* in *The Red Book*. We find, for instance, 'the spirit of the depths' and 'the spirit of this time,' and the other, more abstract oppositional pairs (such as 'life' and 'death,' or 'light' and 'shadow'), and more concrete ones, involving specific personifications or figures, which are described in various ways, either contrasted or reconciled in one way or another. Here I shall consider the figurative pairing of the old prophet, Elijah, and the blind maiden, Salome, both of whom appear in Jung's images throughout *The Red Book*. My description of them will rely on *Liber Primus*, where the relation between the two is expressed particularly clearly.

In Chapter 9 of *Liber Primus*, titled 'Mysterium. Encounter,' Jung meets an old man who lays a black serpent at his feet. There is a house with columns some distance away, and a beautiful maiden steps out of the door. The old man introduces himself as Elijah, and the maiden as his own daughter, Salome. Jung is shocked to hear this, and confused in his failure to understand the meaning of the pair. For, while Elijah is a prophet who appears in the Old Testament, and who could be said to be a symbol of wisdom, Salome had desired the head of John the Baptist in front of King Herod, and thereby seemed for Jung, by contrast, to be 'engendered from heinous seed,' 'vain greed and criminal lust' (Jung 2009, v(v)/ p. 246). Jung cannot understand why Elijah recognizes Salome as his daughter at all.[11] However, Elijah says that her blindness together with his sight have made them companions for all eternity. In addition, Salome says that she loves Jung, and he will come to love her too. Jung complains to Elijah: 'You pose dreadful riddles. How could it be that this unholy woman and you, the prophet of your God, could be one?' (ibid.)

Jung proceeds to amplify these images as follows: 'because I have fallen into the source of chaos, into the primordial beginning, I myself became smelted anew in the connection with the primordial beginning' (*ibid.*, v(v)/ p. 247). What Jung met in the primordial world were two principles of 'forethinking' and 'pleasure,' appearing as Elijah and Salome respectively.[12] According to him, the two principles are indispensable to each other. 'Forethinking needs pleasure to be able to come to form. Pleasure needs forethinking to come to form, which it requires' (ibid.). They presuppose the existence of each other, because 'both are [. . .] in nature intimately one' (ibid.). Therefore, human beings originally could exist only with neither 'forethinking' nor 'pleasure,' and require them both. But it is also impossible to take both attitudes at the same time. Man always puts one side before the other. He says: 'Those who think base the world on thought, those who feel, on feeling. You find truth and error in both' (ibid.). Here, the principle of 'forethinking' is paraphrased in 'those who think,' and 'pleasure' in 'those who feel.' This pairing, of 'those who think' and 'those who feel,' is reminiscent of the pair of rational functions in *Psychological Types*, of 'thinking' and 'feeling.' However, it would be more appropriate to consider the two not as 'thinking' and 'feeling' in their limited meaning, but more flexibly as the pair of two contrasting attitudes to the world, because it was not before *Psychological Types* that Jung gave up identifying 'introversion' and 'thinking,' or 'extraversion' and 'feeling' (Jung 1921, par. 7). In the source of chaos, Jung regarded the undifferentiated forms of the two principles as conflicting with each other at the level of phenomena. It was the primordial form of the two types that his own lecture 'Contribution' or James's *Pragmatism* had regarded as the fundamental opposites. Elijah and Salome, although seeming to conflict at the level of phenomena, should indeed have appeared together as a pair, for they are both essentially inseparable. Nevertheless, a differentiated man cannot live as either of these two alone.

Moreover, Jung also says this: 'It is always the serpent that causes man to become enslaved now to one, now to the other principle, so that it becomes error' (ibid., v(v)/ p. 247). He regarded the serpent lying down between Elijah and Salome as a third principle. If man standing on the one side views the other, he finds a serpent between them. A pleasure for those who think it seems to be alluring and poisonous, and a thought for those who feel it cold and cruel. Man tries to believe, as if the opposite side doesn't exist. The serpent, however, is the thing that combines the both. Jung says:

> The way of life writhes like the serpent from right to left and from left to right, from thinking to pleasure and from pleasure to thinking. Thus the serpent is an adversary and a symbol of enmity, but also a wise bridge that connects right and left through longing, much needed by our life.
>
> (Jung 2009, v(v)/ p. 247)

Because Jung himself was a 'thinker,' and he saw a 'pleasure' embodied by Salome standing on the side of 'forethinking,' she seemed to be poisonous and dreadful. However, accepting the opposite leads one along the way. And here closes Chapter 9 of *The Red Book.*

In the images following this, Jung experiences the 'Mysterium.' Jung rejects Salome and thereby approaches the principle of 'forethinking,' whereupon Elijah becomes dwarflike, unlike himself. As Jung seeks Salome again, he sees the vision of the cross of Christ, and is held fast and spreads his arms wide. The serpent has wound itself around his whole body. When the serpent squeezes his body in its coils, blood streams from his body. Salome bending down to his feet and wrapping her black hair round them, cries, 'I see light!' And truly, her eyes are open and she becomes able to see. She kneels before the light in devotion. Elijah also transforms into a huge flame of white light and the serpent wraps itself, as if paralyzed.

Jung explained the change of Salome as a transition from 'pleasure' to a higher principle, 'love.' For him as a 'thinker,' 'pleasure' had appeared in the figure of the blind maiden at first, but it was freed as 'love' through his inner self-sacrifice. At the same time 'forethinking' also changes into a white flame. In this way, Jung experienced the process of the transition of both principles to the new stage over the human form (ibid., vi(r)–vii(r)/ pp. 248–255).[13]

He says that 'man doesn't only grow from within himself, for he is also creative from within himself' (ibid., vii(r)/ p. 253). Jung experienced the dynamic forming process relating to the opposite principle creatively in the images. For the man who lives according to one of the two principles, the other principle will always seem to exist outside of him and to stand in contradiction to him. But in the world of images that Jung experienced, both principles are presented as one thing at the root, and so the opposite side is also in oneself. He saw the creative transformation of humans, in the process tackling the other side dynamically by the third principle, the serpent.

Could it be said, then, that the soil of his inner experiences in *The Red Book* enabled Jung to develop his typology beyond its simple epistemology, towards a consideration of the issues of creativity as the process of individuation?

Conclusion

The Transformation and the Symbols of the Libido (1911–12), which was a factor that contributed to Jung's parting from Freud, was revised by Jung forty years later as *Symbols of Transformation* (1952). In the Preface of the revision, he wrote about a now-famous episode in which he looked back upon the days of the first edition.

He was driven to ask himself in all seriousness: 'What is the myth you are living?' To which he found no answer. He felt as follows:

> So, in the most natural way, I took it upon myself to get to know 'my' myth, and I regarded this as the task of tasks, for—so I told myself—how could I, when treating my patients, make due allowance for the personal factor, for my personal equation, which is yet so necessary for a knowledge of the other person, if I was unconscious of it?
>
> (Jung 1952, p. xxv)

The problem of the 'personal equation' quoted above was the very theme he addressed in *Psychological Types*. Jung referred to the personal style as recognition of the way in which the world is experienced as distinctive to each person; it is a 'personal equation' that is constructed in terms of the attitudes of extraversion/introversion and the four types of psychological function. *Psychological Types* could be described as a book of methodology, theorizing about the 'personal equation.' Jung's struggle with visions in *The Red Book*, on the other hand, which started in the year following publication of *The Transformation and the Symbols of the Libido*, could be regarded as a practical trial through which he received his own 'personal equation,' namely his own 'myth,' that he himself was living.

The Red Book, as an exploration of individual experiences, and *Psychological Types* as a general theory, are quite different in their ways of expression and direction, but they are also combined inseparably within Jung himself. As in the image of *The Red Book*, the opposites are one at their very core, and the creative formation they bring about is always inevitable, so these two books too, which were created at the same period in Jung's life, must have interacted with each other, dynamically within him. This chaper can only expose the tip of the iceberg of this interaction, and it does so within the context of his particular notion of opposite principles. It therefore encourages a more detailed examination of the relationship between both books in future.

Notes

1 Jung thought back to those days as follows: 'When I had the vision of the flood in October of the year 1913, it happened at a time that was significant for me as a man. At that time, in the fortieth year of my life, I had achieved everything that

I had wished for myself. I had achieved honor, power, wealth, knowledge, and every human happiness. Then [. . .] the vision of the flood seized me and I felt the spirit of the depths' (Jung 2009, ii(r)/ pp. 231f.).

2 His letter announcing the break-up of their personal relationship was dated January 6, 1913 (McGuire 1988, p. 540).

3 According to Shamdasani, Jung was able to maintain a busy therapeutic practice while also struggling with his inner fantasies. Between 1913 and 1914 he had between one and nine consultations per day, five days a week, and moreover, he continued his military service duties at this time. Shamdasani says, 'Thus he maintained his professional activities and familial responsibilities during the day, and dedicated his evenings to his self-explorations. Indications are that this partitioning of activities continued during the next few years' (Shamdasani 2009, p. 201).

4 Eugene Taylor pointed out that Jung had cited James in numerous papers and addresses delivered between 1913 and 1917 (Taylor 1980, p. 164).

5 In 'The Psychology of the Unconscious Processes' (1917), Jung also discussed the problem of types based on the differences between Freud's and Adler's theories. As shown below, the basic idea of the paper is similar to 'Contribution,' and the qualitative change such as seen in *Psychological Types* is hardly recognized.

6 Jung mentioned that Keyserling branded American pragmatism as 'profoundly unspiritual' in his work *La Révolution mondiale et la responsibilité de l'éspri*, and said 'I hope [. . .] he doesn't mean William James!' (Jung 1934, para. 941).

7 For Peirce, however, there was a great difference between his idea of pragmatism and that of James. As a result, Peirce later advocated 'pragmaticism,' in order to discriminate his standpoint from the 'pragmatism' that was coming into fashion (Peirce 1934). For details, refer to Perry (1935).

8 He concluded the lecture with the following sentence: 'The difficult task of creating a psychology which will be equally fair to both types must be reserved for the future' (Jung 1913, par. 882).

9 In his 'Introduction' to *Psychological Types*, Jung referred to this point as follows: 'in my preliminary work on psychological types I did not carry out this differentiation, but identified the thinking type with the introvert and the feeling type with the extravert. A deeper study of the problem has shown this equation to be untenable' (Jung 1921, par. 7). This 'preliminary work' comprises his two works: 'Contribution' and 'The Psychology of the Unconscious Processes.'

10 For instance, there are 'empiricists who are dogmatic, religious, idealistic, intellectualistic, rationalistic, etc., just as there are ideologists who are materialistic, pessimistic, deterministic, irreligious, and so on,' Jung wrote (Jung 1921, par. 538).

11 In the seminar in 1925, Jung referred to this as follows, 'when Elijah told me he was always with Salome, I thought it was almost blasphemous for him to say this. I had the feeling of diving into an atmosphere that was cruel and full of blood' (Jung 1925, p. 93).

12 Although there is no definite statement connecting the two principles to Elijah and Salome in the body text, the editor writes that the draft of *The Red Book* continued: 'Therefore the forethinker approached me as Elijah, the prophet, and pleasure as Salome' (Jung 2009, note 170).

13 It must, however, be added that this image was experienced as the end in view, and therefore it doesn't mean that it had already been accomplished in himself. *Liber Primus* was concluded as follows: 'The mystery showed me in images what I should afterward live. I did not possess any of those boons that the mystery showed me, for I still had to earn all of them' (Jung 2009, vii(r)/ p. 254).

References

Hoeller, S. A. (1982): *The Gnostic Jung and the Seven Sermons to the Dead.* Wheaton, IL: Quest Books.

Homans, P. (1979): *Jung in Context: Modernity and the Making of a Psychology.* Chicago: The University of Chicago Press.

James, W. (1891): *The Principles of Psychology*, in two volumes. New York: Dover Publications, 2000.

James, W. (1898): *Philosophical Conceptions and Practical Results: Pragmatism.* Cambridge, MA: Harvard University Press, 1975.

James, W. (1907): *Pragmatism: A New Name for Some Old Ways of Thinking.* Rockville, MD: ARC Manor, 2008.

Jung, C. G. (1911–12) *Wandlungen und Symbole der Libido*, Munich: Deutscher Taschenbuch Verlag.

Jung, C. G. (1912): *The Theory of Psychoanalysis, Collected Works*, Vol. 4. Princeton, NJ: Princeton University Press, 1961.

Jung, C. G. (1913): *A Contribution to the Study of Psychological Types, Collected Works*, Vol. 6. Princeton, NJ: Princeton University Press, 1971.

Jung, C. G. (1917): *The Psychology of the Unconscious Processes, Collected Works*, Vol. 7. Princeton, NJ: Princeton University Press, 1953/1966.

Jung, C. G. (1921): *Psychological Types, Collected Works*, Vol. 6. Princeton, NJ: Princeton University Press, 1971.

Jung, C. G. (1925): *Analytical psychology: Notes of the Seminar Given in 1925.* W. McGuire (ed.), Princeton, NJ: Princeton University Press.

Jung, C. G. (1934): *La Révolution mondiale et la responsibilité de l'ésprit.* Collected Works, Vol. 10. Princeton, NJ: Princeton University Press, 1964/1970.

Jung, C. G. (1952): *Symbols of Transformation. Collected Works*, Vol. 5. Princeton, NJ: Princeton University Press, 1956/ 1967.

Jung, C. G. (2009): *The Red Book: Liber Novus.* S. Shamdasani (ed.), New York: W.W. Norton.

Jung, C. G. /Jaffé, A. (1962): *Memories, Dreams, Reflections.* London: Vintage Books, 1989.

McGuire, W. (1988): *The Freud/Jung Letters: The Correspondence between Sigmund Freud and C. G. Jung.* R. Manheim and R. F. C. Hull (trans.), Cambridge, MA: Harvard University Press.

Peirce, C. S. (1934): *Pragmatism and Pragmaticism*, in *Collected Papers of Charles Sanders Peirce*, Vol. 5, Charles Hartshorne and Paul Weiss (ed.), Cambridge, MA: Harvard University Press.

Perry, R. B. (1935): *The Thought and Character of William James: As Revealed in Unpublished Correspondence and Notes, Together with His Published Writings*, vols. 1 and 2, Boston, MA: Little, Brown.

Shamdasani, S. (1995): Memories, Dreams, Omissions. Spring 57. New York: Spring Publications.

Shamdasani, S. (2003): *Jung and the Making of Modern Psychology.* Cambridge, MA: Cambridge University Press.

Shamdasani, S. (2005): *Jung Stripped Bare by his Biographers, Even.* London: Karnac.

Shamdasani, S. (2009): *Liber Novus: The 'Red Book' of C. G. Jung. The Red Book: Liber Novus.* S. Shamdasani (ed.), London: W. W. Norton.

Taylor, E. (1980): William James and C. G. Jung. Spring 20. New York: Spring Publications.

12

ARCHETYPAL ASPECTS OF TRANSFERENCE AT THE END OF LIFE

Isabelle DeArmond

> I feel it is rewarding to help patients and families during the dying process. I like to watch the interaction when one stops protecting the other and I can sense love flowing.
>
> (Hospice worker)

Introduction

My encounters with pain and loss at the end of life stem mostly from my past experiences as a medical practitioner. A few images seem to superimpose themselves on diverse experiences of attending to patients at very critical stages of their illnesses. I see Cathy in her twenties—my age at the time—dying slowly of a terminal congenital cardiac disease. I see her progressive detachment from the world and, despite our best efforts, the body of this beautiful woman changing. I held a loving attention to her body, and my focus centered on her breath. As days went by, fewer words were spoken so as not to disturb the peace progressively growing in the room. I could never face the gravity of her mother's grief. Later, my other experiences came as a result of working in a neonatal intensive care unit. I put all my heart into my hands, manipulating the seriously sick neonates and tending to their bodies as though they were delicate plants, in full awe of their impetuous will to live and of how soon their physical condition could become unpredictable. In that time, I remember meeting the eyes of some fathers who were standing in the corridors, having asked quietly to be allowed to stay and hold their pain behind the glass doors. I strongly identified with the pain of the parents. Most of my attention during these years had been on the gentle care of the bodies, on the silent connection established with human beings when the material dimensions of their life were getting smaller, and on lovingly sharing their journey. The experience of this silent and deep connection motivated me to explore further the experience of caregivers facing the bodily and spiritual pain of end-of-life.

In his essay 'The Soul and Death', Jung commented on the resistance to aging and death as being a resistance to a normal demand of life. He wrote: 'We are so convinced that death is simply the end of a process that it does not ordinarily occur to us to conceive of death as a goal and fulfillment, as we do without hesitation the aims and purposes of youthful life in its ascendance' (Jung 1934/1969: para. 797).

Jung also insisted on how the psyche prepares for death and noted that 'thoughts of death pile up to an astonishing degree as the years increase' (ibid.: para. 808). In addition, death is very often indicated by symbols, which in normal life would accompany changes of psychological conditions such as symbols of rebirth. The psyche prepares consciousness for death. For Jung, 'it seems that the unconscious is all the more interested in *how* one dies; that is, whether the attitude of consciousness is adjusted to dying or not' (ibid.: para. 809). Therefore, it is critical to communicate to the dying person that when, during the dying process, one's autonomy is removed, the developmental process of growth and learning continues and sometimes intensifies through dreams and forgiveness of self and others. This developmental process of growth includes a spirituality that is concerned with the purpose and meaning of life, and is an ontologically driven impulse toward union or relationship with God, or ultimate transcendent reality (Heyse-Moore 1996; Hodge 2006; Rousseau 2000). While physical suffering is under control, spiritual pain has been consistently described at the end of life and communicated through the emotional realm in terms 'despair', 'regret', or 'anxiety' (Gijsberts *et al.* 2011; Hermann 2006; Mako *et al.* 2006; Vachon *et al.* 2009). Addressing spirituality at the end of life is also under scrutiny because of the relationship between spiritual well-being and physical well-being (Ironson *et al.* 2002).

The general approach for the treatment of spiritual suffering, after having controlled physical symptoms, is to provide supportive presence, encourage a life review, and explore guilt, loss, and forgiveness. There have been some recent attempts to develop short-term psychotherapeutic interventions aiming to relieve spiritual pain (Breitbart and Heller 2003; Breitbart e*t al.* 2004; Chochinov *et al.* 2006; Montross *et al.* 2011). The spiritual dimension is an integral component of the dying process and healthcare professionals are challenged to include the spiritual dimension for whole-person care (Rousseau 2000; Puchalski 2007/2008). The religious and existential aspects of care are now fully integrated into palliative care guidelines (Ferrell *et al.* 2007). For example, cancer pain is best managed by a multidisciplinary approach integrating the psychosocial and spiritual aspects of cancer pain and the needs of patients (Otis-Green *et al.* 2002). The role of clinical psychologists at the end of life is growing in America (Haley *et al.* 2003; Nydegger 2008). While several psychologists have described their experience of working with patients at the end of life (Carvalho 2008; Kearney 2007; Wheelwright 1981), there is overall a paucity of research on the experience of caregivers witnessing death and dying with its spiritual pain and on the nature of the transference–countertransference – that is, the union of unconscious elements from the psyche of the analysand and from the psyche of the analyst. Schaverien (2002) related her experience of working with a dying male patient and the nature of the bond between them. Both recognized the need to maintain the analysis going until the end to help the analysand make sense of his present experience.

The purpose of this chapter is to discuss the archetypal aspects of the relationship of professional caregivers such as hospice workers with patients at the end of life, based on their reported experience in a previous study (DeArmond 2012/2013). The experience of hospice workers is assumed to be similar to that of medical personnel, therapists, volunteer and employed caregivers working in similar situations, and the discussion will make no differentiation based on professional occupation. The term of caregiver is generally applied throughout the chapter. A Jungian perspective on spiritual pain will be discussed.

Experiences of hospice workers

DeArmond (2012/2013) conducted a hermeneutic Jungian case study to explore the psychological experience of hospice workers during encounters with death and dying. Seventeen hospice workers of a large hospice in California, USA, were interviewed and the presence of personal growth was found in the large majority of the sample, sometimes with a transcendent experience. One participant said: 'There is something magnificent about death. It gives meaning to life. It becomes easier to appreciate some parts of life. It is special to see someone to die. It is an intimate gift.' While the experience of hospice workers and the themes that emerged from their narratives during encounters with death and dying are presented elsewhere (DeArmond 2012/2013), the themes can be summarized as interconnectedness, suffering and sacrifice, and birth and rebirth.

Participation, empathy, and compassion were the affective components involved in the experience of interconnectedness. One participant said: 'I have intense feelings when I take care of the dying. I can sense a sacred interconnectedness between all beings.' By witnessing the death of the other, the participants experience a tragic emotion. They experience changes of personality and spirituality. They become intimate with death. For one participant, 'The experience of being with the dying is calming, authentic, intimate, and loving.' They manifest a form of devotion in their care to the dying, which is an aspect of the relation to the sacred. The dying person becomes a symbolic other.

Witnessing a transformation, the participants experience a tragic compassion for the pain of the dying and the family. One hospice worker shared, 'When I talk to parents, I always tell them I lost a child, and I say I am glad, grateful they brought the child to the hospice.'

The dying person becomes a symbol of suffering, sacrifice, and transformation. The participation of the hospice workers in the tragedy is a form of 'understanding' that is an assimilation of the experience of the other. One hospice worker said: 'I feel it is rewarding to help patients and families during the dying process. I like to watch the interaction when one stops protecting the other and I can sense love flowing.' By taking part in the tragic event, the hospice workers are delivered from it. For example, one of them noted: 'When dying, patients give up; they are in peace, joining something bigger. I share the feeling when sitting with dying patients. It is a spiritual experience. It is not boring; I meditate and I often have some insight. I feel more connected.'

To be a witness of some rite of transformation is to participate in a process of transformation and rebirth oneself. The hospice workers are guiding the dying and guiding themselves. One said: 'I have images, flashbacks, of people who died. It makes me feel peaceful. I carry with me a little bit of each of them.' They use the experiences as an initiation into life. Another hospice worker noted: 'I am in better touch with the oneness of people, the oneness of humanity. I want to continue to work in a hospice. I feel I make a difference. It is a privilege and an honor to work with the dying. It rejuvenates me. It gives to me.' Caring for the dying becomes an indirect form of renewal and rebirth, and a way to practice for their own death.

Archetypal aspects of transference

Several factors could explain the experience of the hospice workers and how they related to the inward journey and spiritual pain of the dying person. First, an archetype of transformation may be constellated. Moreover, the enlargement of personality possibly has inner compassion as a source. For the caregiver, the broadening of consciousness underlying their personal growth may result from assimilation and integration of the experience of the other. Ultimately, the situation of witnessing death and dying may very well stimulate the feeling function of the caregivers through empathy.

Activation of an archetype of transformation

Archetype of transformation

Jung thought that images or situations could activate, or constellate, archetypes and enhance consciousness. For Jung, 'Any activated archetype can appear in projection, either into an external situation, or into people, or into circumstances—in short, into all sorts of objects' (Jung 1936/1976: para. 324). Jung defined the archetypes of transformation as 'typical situations, places, ways and means, that symbolize the kind of transformation in question' (Jung 1934/1954/1968: para. 80). With this definition, specific environments could activate the archetype of transformation, although the characteristics of an environment necessary to activate the archetype, the role of idiosyncratic or cultural factors, or the symbolic expression of the archetype have not been described. In addition, Jung described the existence of an archetype of death involved in the religious celebrations of catastrophic events. He said:

> Death means the total extinction of consciousness and the complete stagnation of psychic life, so far as this is capable of consciousness. So catastrophic a consummation, which has been the object of annual lamentations in so many places (e.g. the laments for Linus, Tammuz, and Adonis) must surely correspond to an important archetype, since even today we have our Good Friday.
>
> (Jung 1946/1966: para. 469)

Contemporary authors have built on Jung's definition of archetype and remained consistent overall with a shaping role on consciousness of the activation of archetypes. Kalsched built on Jung's model of the psyche's dissociability into many different complexes, each containing a set of archetypal images at its core (Kalsched 1996: 72). According to Knox (2003), the archetype is an emergent structure, an early product of self-organization. For Hollis (2000), the archetypal function has a centering effect. The psyche 'archetypes'—that is, it transforms and structures life experiences, and gives meaning to them (Hollis 1995: 21).

Activation of archetype of transformation

The role of attending to the dying and the environment of the hospice represent typical situations that activate the archetype of transformation in the caregiver because of the remarkable resonance between death and transformation through transference and counter-transference, and through indirect participation in a process of transformation. Caregivers focus their attention, their consciousness, on the dying process. Simultaneously, they project their own unconscious contents and are the receivers of the projection of unconscious contents from the dying. As mentioned above, Jung (1946/1966: paras. 353–449) commented on the alchemical treatise, the *Rosarium Philosophorum*, where the images of death and birth are present and highly symbolic of personal transformation. The alchemical union of the spirit and the soul in the *unio mentalis* corresponds, in psychological language, to the ego-personality confronting and integrating the shadow, the dark side of the personality (Jung 1955/1970: para. 707). This may be the task of the caregiver; in facing the dying person, the caregiver may be facing a symbolic image of transformation. The hospice worker may also face the shadow, this other complementary part of oneself and existence that one avoids. Death is the other and hidden face of existence.

The relationship between the caregiver and the dying person is also an example of a relationship between a healer and a wounded person. Caring for the dying is a way for the caregivers to attend to the wounded side of their own personalities. The myth of Asklepios is reflected in the doctor–patient relationship as an archetypal aspect of the transference (Groesbeck 1975). In this case, the patient looks for a healer, or physician, and the physician-healer looks for patients. Because of their illnesses, the patients unconsciously activate their 'inner healer'—and vice versa, the inner wounded side of the physician is activated by contact with the sick person.

Lastly, the symbols of birth and rebirth have been described as symbols of personal growth and are, with death, important symbols of transformation (Jung 1915/1950/1967). In his essay 'Concerning Rebirth', Jung described many forms of rebirth (Jung 1950a/1968: paras 199–205) including indirect rebirth, where the transformation is brought about not by passing directly through death and rebirth oneself but indirectly by participating in a process of transformation. Participating in a process of transformation is both witnessing and ultimately taking an active part in it. For example, this is the case for the rites of transformation of the Christian Mass and of the Eleusinian mysteries (ibid., para. 205). For Jung, 'the parallel to the motif of dying and rising again is that of being lost and found again' (1915/1950/1967, para. 531). In both cases of the Christian Mass and the Eleusinian mysteries, there is a celebration of some form of disappearance: death or journey in the underworld.

Understanding and broadening of consciousness

Empathy

For Jung, empathy is 'a readiness to meet the object halfway, a subjective assimilation that brings about a good understanding between subject and object, or at least stimulates it' (Jung 1921/1971, para. 489). For the caregiver, empathy is a participation that brings understanding, a broadening of consciousness. Another mechanism for understanding may be the internal fire created by the encounter with death and dying. Assagioli (1969) defined different stages in the development of the transcendent: (a) crises preceding spiritual awakening; (b) crises caused by spiritual awakening; (c) reactions to spiritual awakening; and (d) phases in the process of transmutation. The enlargement of personality has possibly inner compassion as a source. For the caregiver, the broadening of consciousness underlying their personal growth may result from assimilation and integration of the experience of the other. Ultimately, the situation of witnessing death and dying may very well stimulate the feeling function of the caregivers through empathy.

Interconnectedness

Interconnectedness is a participation and a form of oneness with the other. Through the connection with the other, interconnectedness may reach a spiritual dimension. Many scholars have established a parallel between the relationship with the other and the relationship with God. Otto posited in 'The Idea of the Holy: An inquiry into the non-rational factor in the idea of the divine and its relation to the rational', that God is 'the wholly other' (Otto 1923/1958: 25–30) and experienced as a *mysterium tremendum*. For Buber, the relationship between the I and the You, the other, is a relationship with the sacredness of the other. In addition, according to Buber, the relationship between the I and the You is inherent in the development of the person:

> The basic word I–You can be spoken only with one's whole being. The concentration and fusion into a whole being can never be accomplished by me, can never be accomplished without me. I require a You to become; becoming I, I say You.
>
> (Buber 1923/1970: 62)

In the context of end-of-life care, the caregivers establish relationships with the dying persons, who become, for them, a symbolic other. Thus they become more of an I, as conceptualized by Buber, because the dying person represents more than just one person.

Transcendence

In addition to the increased capacity to relate, for the caregivers, the experiences of death and dying influence the transcendence of the ego in its effort to reach the numinosum. Maslow discussed the various meanings of transcendence. He noted that transcendence is:

> the same kind of self-forgetfulness which comes from getting absorbed, fascinated, and concentrated. In this sense, meditation or concentration on something outside one's own psyche can produce self-forgetfulness and therefore loss of self-consciousness in this particular sense of transcendence of the ego or of the conscious self.
>
> (Maslow 1969: 56)

Another aspect of the transcendent experience is that some caregivers may have an encounter with the Self when caring for the dying. In the pair of opposites of the dying and the living, the ego may be thought of as represented by the caregiver, while the dying person could be conceived as a symbolic image of the Self and a symbolic image of the transcendent. For Jung, a balance between consciousness and the unconscious is needed for individuation (Jung 1946/1966: para. 395; 1939/1968: paras 489–524). The living needs the dying just as the ego needs the Self. In this sense, the relationship of the caregiver with the dying person symbolically mirrors the relationship of the ego with the Self.

Redemption through suffering and sacrifice

The activation of the transcendent function, a psychological function facilitating and arising from the union of conscious and unconscious contents, and the redemption through suffering and sacrifice are other avenues for a transformation.

Transcendent function

According to Jung (1934/1969: paras 796–815), the psyche spontaneously prepares for death. After middle life, consciousness progressively detaches itself from the world and turns inward. This turning inward gives rise to a personal transformation. In the context of witnessing death and dying, the dying is a symbolic image of transformation. The alchemists were projecting upon matter and proceeding to a transformation of their own psyches. Similarly, the caregivers may also project unconscious contents and, in the process, be transformed themselves through the activation of the transcendent function.

For Jung, the crisis of illness can also be the source of psychological growth through the activation of the transcendent function:

> It is as though, at the climax of the illness, the destructive powers were converted into healing forces. This is brought about by the archetypes awaking to independent life and taking over the guidance of the psychic personality, thus supplanting the ego in its futile willing and striving.
>
> (Jung 1933/1969: para. 534)

It is possible that, through participation, the caregivers assimilate the transformation of the other and that the constellation of the archetype of transformation activates the transcendent function.

Suffering and sacrifice

Witnessing death and dying has the character of a sacred celebration. Jung identified sacrifice as a symbol of transformation (1915/1950/1967: paras 613–682). Alchemists emphasized sacrifice as part of the work (opus), especially the self-sacrifice of intellectualism and rationalism, the *sacrificium intellectus* (Jung, 1944/1968: para. 59). Elsewhere, Jung described the psychological aspects of the symbolism of transformation in the Christian Mass, in which the Divine Child, the image of God, is eaten (Jung 1954/1969: paras 376–448). Attending a transformational event fosters a personal transformation by assimilation. The hospice workers, through empathy, participate in the transformation of the dying process and are themselves transformed.

Suffering is an opening to redemption, described by Jung in the Introduction to the *Tibetan Book of the Dead*, as 'a separation and deliverance from an earlier condition of darkness and unconsciousness' (Jung 1953/1969: para. 841). Redemption leads to 'a condition of illumination and releasedness, to victory and transcendence over everything "given"' (ibid.). Redemption, in the case of witnessing death and dying, pertains to the dying, on one hand, and to the caregiver, on the other hand. Caregivers are both the redeemed and the redeemers. They have a passive role when offering their presence, but also an active role when making the choice to be present and actively witness the dying process. Jung insisted on the duality of human nature to be both the redeemed and the redeemer. Whereas being redeemed is part of the Christian tradition, being a redeemer has an alchemical character. Being a redeemer is taking responsibility for carrying out the redeeming opus: redemption from the imprisonment of the *anima mundi* in matter (Jung 1944/1968: para. 414). By being both redeemed and redeemer, having both a passive and an active role, the caregiver may process suffering, transform it, and be redeemed.

Suffering and sacrifice can lead to redemption, and this gives suffering meaning. In the case of the caregiver, suffering is the assimilation of the suffering of the dying person. Death and dying are aspects of a heroic journey, and the caregivers feel its tragic quality. The hero, the dying person, is powerless. Death is the total defeat of the ego. Jung noted that to experience the Self, one has to sense the finitude of the conscious will to give room for the Self to grow (Jung 1955/1970: para. 778). Death and dying may be an experience of the Self for the dying and, by assimilation, for the caregiver, too. Witnessing death and dying is for the caregivers a reenactment of death that leads indirectly to rebirth. In caring for the dying, the caregivers become aware of their own finitude, their own deaths. For Jung, the integration of unconscious contents into consciousness, the continuous conscious realization of them, brings a change (Jung 1928/1966: paras 358–359). The experiences of the caregivers are partly conscious and partly unconscious. For the caregiver, a change in personality may be the result of the assimilation of the other and the integration of unconscious contents.

Discussion: a Jungian approach of spiritual pain

In *Memories, Dreams, Reflections*, Jung reported the visions he had during a near-death experience and said:

> It is impossible to convey the beauty and intensity of emotion during those visions . . . And what a contrast the day was: I was tormented on the edge; everything irritated me; everything was too material, too crude and clumsy, terribly limited both spatially and spiritually.
>
> (Jung 1963/1989: 295)

In Jung's case, it seems that visions, dives into the unconscious, and irruption of the numinosum cohabit with an ego frustration.

He added later, 'there was a pneuma of inexpressible sanctity in the room, whose manifestation was the *mysterium coniunctionis*' (ibid.). Jung described the *coniunctio* as the 'union of two figures, one representing the daytime principle, i.e., lucid consciousness, the other a nocturnal light, the unconscious' (Jung 1946/1966: para. 469). In a touching letter he sent to Kristine Mann who was dying of cancer, Jung shared his experience of the dying process during his near-death experience:

> The only difficulty is to get rid of the body, to get quite naked and void of the world and the ego-will. When you can give up the crazy will to live and when you seemingly fall into a bottomless mist, then the truly *real* life begins with everything which you were meant to be and never reached.
>
> (Jung 1973, 1 February 1945, italics in text)

In addition, Jung insisted on strong and even causal connections between the psyche and the body (Jung 1955/1970: paras 767–768).

What is spiritual pain from a Jungian perspective? The different facets of spiritual pain here discussed include: (1) a frustration of not having spiritual needs met; (2) a nigredo phase of individuation; and (3) a pessimistic expression of spirituality.

A frustration of not having spiritual needs met

Spiritual pain may come from a real frustration of not having spiritual needs attended to or as a call for further attention. This is a pragmatic facet of end-of-life that should not be overlooked since there is a possibility to base the therapeutic approach directly on the satisfaction of unmet needs. If spiritual pain stems primarily from a frustration of not having spiritual needs attended to, spiritual pain would be further exacerbated in an environment unsupportive of spiritual development as are, for example, some medical environments where the emphasis is exclusively on the fight for life at the expense of the sustainment of spiritual life. Very often also in terminal care, patients have difficulty in communicating their needs because of physical limitations and this could further aggravate the frustration of the patients. Amplifying the symbolic life, tapping into the resources of creativity, and co-creating with the patient through narratives, poetry, and painting open a channel of communication in terminal care (Bolton 2008; Miller and Cook-Greuter 2000). These artistic experiences can be used to enable insight and healing but also to support practitioners professionally as a form of reflective practice.

A nigredo phase of individuation

Death is a physical and psychic transformation that starts well before the final moment. If death is imminent, as for example in terminal care, and assuming a strong mind–body relationship, there is in all likelihood an opportunity for a spiritual change in the midst of considerable organic changes. Spiritual suffering, a painful expression of a transformation to come, may be related to the nigredo phase of individuation, a dark crisis. Jung noted the foreknowledge of the psyche to death and dying (1934/1969). I posit that, in some instances, spiritual pain expressed as nigredo may come as an anticipation and preparation of the psyche for death.

The triangular relationship between spirituality, suffering, and death is further supported by the common presence of death and suffering within the symbolism of individuation. As emphasized by Jung (1955/1970, 1950b/1968), alchemy and religious symbolism are very evocative of the process of individuation and both frequently include pain and death. Regarding alchemy, there is a strong relationship between alchemy and death, between organic and psychic transformation. Jung said:

> This process underlies the whole *opus*, but to begin with it is so confusing that the alchemist tries to depict the conflict, death, and rebirth figuratively, on a higher plane, first—in his *practica*—in the form of chemical transformations and then—in his *theoria*—in the form of conceptual images.
>
> (Jung 1954/1966: para. 471, italics in text)

In his essay 'The Psychology of the Transference,' Jung posited that the images of the alchemical treatise '*Rosarium Philosophorum*' symbolize the union of opposites and the process of individuation, and noted that death follows the reconciliation of opposites, the *coniunctio oppositorum* (Jung 1946/1966: para. 467). The alchemists thought that the *lapis philosophorum*, the philosophical stone, could heal physical disharmonies, and psychic and spiritual conflicts. In order to obtain the lapis, the alchemists had to loosen the attachment of the soul to the body. This operation is a figurative death, acknowledging one's projections and the influence of anima or animus (Jung, 1955/1970: para. 673). Therefore, alchemical symbolism, with its insistence on the interrelationship between body and mind, is very significant for tracing the psychic transformations of the end of life.

On the side of religious symbolism, spiritual pain at the end of life presents similarities with the despair and spiritual crisis experienced by the biblical Job. Jung noted a parallel between the story of Job and the process of individuation. When confronted with unconscious contents, Job becomes more conscious, but God's consciousness also increases. It is a reciprocal process. For Jung, 'existence is only real when it is conscious to somebody'

(Jung 1953/1969: para. 575). This already points to the importance of the role of a caregiver, containing and mirroring the pain, for a process of increasing consciousness. Another example of the religious symbolism of pain, death, and transformation is the crucifixion of Jesus. Jung asserted that Jesus is a symbol of the Self (Jung 1948/1969: paras 226–233). For Jung, 'Christ exemplifies the archetype of the self' (Jung 1950b/1968: para. 70). Jesus's death has a redemptive effect on the community. Jung established a parallel between individuation, or self-realization, and the passion of Christ. He said:

> The human and the divine suffering set up a relationship of complementarity with compensating effects. Through the Christ-symbol, man can get to know the real meaning of his suffering: he is on the way towards realizing his wholeness. As the result of the integration of conscious and unconscious, his ego enters the 'divine' realm, where it participates in 'God's suffering.'
>
> (Jung 1948/1969: para. 233)

There are other multiple examples of dying gods or dying mythological figures often as a part of a heroic journey. In mythology or religion, venerating the death of god brings a renewal of the personality and salvation. The transcendental nature of death is emphasized and in the past these dying gods were especially venerated for their knowledge of the underworld. Osiris and Horus were grieved by Isis, and their deaths were followed by resurrection and renewal. Wholeness also followed death in the Eleusinian mysteries that celebrated the spring return of Persephone, the daughter of Demeter, from the underworld.

A pessimistic expression of spirituality

Spiritual pain may also be a natural form of expression of spirituality, the expression of religious feelings where there is a dominance of sadness. In medical terms, pain has often a negative connotation and is the sign of a dysfunction. Pain, in the Christian sense, is a mark of defilement. This polarized definition of pain is misleading for spirituality. William James described some pessimistic expressions of religious experience. For James, the three forms of melancholy are vanity of mortal things, sense of sin, and fear of the universe (James 1902/2002: 129). James viewed the personal experience of humiliation as critical to engender a deep sense of life significance (ibid: 111). For Tolstoy, mid-life crisis is a painful depression. Tolstoy's attack of melancholy led him to develop his own religious conclusions and to experience conversion. James noted that in Tolstoy's case, the sense that the meaning of life was for a moment totally withdrawn (ibid: 121). Spirituality may therefore have painful, sad expressions. However, caution is needed when the focus is exclusively on spiritual pain, and the personal history and the role of interpersonal relationships recedes into the background; for spiritual pain may also be the result of an exacerbation of a pre-existent malaise. Sadness at the end of life may be related to the closure of personal relationships and to the fearful anticipation of a final transition.

Overall, spiritual pain at end-of-life may be the expression of religious feelings with a dominance of sadness and an urge for individuation. The anguish and spiritual pain of end-of-life may not require an approach any different from the general one used in Jungian psychotherapy. However, some elements specific to the situation of death and dying are to be taken into consideration. Time is limited. A dialogue may be difficult to establish in the presence of physical symptoms and limited physical strength. The environment of the hospice or home is more or less favorable to the conduct of the psychotherapy. At the end of life, there is often a marked existential or religious anguish of facing one's limitedness. These circumstances are challenges for the therapy, but are also very likely to influence the psychotherapist and engender a marked transference.

Conclusion

As one of the hospice workers in DeArmond's study said: 'Every death changes you.' Based on the themes emerging in the reported experience of hospice workers and on the themes emerging from their narratives, the role of attending to the dying and the environment of the hospice may represent typical situations that activate the archetype of transformation in the caregiver through transference and counter-transference and through indirect participation in a process of transformation. I suggest that the main elements of the experience of being an engaged witness of death and dying include the following: (a) an archetype of transformation is constellated—in this context, the dying person is a symbolic image of transformation, of the Self and of the shadow, and constellates an archetype of transformation such that caring for the dying is practicing for one's own death and a form of indirect rebirth; (b) the empathy and compassion for the dying person leads to greater understanding and a broadening of consciousness for the caregiver; and (c) the suffering of witnessing death and dying leads to redemption. The dying person may operate as a trigger for the activation of unconscious contents of the caregivers. The hospice worker/caregiver has a role in holding, helping to find meaning, and validating the experience.

This discussion on the dynamic of the archetype of transformation, the role of suffering and redemption in personal growth, and the symbolism of the dying person is a contribution to a Jungian approach of the spiritual pain of end-of-life that has been tentatively defined as the combination of a frustration of not having spiritual needs met, a nigredo phase of individuation, and a pessimistic expression of spirituality. As more focused studies of the experience of caregivers and psychologists with death and dying become available, a better appreciation of the transference and countertransference involved in the care of end-of-life will likely support the increased involvement of psychotherapists in this setting, a deeper relationship to spiritual pain, and an improved care of end-of-life.

References

Assagioli, R. (1969) 'Symbols of transpersonal experiences', *The Journal of Transpersonal Psychology*, 1: 33–45.

Bolton, G. (ed.) (2008) *Dying, bereavement, and the healing arts*, Philadelphia, PA: Jessica Kingsley Publishers.

Breitbart, W. and Heller, K.S. (2003) 'Reframing hope: meaning-centered care for patients near the end of life', *Journal of Palliative Medicine*, 6: 979–988.

Breitbart, W., Gibson, C., Poppito, S.R. and Berg, A. (2004) 'Psychotherapeutic interventions at the end of life: a focus on meaning and spirituality', *Canadian Journal of Psychiatry*, 49: 366–372.

Breitbart, W., Rosenfeld, B., Gibson, C., Pessin, H., Poppito, S., Nelson, C., Tomarken, A., Timm, A.K., Berg, A., Jacobson, C., Sorger, B., Abbey, J. and Olden, M. (2010) 'Meaning-centered group psychotherapy for patients with advanced cancer: a pilot randomized controlled trial', *Psycho-Oncology*, 19: 21–28.

Buber, M. (1923/1970) *I and thou*, trans. W. Kaufmann, New York: Simon & Schuster.

Carvalho, R. (2008) 'The final challenge: Ageing, dying, individuation', *The Journal of Analytical Psychology*, 53: 1–18.

Chochinov, H.M., Krisjanson, L.J., Hack, T.F., Hassard, T., McClement, S. and Harlos M. (2006) 'Dignity in the terminally ill: revisited', *Journal of Palliative Medicine*, 9: 666–672.

Chochinov, H.M., Kristjanson, L.J., Breitbart, W., McClement, S., Hack, T.F., Hassard, T. and Harlos, M. (2011) 'Effect of dignity therapy on distress and end-of-life experience in terminally ill patients: a randomised controlled trial', *Lancet Oncology*, 12: 753–762.

DeArmond, M.I. (2012/2013) 'The psychological experience of hospice workers during encounters with death', *Omega: Journal of Death and Dying*: 66, 4: 281–299.

Ferrell, B., Connor, S.R., Cordes, A., Dahlin, C.M., Fine, P.G., Hutton, N., Leenay, M., Lentz, J., Person, J.L., Meier, D.E. and Zuroski, K., The National Consensus Project for Quality Palliative Care Task Force Members (2007) 'The National agenda for quality palliative care: the national consensus project and the national quality forum', *Journal of Pain and Symptom Management*, 33: 737–744.

Gijsberts, M.J., Echteld, M.A., van der Steen, J.T., Muller, M.T., Otten, R.H., Ribbe, M.W. and Deliens, L. (2011) 'Spirituality at the end of life: conceptualization of measurable aspects—a systematic review', *Journal of Palliative Medicine*, 14: 852–863.

Groesbeck, C.J. (1975) 'The archetypal image of the wounded healer', *The Journal of Analytical Psychology*, 20: 122–145.

Haley, W.E., Kasl-Godley, J., Larson, D.G. and Neimeyer, R.A. (2003) 'Roles for psychologists in end-of-life care: emerging models for practice', *Professional Psychology: Research & Practice*, 34: 626–633.

Hermann, C.P. (2006) 'Development and testing of the Spiritual Needs Inventory for patients near the end of life', *Oncology Nursing Forum*, 33: 737–744.

Heyse-Moore, L.H. (1996) 'On spiritual pain in the dying', *Mortality*, 1: 297–315.

Hodge, D.R. (2006) 'A template for spiritual assessment: a review of the JCAHO requirements and guidelines for implementation', *Social Work*, 5: 317–326.

Hollis, J. (1995) *Tracking the gods: the place of myth in modern life*, Toronto: Inner City Books.

—— (2000) *The archetypal imagination*, College Station, TX: Texas A&M University Press.

Ironson, G., Solomon, G.F., Balbin, E.G., O'Cleirigh, C., George, A., Kumar, M., Larson, D. and Woods, T. (2002) 'The Ironson-Woods Spirituality/Religiousness Index is associated with long survival, health behaviors, less distress, and low cortisol in people with HIV/AIDS', *Annals of Behavioral Medicine*, 24: 34–48.

James, W. (1902/2002) *The varieties of religious experience: a study in human nature*, New York: Routledge.

Jung, C.G. (1915/1950/1967) *Symbols of transformation, Collected Works*, Volume 5, Princeton, NJ: Princeton University Press.

—— (1921/1971) *Psychological types, Collected Works*, Volume 6, Princeton, NJ: Princeton University Press.

—— (1928/1966) 'The relations between the ego and the unconscious', in *Collected Works*, Volume 7, Princeton, NJ: Princeton University Press.

—— (1933/1969) 'Psychotherapy or the clergy', in *Collected Works*, Volume 11, Princeton, NJ: Princeton University Press.

—— (1934/1954/1968) 'The archetypes of the collective unconscious', in *Collected Works*, Volume 9, Part I, Princeton, NJ: Princeton University Press.

—— (1934/1969) 'The soul and death', in *Collected Works*, Volume 8, Princeton, NJ: Princeton University Press.

—— (1936/1976) 'The Tavistock lectures: On the theory and practice of Analytical Psychology', in *Collected Works*, Volume 18, Princeton, NJ: Princeton University Press.

—— (1939/1968) 'Conscious, unconscious, and individuation', in *Collected Works*, Volume 9, Part I, Princeton, NJ: Princeton University Press.

—— (1944/1968) *Psychology and alchemy, Collected Works*, Volume 12, Princeton, NJ: Princeton University Press.

—— (1946/1966) 'The psychology of the transference', in *Collected Works*,Volume 16, Princeton, NJ: Princeton University Press.

—— (1948/1969) 'A psychological approach to the dogma of the Trinity', in *Collected Works* Volume 11, Princeton, NJ: Princeton University Press.

—— (1950a/1968) 'Concerning rebirth', in *Collected Works*, Volume 9, Part I, Princeton, NJ: Princeton University Press.

—— (1950b/1968) *Aion: Researches into the phenomenology of the self, Collected Works*,Volume 9, Part II, Princeton, NJ: Princeton University Press.

—— (1952/1969) 'Answer to Job', in *Collected Works*, Volume 11, Princeton, NJ: Princeton University Press.

—— (1953/1969) 'Psychological commentary on *The Tibetan Book of the Dead*', in *Collected Works*, Volume 11, Princeton, NJ: Princeton University Press.

—— (1954/1969) 'Transformation symbolism in the Mass', in *Collected Works*, Volume 11, Princeton: Princeton University Press.

—— (1955/1970) *Mysterium Coniunctionis, Collected Works*, Volume 14, Princeton, NJ: Princeton University Press.

—— (1963/1989) *Memories, dreams, reflections*, A. Jaffe (ed.), New York: Vintage, Random House.

—— (1973) *Letters* 1: 1906–1950, G. Adler and A. Jaffé (eds.), Princeton, NJ: Princeton University Press.

Kalsched, D. (1996) *The inner world of trauma: archetypal defenses of the personal spirit*, New York: Routledge.

Kearney, M. (2007) *Mortally wounded: stories of soul pain, death, and dying*, New Orleans, LA: Spring Journal Books.

Knox, J. (2003) *Archetype, attachment, analysis*, New York: Brunner-Routledge.

Mako, C., Galek, K. and Poppito, S.R. (2006) 'Spiritual pain among patients with advanced cancer in palliative care', *Journal of Palliative Medicine*, 9: 1106–1113.

Maslow, A.H. (1969) 'Various meanings of transcendence', *Journal of Transpersonal Psychology*, I: 56–66.

Miller, M.E. and Cook-Greuter, S.R. (eds) (2000) *Creativity, spirituality, and transcendence: paths to integrity and wisdom into the mature self.* Stamford, CT: Ablex Publishing.

Montross, L., Winters, K.D. and Irwin, S.A. (2011) 'Dignity therapy implementation in a community-based hospice setting', *Journal of Palliative Medicine*, 14: 729–734.

Nydegger, R. (2008) 'Psychologists and hospice: where we are and where we can be', *Professional Psychology: Research & Practice*, 39: 459–463.

Otis-Green, S., Sherman, R., Perez, M. and Baird, P. (2002) 'An integrated psychosocial-spiritual model for cancer pain management', *Cancer Practice*, 10: S58–S65.

Otto, R. (1923/1958) *The idea of the Holy: an inquiry into the non-rational factor in the idea of the divine and its relation to the rational*, trans. J. W. Harvey, New York: Oxford University Press.

Puchalski, C. M. (2007–2008) 'Spirituality and the care of patients at the end-of-life: An essential component of care', *Omega: Journal of Death & Dying* 56: 33–46.

Rousseau, P. (2000) 'Spirituality and the dying patient', *Journal of Clinical Oncology*, 18: 54S–56S.

Schaverien, J. (2002) *The dying patient in psychotherapy: desire, dreams, and individuation,* New York: Palgrave Macmillan.

Vachon, M., Fillion, L. and Achille, M. (2009) 'A conceptual analysis of spirituality at the end of life', *Journal of Palliative Medicine*, 12: 53–59.

Wheelwright, J.H. (1981) *The death of a woman: how a life became complete*, New York: St Martin's Press.

13

IN CONSIDERATION OF DISQUIET AND LONGING FOR OUR CHANGING WORLD

Perspectives from the poetry and prose of Fernando Pessoa

Cedrus Monte

I am the escaped one.
After I was born
They locked me up inside myself
But I left . . .
My soul still seeks me
Over hills and valley.
I hope my soul
Never finds me.[1]

(Pessoa 2006a, p. 315)

Fernando Pessoa: a brief biography

Fernando Pessoa is considered Portugal's greatest contemporary writer. He was born Fernando António Nogueira de Seabra Pessoa in Lisbon on June 13, 1888. He died on November 30, 1935, in the same city at the early age of 47. Pessoa's mother, Maria Madalena Pinheiro Nogueira, originally from the Azores, was interested in both music and literature. His father, Joaquim de Seabra Pessoa, was a civil servant and a music critic for Lisbon's daily newspaper, *O Diário de Notícias*. On July 13, 1893, when Pessoa had just turned five, his father died of tuberculosis. The following year, on January 2, Pessoa's younger brother, Jorge, also died. He was only a year old (Pessoa 2003).

Surrounded by death, Pessoa created his first literary companion, a pen pal by the name of *Chevalier de Pas*. Not only did Pessoa write to *Chevalier de*

Figure 13.1 Fernando Pessoa (author unknown, 1914, creative commons attribution)

Pas, but his imaginary pen pal wrote back, acknowledging Pessoa's contact. These were the early beginnings of Pessoa's experience of the written word taking the form of reality, and the first of many characters to appear in his literary world. Through his writing, Pessoa began to create and re-create a world that would not only sustain him for the remainder of his life, but would create in literature a unique and completely original way of expressing and articulating the many dimensions of psyche.

In December of 1895, Pessoa's mother remarried João Miguel dos Santos Rosa, a military officer. The family moved to Durban, South Africa, where Pessoa's stepfather had been appointed the Portuguese consul. Pessoa attended the English-speaking schools there and continued to develop his desire for writing. However, at the age of 17 after his early education in South Africa, Pessoa decided to come back to Lisbon and enrolled at the university. After his return, he rarely left the city.

Pessoa was a brilliant student, but due to difficult personal and political circumstances that ensued, he dropped out of the university not long after his seventeenth birthday and began to study on his own. He went to the National Library of Lisbon, where he systematically read major works of philosophy, theology, history, sociology and, of course, literature, especially Portuguese literature (Zenith 2008).

In 1916, one of Pessoa's closest friends and fellow poet, Mário de Sá-Carneiro, committed suicide. His friend's death affected him profoundly. It was at this point that Pessoa began to look for spiritual answers. To that end, he studied the cabala, alchemy, theosophy and other disciplines within the occult. He also became especially interested in astrology. Astrology was part of Pessoa's everyday life and he kept that interest until his death.

During his lifetime, Pessoa lived in rented rooms and later in a common residence with other members of his family. In 1920, Pessoa's mother returned to Lisbon from Durban after the death of her second husband. It was at this time that Pessoa rented living quarters for the reunited family – his mother, his half-sister and half-brothers and himself. The house is located in Lisbon on Rua Coelho da Rocha, 16. Today, this house is known as the *Casa Fernando Pessoa*. It houses a library, a bookstore, a museum, an art gallery and a lecture room, all open to the public. Admission is free. The world is fully and generously invited to participate in this extraordinary poet's life and work. Pessoa lived in this house for the last fifteen years of his life (Zenith 2006).

From the website of *Casa Fernando Pessoa*, we find the following:

> **A plural universe**
>
> Opened in November 1993, the cultural centre Casa Fernando Pessoa was conceived by the Lisbon City Council as a tribute to Fernando Pessoa and his memory; in the city where he lived and the area in which he spent the last fifteen years of his life . . .
>
> With its auditorium, garden, exhibition rooms, works of art, a library exclusively dedicated to poetry, in addition to part of the poet's estate (furniture and personal items that are now municipal heritage), the Casa Fernando Pessoa is a small but multifarious world. Its three floors host colloquiums, poetry readings, meetings with authors, concerts and theatre, lectures, workshops, art exhibitions, book launches and children's ateliers in a programme of events which is as widely diversified as possible.

Pessoa was solitary by nature, having a limited social life and virtually no love life. He was, however, an active leader of Portugal's Modernist movement in the early 1900s. In Lisbon, he was respected as an intellectual and a poet yet, sadly, most of Pessoa's work was not published in his lifetime. He did publish his work in several magazines, some of which he helped to found, but his genius was essentially unrecognized by the world-at-large until after he died (Zenith 2006).

At his death, his friends opened a large trunk in his apartment, discovering an estimated 25,000 pages of poems, essays, short stories and plays. Most of what we know of Pessoa's literary life comes from that trunk. More than ten decades after his death, Pessoa's vast body of writing has not yet been fully chronicled by researchers, and much of his prose is still to be published.

Pessoa was able to support himself financially as a commercial correspondent by writing letters in English and French for Portuguese companies that had business dealings abroad. Up until his death, he was largely employed as an independent commercial correspondent, working for individual companies on a contractual basis. He died without having acquired any material means beyond that which was needed for a simple existence.

The soul of the poet

After his death, Pessoa became a national treasure. In 1988, 100 years after his birth, Pessoa was entombed at the Monastery of São Jeronimo in Lisbon, now a UNESCO World Heritage Site. Along with Luís Vaz de Camões, Portugal's much loved and celebrated 16th-century poet, Pessoa also presides here with Vasco de Gama, the fearless oceanic explorer from Portugal's Age of Discovery.

Pessoa was also a fearless explorer of inner worlds. The fact that this inner fearlessness is also recognized as greatness pays tribute not only to Pessoa, but to the culture and the people of Portugal who have honored this shy, eccentric and introverted artist.

An inscription on his tomb at São Jeronimo reflects the soul of Pessoa in four lines:

> I am nothing.
> I shall always be nothing.
> I cannot want to be anything.
> But I have in me all the dreams of the world.
>
> (Alvaro do Campos; translation mine)

Since his death, Pessoa's reputation has grown throughout the world. He is recognized internationally as one of the major poets of the 20th century. To a certain audience within the general public, this modest and melancholy poet is something of a rock star, a cult figure who allows for the exploration of the deeper layers of the psyche, of life itself, life that is so often accompanied by quiet despair.

> I'm having one of those days when I feel I never had a future. There is only the present, fixed and encircled by a wall of anguish. The other bank of the river, because it is the other bank, is never the bank we are standing on: and that is the intimate reason for all my suffering.

> There are ships sailing to many different ports, but not a single one goes where life is not painful . . . All of this happened such a long time ago, but my sadness began even before then . . .
>
> (Pessoa 1998b, pp. 21–22, xxv)

Much of Pessoa's most famous work is attributed to four of his many heteronyms – Alberto Caeiro, Ricardo Reis, Álvaro de Campos and Bernardo Soares. The word 'heteronym' was a term that Pessoa used rather than 'pseudonym' (a name that one hides behind) in that each heteronym was, by design, an individual writer with a unique personality. Although it can be said that each writer reflects a dimension of Pessoa's multifaceted way of perceiving the world, as a heteronym each poet or writer speaks as a self-contained autonomous individual, unhindered or uncompromised by what might be interpreted as contradictions within the complex structure of Pessoa's nature and his vision of reality.

The apparent contradictions within Pessoa are, in fact, not contradictions. His need to express truth needed to come through the multiplicity of distinct voices. The invention of the many heteronyms allowed for each truth to unfold without the need to compromise or 'relativize.' Pessoa's heteronyms have their own separate personalities, their own biographies, individual signatures, and even their own astrological charts. They were each given their time to speak.

If we look at Pessoa's chart we learn that he was born with the sun in Gemini. He also has three other planets in Gemini, Gemini being the sign of the twins. For Pessoa, with four planets in the sign of twins, this quaternity of couplets creates much more than the sum of eight figures . . . it creates a virtual galaxy of heteronyms, over 70 in total, including one woman.

Pessoa could become whole only by giving voice to figure after figure within him. It was not only a matter of literary genius, it was also an act of following the soul: of living and expressing that constellation of energies that is intrinsically who we are, and is always calling us toward its fulfillment in and through our life experiences. Pessoa writes:

> I don't know how many souls I have . . .
> I've changed at every turn.
> I always feel like a stranger.
> I've never seen or found myself.
> From being so much, I am only soul . . .
>
> Attentive to what I am and to what I see,
> I become them. I stop being I.
> Each of my dreams and each desire
> Belongs to whoever had it, not to me . . .
>
> (Pessoa 1998a)

Here again, from another perspective, he speaks of the multiplicity of being:

> I created myself, echo and abyss, by reflecting. I multiplied myself, by going deeply into myself. The smallest episode – a change of light, the crumpled fall of a dead leaf, the petal that drops off and commits yellowcide, the voice on the far side of the wall . . . the half-open gate to the old estate, the patio that opens with an arch onto the houses heaped up in the moonlight – all these things, which do not belong to me, tie up my sensory reflections with chords of resonance and nostalgia. In each one of these sensations I am someone else, I renew myself painfully in each indefinite impression.
>
> I live on impressions that don't belong to me, reckless with renunciations, just another version of myself.
>
> (Pessoa 1998b, pp. 21–22)

Continuing with Pessoa's astrological portrait, one finds that he also had a strong emphasis in what is known as the eighth house of the astrological chart. (Each chart is divided into twelve houses or aspects of life, corresponding with the twelve signs of the zodiac.) In large part, the eighth house represents the dimension of the psyche that is involved with death and rebirth, with deep transformational forces that regulate and demand the repeated release of established forms and structure, allowing for continual rebirth. The mythical phoenix is an appropriate image of this process.

The eighth house also delineates the area of the psyche that is most related to depth analytical psychology: transformation through the death of the lesser ego through the constant integration of the unconscious and its vivifying effects. Apropos to this particular expression of transformation, when speaking of the integration of the unconscious in relation to the ego, Jung says: 'The secret is that only that which can destroy itself is truly alive' (Jung 1968, par. 93). Jung was suggesting that for every insight that arises from the unconscious and integrated into conscious life, that integration is experienced as a death by the ego – that is, the ego must relinquish its more limited and confined vision to a wisdom that is greater than itself.

It is only by accepting the death of what is no longer viable that we can be truly alive. From the piece of the cosmos that Pessoa was given to explore, astrologically speaking, one can say that Pessoa had been given an open account with the unconscious (also an eighth house concern), forever venturing into and integrating new territory through character after character, heteronym after heteronym. In this, Pessoa was a companion with his fellow compatriots, those mariners and navigators who for centuries crossed what was indeed the great unknown in their numerous *caravelas*, swift and highly nimble ships, carrying them across uncharted waters, making the unknown, 'unconscious' world known.

To venture into the outer unknown, we need to confront our physical death. To venture into the inner unknown, the ego must die to the deeper wisdom of the unconscious, again and again. It was this inner venture that Pessoa helped to chart for us through his vision and through his literary opus.

Thus, from his astrological destiny, as well as for other reasons, Pessoa had a natural inclination toward the impulses in life that request our acceptance of death as the fundamental road toward a fuller life. He lived with this paradox intimately every day, from early childhood until his physical death, as the core and essence of his life and work as an artist. This natural inclination would be no small factor in Pessoa's influence as one of the greatest contemporary writers of Portugal, and beyond. He speaks and writes of the taboos held within the underbelly of life and death. In his psychological sensitivity and literary skill he allows us to claim our own fears and unlived life forces, helping us to confront our uncertainties about death, and to accept them without flinching.

The Book of Disquiet

'To understand I had to destroy myself. To understand is to forget about loving' (Pessoa 2006b, section 48). This quotation appears in what is perhaps Pessoa's greatest sustained individual work, *The Book of Disquiet,* penned by Bernardo Soares. Soares is the heteronym that was most like Pessoa himself. He was a quiet clerk in Lisbon, an accountant working in an office. This is a world that Pessoa knew quite well due to his long career as a correspondence translator.

The Book, as it is also known, was first published 47 years after Pessoa's death. Now published in 37 languages, *The Book* is a bestseller, especially in German, with 16 editions. The *Book of Disquiet* is a haunting mosaic of dreams, psychological reflections and autobiographical vignettes. Listed as one of the top 100 books of all time, Pessoa's *Book of Disquiet* was discovered in the trunk in his apartment after his death.

In a period of over two decades, Pessoa recorded his reveries and impressions. It is an exploration of paradox, an expression of his astute and penetrating melancholy.

> In its essence all life is monotonous. Happiness therefore depends on a reasonably thorough adaptation to life's monotony. By making ourselves monotonous, we make ourselves the same as life. We thus live to the full. And living to the full is to be happy.
>
> I always acted on the inside . . . I was never able to touch life . . . I enjoyed strolling alone through green parks and down wide corridors . . . In the broad and dusky corridor at the back of the palace, I often strolled with my fiancée . . . though I never had a real fiancée . . . I never knew how to love . . . I only knew how to dream of loving . . . If I liked to wear ladies' rings on my fingers, it's because I

> sometimes supposed that my hands belonged to a princess and that I, at least in the movements of my hands, was the woman I loved . . . It isn't me who's telling you this . . . Who's speaking is what's left of me.
>
> (Pessoa 2006b, section 342)

> I turned myself into a fiction of myself to such a degree that any natural feeling I have, of course, from the moment it's born, becomes a feeling of the imagination – the memory in dreams, the dream of forgetting about the dream, knowing myself by not reflecting on myself.
>
> I stripped off my own being to such an extent that existing means dressing up. Only when I'm disguised am I truly myself. And around me all unknown sunsets as they die, make golden the landscapes I shall never see.
>
> (Pessoa 1998b, p. 55)

Disquiet and longing for our changing world

So how does this shy, introverted man become one of Portugal's greatest artists? How does he become a rock star of the soul in the world-at-large? I would suggest it is because humanity desperately longs for what Pessoa gives voice to; it longs to feel what we have largely rejected in the pursuit of what we think is perfect happiness and worldly success. We long to feel the disquiet and despair that we lock away in our closet of skeletons; we long for the release of our tightly withheld lament. And, I would suggest, humanity longs to understand the deeper meaning of longing, which mystical traditions recognize as the homesickness of the soul yearning for its true Home.

The Sufi mystics understood this longing as the core of the spiritual quest (and mystic Islam would not be foreign to the Portuguese psyche, with the Moors having ruled in the Iberian Peninsula from approximately AD 700 to AD 1200).

Llewellyn Vaughan-Lee, Sufi mystic and lineage successor in the Naqshbandiyya-Mujaddidiyya Sufi Order, writes:

> Longing is the central core of every mystical path, as the anonymous author of the fourteenth-century mystical classic, The Cloud of Unknowing, simply states: 'Your whole life must be one of longing.' Yet our present Western society is so divorced from this mystical thread that underlies every spiritual path that we have no context within which to appreciate the nature of the heart's desire for Truth. There are many people who feel the unhappiness of a homesick soul and yet do not know its cause. They do not realize the wonder of their pain, that it is their heart's longing that will take them Home.
>
> (Vaughan-Lee Summer 1999)

Longing and lament, disquiet and despair are largely marginalized in the greater collective and often seen as pathological in the more extroverted, success-driven world. A place and time to lament what has been lost, space to experience our longing for that which is beyond temporal fulfillment, finds little place or recognition. Pessoa's quest compels us to ask what we can redeem in psychic wholeness by making a place for these abandoned soul forces.

Pessoa did not turn away from his sense of desolation. Paradoxically, fragilely, even at great cost to his own physical being, he discovered and recreated himself within it. Perhaps it is this fragile, yet fierce and fearless search that the Portuguese, and in fact the world at large, have understood as greatness.

Pessoa was talented, yes, but his genius goes beyond literary talent. In his experience of marginalization, he created a meaningful center, no matter its vulnerability. Through his writing he created a center for himself, for himself and for others who feel a sense of longing and disquiet that can never be fully eased. Pessoa's life was in constant tension with no apparent resolution. He was often tormented. But that he searched and endured and wrote as he did was itself the resolution.

'Everything I wanted in life, I abandoned for the sake of the search' (Pessoa 2006b, section 342). Pessoa's life-long search for meaning, stemming from a continual sense of disquiet and despair, from an ever-present experience of longing and lament, gives us a template from which to better understand the redemptive nature of disquiet and longing for our changing world.

We cannot give in to despair, yet we cannot move forward without acknowledging it. To continuously re-create our world, to survive, we must learn how to live within the tensions of paradox: peace is the partner of disquiet; to learn about wholeness, we must invite that for which we long; without time for lament, our happiness becomes frenetic, empty.

In Pessoa's writing, we find clues to holding the tension of opposing energies and to finding meaning in the haunting sense of meaninglessness that can spur the disconsolate soul forward into the search, toward the journey Home.

Pessoa also writes from a sense of hopelessness that is just as paradoxical as the sense of despair and longing that he communicates:

> In those slow empty hours there arises from my soul to my mind a sadness that encompasses my entire being, the bitterness of all being . . . which is not within my power to change . . . The peace of anguish is in my heart, and my serenity is made of resignation.
>
> (Pessoa 1998b, p. 45)

Although Pessoa did not live in the same time historically as Tibetan Buddhist nun and teacher, Pema Chödron, they would have no doubt understood each other. To understand the sense of hopelessness and uncertainty from a spiritual perspective, Chödron offers her teachings. She says, 'If we're willing to give up hope that insecurity and pain can be exterminated, then we can have the courage to relax with the groundlessness of our situation' (Chödron 1997, p. 38). She continues further by explaining

> that turning our mind toward spiritual teachings does not bring security or confirmation of hope. It does not bring any ground to stand on. In fact, when one's mind turns toward spiritual teachings, one begins to fearlessly acknowledge impermanence and we begin to get the knack of hopelessness.
>
> (ibid.)

We begin to acknowledge that we cannot hide from a life that includes chaos, death and uncertainty. While Chodrön is not suggesting that life is hopeless, she does offer that if we do not include chaos, death and impermanence in our lives we will be denying the intrinsic nature of life itself.

Chödron continues:

> In the process of discovering bodhichitta [an awakened heart], the journey goes down, not up. It's as if the mountain pointed toward the center of the earth instead of reaching into the sky. Instead of transcending the suffering of all creatures, we move toward the turbulence and doubt. We jump into it. We slide into it. We tiptoe into it. We move toward it however we can. We explore the reality and unpredictability of insecurity and pain, and we try not to push it away. If it takes years, if it takes lifetimes, we let it be as it is . . . Right down there in the thick of things, we discover the love that will not die.
>
> (Chödron 1997, p. 39)

This was also Pessoa's search and struggle, to understand this perspective in his own way in his own time and in his own system of belief, and in particular through his explorations in the *Book of Disquiet*. He may not have experienced these paradoxical truths as fully integrated into his personal life – he most likely would not have chosen to go down this path of engaging the darker areas of longing and despair of his own accord, but it is apparently certain that Pessoa's *daimon* had set sights on the exploration of this shadowy territory. Thus, with the trembling of hopelessness coupled with a persistent lack of fear, Pessoa ventured into the uncertainty of these unknown forces as a navigator of the depths, showing the way for those willing to follow.

In addition to his ventures in the *Book of Disquiet*, Pessoa's search continues in the only book he published in Portuguese, *Mensagem,* or *Message.*

Pessoa's *Message* and the Age of the Holy Spirit

Message

It is not only the redemptive powers of disquiet, longing and uncertainty that Pessoa called forth within the hearts of others. He also sent us a message of another kind. Published just one year before his death, *Mensagem*, or *Message*, was the only book Pessoa published in Portuguese. *Message* is a three-part, multi-layered complexity of forty-four short poems, a symbolist epic interconnecting nation with the individual self, calling the reader forward to a spiritual quest.

The first section of *Mensagem,* entitled *Brasão*, or *Coat-of-Arms*, speaks of both the material and spiritual dimensions of Portugal, all leading to the Golden Age of Discovery that started in the early 15th century and continued up to the 17th century.

The second section of the epic is entitled *Mar Português*, or *Portuguese Sea.* It starts with the time of the Discoveries and the empire that was built through Portuguese oceanic exploration, and ends with the demise of Portugal's young king, Sebastian (January 20, 1554–August 4, 1578). One of the most famous of Pessoa's poems is in this second section and has the same name, *Mar Português.* It describes the perils of these oceanic adventures into the unknown as well as the costs for global expansion. As such, one may understand that Pessoa was speaking not only of the outer journey but also, symbolically, of the inward voyage one must undertake for an expanded experience of consciousness.

> Portuguese Sea
> Salt-filled sea, how much of your salt
> Is tears of Portugal!
> For us to cross you, how many mothers wept
> How many sons kept Vigil in vain!
> Lived as old maids how many brides-to-be
> Till death, so that you might be ours, sea!
> Was it all worth while? It is worth while, all,
> If the soul is not small.
> Whoever intends to sail beyond the Cape
> Must double sorrow – no escape.
> God to the sea has given peril and abyss
> But has yet made it the mirror of heaven.
>
> (Pessoa 2007, p. 73)

Finally, part three of *Mensagem*, *O Encoberto*, or *The Hidden One*, refers to the return of the lost king (in this case, King Sebastian). *The Hidden One* speaks of the fulfillment of humanity's destiny, which is predestined or designed by God, and of Portugal's implied role in this destiny. The return of the lost king, Sebastian, follows the archetypal 'return of the king' (such as found in the legend of King Arthur) whereupon the king returns in the darkest hour to help his people. For the Portuguese, *The Hidden One* would return on a foggy morning to save Portugal.

In *Message*, the historical human figures from Portugal's past are symbols for the spiritual quest, and the ordeals of the ocean mariners describe the need for individual resolve and perseverance. The quest is to reconnect not only the individual but also Portugal back to historical, mystical roots. As such, Pessoa interjects an underlying current in the poem that refers to the prophetic tradition of the Age of the Holy Spirit, wherein a new epoch of peace and concord begins. This era would coincide with the return of the lost king.

The Age of the Holy Spirit

Portugal's history is particularly connected to the Age of the Holy Spirit. Before describing that history and its deeper meaning, however, a brief explanation of the Holy Spirit and the Age of the Holy Spirit will serve as an introduction.

Theologically, the Holy Spirit, often represented as a white dove, is the third person of the Christian Trinity with God the Father and God the Son. This third is known equally as the Holy Spirit, the Holy Ghost, or the Paraclete (meaning 'comforter' in Greek). In the Old Testament, the Holy Spirit is shown as the life-giving breath of God. In the New Testament, Christians believe that the Holy Spirit is God working in the world, the *activity* of God on earth. Contemporary theologians, Shults and Hollingsworth, describe the Holy Spirit 'as both the divine ground of all life . . ., as well as the presence that engenders experiences of transformed life,' for example, healing and prophetic insight (Shults and Hollingsworth 2008, pp. 2, 3).

Historically, the medieval theologian Joachim de Fiore (*c.*1135 to March 30, 1202), wrote about The Age of the Holy Spirit as an age in which the necessity for texts, church structures and organizations would be overcome and be drawn into the living spirit, living not by texts or hierarchical authorities. Organizations would be left behind and people would be able to tune into spiritual life on their own. Joachim de Fiore was the founder of the monastic order of San Giovanni in Fiore (in Italy). He was a mystic and a theologian, born in a small village in Calabria, at that time part of the Kingdom of Sicily.

> He theorized the dawn of a new age in which the hierarchy of the church would be unnecessary. Members of the *spiritual* wing of the *Franciscan* order acclaimed him as a prophet. Though theoretically controversial according to some, the holiness of his life was widely known: *Dante* affirmed that miracles were said to have taken place at his tomb, and, though never officially beatified, he is still venerated on May 29.
>
> (Wikipedia)

The mystical basis of Fiore's Theory of the Three Ages is founded on his interpretation of the biblical text, The Book of Revelation. He believed that history, by analogy with the Trinity, was divided into three fundamental epochs: The Age of the Father, corresponding to the Old Testament and the obedience of humanity to the letter of the law; The Age of the Son, when Man becomes the son of God; and the Age of the Holy Spirit wherein humanity has a direct relationship with God and has the full understanding and experience of universal love. Fiore believed that only in the Age of the Holy Spirit would it be possible to understand the writings of God in their deepest meaning, not just in the literal sense. And, rather than the Second Coming of Christ, an era of peace and harmony would reign, making the hierarchy of the Church unnecessary.

Unfortunately, it would seem, Fiore was a man far ahead of his time. He saw this all coming to pass in the 13th century. He concluded that this age would begin in 1260 based on The Book of Revelation, verses 11:3 and 12:6, which mention 'one thousand two hundred and sixty days' (Wikipedia: website).

Not incongruent with Fiore's theory, Jung saw the Age of the Holy Spirit as a time when the individual would live spiritual life independent of sacred texts or dogma. He saw it as a time when we would be able to experience the numinous in direct communion, not through the hierarchy of religious authority.

During a seminar with Murray Stein, Jungian analyst, Stein was asked what Jung meant when he said, 'Things will be resolved in the age of the Holy Spirit.' Stein's response (paraphrased) was that Jung understood that the psyche works through polarities that require us to hold tension or conflict, out of which comes the third, resolved thing. In the development of the doctrine of the Trinity, the third – the Holy Spirit – comes out of the two, the Father and the Son and the third unites the two. The development of the doctrine of the Trinity is this dialectic that leads to a third. The Age of the Holy Spirit is not a collapse of the difference between one polarity and the other, but the resolution of the polarities by holding them in a container that is big enough to lift both opposites into wholeness . . . this would be considered the Age of the Holy Spirit.

Stein also noted that the Age of the Holy Spirit is an age in which necessity for texts is overcome; people are drawn into life through the living spirit, not through Church authorities. Jung, Stein said, saw this as an essential need in the psyche, and that individuals are capable of accessing spiritual life on their own through dreams and active imagination – for example, independent of sacred texts.

Stein continues by saying that Jung encouraged the making of one's own sacred text out of personal material, not handed down by outer authority (*The Red Book* being the primary example of this). He saw the spiritual future as an age of the individual, of freedom, where the need for Church and doctrines would be left behind, tuning into a spiritual life where we are capable of experiencing the numinous individually, not through external authorities. Jung saw this as the future for religion on this planet, just as the medieval theologian Joachim de Fiore did centuries before (Asheville Jung Center: website).

As mentioned above, Portugal is especially attuned to the Age of the Holy Spirit as a result of its own mystical, historical roots. It is a subject too complex to fully cover within the limitations of this chapter, but a brief description will help reveal the depth of the *Message* that Pessoa leaves with us.

The members of the Knights Templar built many castles, churches and towns in Portugal. In 1307, King Philip IV of France, in debt with the Order, arrested and burned the Knights Templar at the stake. In 1312 Pope Clement V disbanded this powerful and rich order. After the extinction of the Order in 1312, King Dinis of Portugal (1261–1325) renamed the Portuguese branch, calling it the Order of Christ and left it to go about its business as usual. Prince Henry the Navigator (1394–1460), mastermind of the 16th-century discoveries, was himself a leader of this Order. The ships that sailed from Portugal carried the flag of the cross of the Order of Christ. These facts and developments are the foundation of a vast literature of mystic nationalism that speculates on the real aim of the Portuguese discoveries (Santos and Farias 2002).

In the early 1300s, during the same period that King Dinis created the Order of Christ, Joachim de Fiore's Theory of the Three Ages began to spread throughout Portugal. Cistercian and Franciscan monks were the first to take the theory seriously, but the royal family, King Dinis and his Queen, Isabel, were also moved. As we read above, Fiore's vision proclaimed the imminent rise of an Age of the Holy Spirit. In this new age, humanity would receive a gospel by direct dispensation from the Holy Spirit and the ideal of universal brotherhood would finally become a reality (Santos and Farias 2002).

The celebrations and festivities of the Holy Spirit, or the Holy Ghost, began during the reign of King Dinis and Queen Isabel (1270–1336) at about 1305. The widespread popular adherence that quickly followed spread the celebrations throughout the mainland and subsequently to the overseas possessions, constituting a phenomenon unparalleled in other Christian countries. The main features of these festivities were, and largely still are, the coronation of a child or man, usually of low social standing, symbolizing that the Empire of the Spirit belongs to the simple and innocent ones – those without cunning or guile or worldliness; a ritualized, collective banquet for hundreds of people in each village or locale, symbolizing generosity for the common good, supporting brotherhood and sisterhood among all people; and (then, but not now) the unchaining of certain (non-violent) prisoners, symbolizing the liberation of humankind.

Prohibitions by the Catholic Church contributed to the progressive deterioration of these festivities on the Portuguese mainland, but they are still very much alive in the Atlantic Azorean Archipelago, and in many Azorean emigrant communities in the USA and Canada.

The festival of the Holy Ghost is a unique Portuguese feast for those of Portuguese-speaking countries or communities to experience as a Pentecostal act. Although the festival takes place over many weeks, the main events take place on Pentecost Sunday, the day the Paraclete, the Holy Spirit, came down in flames over the heads of the apostles inspiring them to go out and bring the teachings and prophesies of God into the world.

The Age of the Holy Spirit would re-emerge as a concept throughout the history of Portuguese mystical thought (Santos and Farias 2002).

In their book *The Holy Spirit,* Shults and Hollingsworth give the following examples of what the Holy Spirit was and is considered to be in Christian theology. The italics are mine, calling the reader's attention to those ideas that relate directly to the Age of the Holy Spirit prophesied by Fiore, and which the Portuguese festivals are intended to commemorate. They also call attention to the archetypal elements included in the mystical, historical roots of Portugal, its culture and its people.

> Paul connects the experience of the Holy Spirit to the flourishing of the community in his letter to the Romans. God's love 'has been poured into our hearts through the Holy Spirit' (Prov 5:5). *The Spirit is the source of the community's love, freedom, and hope for renewal.*
>
> (Shults and Hollingsworth 2008, pp. 4, 5)

> One of Paul's central themes is the way in which the Holy Spirit creates, upholds, and enlivens the community of believers. *The 'gifts' of the Spirit, which are manifested through individual voices, are primarily intended for communal contexts and for the common good of everyone* (Cor 1:12).
>
> (ibid.)

> Those who are led by the Spirit are not subject to [the letter of the] law, but *Spirit-filled living results in loving, patient,* gentle *attitudes and actions toward others* (Gal 5:18–23).
>
> (ibid.)

> The Holy Spirit not only anoints bodies and enlivens voices, but also *calls them outward toward serving others, into the world to do the work of the divine kingdom of peace and justice.*
>
> (ibid.)

Returning now to Pessoa's poetic epic, *Message* is a call to the soul, the individual soul and the soul of a nation. It is a call to fulfill a certain destiny: the embodiment of a mystical consciousness that engenders profound experiences of transformed life in service to the common good, a consciousness that is embedded in the greater collective soul of a nation and of humanity as a whole. It is a call to enter into the essence of the Age of the Holy Spirit, the dimension of life that embodies the mystical nature of the psyche.

In the last poem of *Message*, Pessoa refers to Portugal as Portugal itself, and also, perhaps, as yet another heteronym, as another figure within him, and also, perhaps, within us:

Fog
Neither king nor law, neither peace nor war
Can define the outline and the truth
Of, look!, that radiant gleam of the earth
That's Portugal, breaking the heart –
A flaring without light or heat,
Like the core of an ethereal flame.

No one knows what she desires.
No one understands what soul is hers,
Not what is bad, nor what is good,
(What distant agony mourning near?)
All's uncertain and is at the end,
All is scattered, nothing entire.
O Portugal, fog you are . . . and yet

It is the Hour!

(Pessoa 2007, p. 107)

Epilogue

Comes the hour . . . from out of a foggy morning comes the 'lost king,' *The Hidden One*, a hidden consciousness now coming to light, returning to redeem what has been lost, what we have lost. To remind us that a new Empire of the Spirit, a Holy Spirit, is to be built from a consciousness that can embrace the complexity of paradoxical truths and lead us out of the polarization of fundamentalism and hatred. To remind us that a world can be built from a consciousness crafted for and in service to the common good, a consciousness that can hold the tensions of life's natural polarities and lift them into wholeness.

It is indeed the hour in our critically changing world not to marginalize the more difficult dimensions of a life fully lived. It is the hour to embrace both joy *and* despair, to accept both peace *and* disquiet, to rejoice *and* to openly lament. Most importantly, it is the hour to embrace our greater destiny, the mystical Oneness that forever holds and re-creates our scattered, uncertain and fragmented lives.

Fernando Pessoa, the one in whom *all the dreams of the world* exist, helps guide us to this embrace.

Note

1 Although the translations of Pessoa's poems are my own, for ease of reference for the reader, I cite the passages as they appear in the familiar translations by Richard Zenith, published by Grove (1998) and Penguin (2006), and by Jonathan Griffin, published by Shearsman.

References

Asheville Jung Center (website). 'The Age of the Holy Spirit: Transcending the polarities of God the Father and God the Son,' seminar. Online. Available: http://ashevillejungcenter.org/2010/06/age-of-holy-spirit-transcending-polarities-of-god-father-god-son/ (accessed 24 May 2011).

Casa Fernando Pessoa (website). Online. Available: http://casafernandopessoa.cm-lisboa.pt/index.php?id=2258&L=4 (accessed 22 September 2012).

Chödron, P. (1997) *When Things Fall Apart: Heart Advice for Difficult Times*, Boston, MA and London: Shamballa.

Jung, C.G. (1968) *Psychology and Alchemy. Volume 12. The Collected Works of C. G. Jung*, trans. R.F.C. Hull, Bollingen Series XX, Princeton, NJ: Princeton University Press.

Pessoa, F. (1998a) *Fernando Pessoa & Co. – Selected Poems*, trans. R. Zenith, New York: Grove Press. Online. Available: www.poetryinternationalweb.net/pi/site/poem/item/7084 (accessed 9 September 2012).

Pessoa, F. (1998b) *The Book of Disquiet*, composed by Bernardo Soares, Assistant Bookkeeper in the City of Lisbon, trans. Alfred Mac Adam, Boston, MA: Exact Change.

Pessoa, F. (2003) *Escritos Autobiográficos, Automáticos e de Reflexão Pessoal*, Assírio and Alvim, 'Chronology established by R. Zenith and corrected by him for inclusion on our site. Sources for the information can be found in the cited edition.' Online. Available: http://casafernandopessoa.cm-lisboa.pt/index.php?id=4285&L=4 (accessed 15 September 2012).

Pessoa, F. (2006a) *A Little Larger than the Entire Universe: Selected Poems,* trans. R. Zenith, New York and London: Penguin.

Pessoa, F. (2006b) *The Book of Disquiet*, 'A Factless Autobiography,' Richard Zenith Edition, Lisbon.

Pessoa, F. (2007) *Message/Mensagem*, trans. Jonathan Griffin, Exeter and London: Shearsman Books and The Menard Press.

Santos, T. and Farias, M (2002) 'Religion in Portugal,' in Dr. J. Gorden Melton (ed.) *The 21st Century Encyclopedia of World Religion,* Santa Barbara, USA: 2002. Online. Available: www.prolades.com/cra/regions/ibero/port-eng/Portugal,%20Religion%20in.htm (accessed 5 September 2012).

Shults, F. and Hollingsworth, A. (2008) *The Holy Spirit,* Grand Rapids, MI/Cambridge, UK: William B. Eerdmans Publishing Company.

Vaughan-Lee, L. (Summer 1999) 'Love and Longing: The Feminine Mysteries of Love.' *Personal Transformation*. Online. Available: http://goldensufi.org/a_love_and_longing.html (accessed 15 September 2012).

Wikipedia (website). Online. Available: http://en.wikipedia.org/wiki/Joachim_of_Fiore (accessed 14 September 2012).

Zenith, R. (2006) *The 'Real' Fernando Pessoa: a biographical sketch.* Online. Available: www.poetryinternationalweb.net/pi/site/cou_article/item/7098/The-Real-Fernando-Pessoa-a-biographical-sketch (accessed 22 June 2012).

Zenith, R. (2008) *Fernando Pessoa (Fotobiografias Século XX),* Lisboa: Círculo de Leitores. Online. Available: http://en.wikipedia.org/wiki/Fernando_Pessoa (accessed 20 September 2012).

14

FERNANDO PESSOA AND ALBERTO CAEIRO'S 'LESSONS IN UNLEARNING'

Living in a changing world

Terence Dawson

Although C. G. Jung (1875–1961) considered individuation to be the crucial concern of analytical psychology, he was often embarrassed as to how to define exactly what he meant by it. His younger contemporary, the Portuguese poet Fernando Pessoa (1888–1935), lived an unassuming, introverted life, almost entirely devoted to analysing his various inner experiences. His sustained exploration of his inner journey might be described as a process of individuation. Jung and Pessoa had much in common. They both sought to understand the apparently irrational nature of inner experiences, including the nature and function of dreams and the implications of astrology, alchemy, and mysticism. They belonged, however, to different psychological types, which meant that they experienced and responded to their inner worlds in remarkably different ways. And yet, in spite of these differences, they agreed on one of the major objectives of individuation.

In this chapter, I shall be looking at a number of poems that Pessoa attributed to Alberto Caeiro, one of his heteronyms (i.e. the alter-ego or persona-like figures to which he ascribed much of his work). Pessoa first experienced Caeiro in 1914, an event that triggered his artistic maturity. For this reason, both Caeiro and Pessoa's two other major heteronyms, Ricardo Reis and Álvaro de Campos, referred to him as their 'Master'. My purpose is to explore the significance of the views given expression in Caeiro's poems both in their own right *and* as they relate to Pessoa. It is to show how the poems attributed to Alberto Caeiro help us to understand Jung's concept of individuation. In the course of addressing this issue, I shall also be exploring the tension that exists between being a Jungian and being an individual, and reflecting on how one can best live in a world characterised and governed by increasingly hectic change.

Taking the dream for what it is

Following his break with Freud, instead of seeing the dream as a disguise, Jung argued that it represents the best possible representation of an issue pertinent to the subject at the time of its experience: 'I take the dream for what it is. [. . .] The dream is a natural occurrence, and there is no earthly reason why we should assume that it is a crafty device to lead us astray' (1937, par. 41).

Instead of assuming, as Freud did, that he knew the meaning not only of an image but also of its associations, he asked the patient to provide his or her associations for each and every element in the dream—and he used these associations as the basis for his interpretation. In other words, he sought an explanation for the images actually experienced by the dreamer. He argued that the amplification of a subject's *associations* could reveal the nature of an impasse or disturbance and thus suggest how it might be resolved. His position lies open to the charge that our associations might not always be as 'authentic' as Jung assumed them to be.

From 1912, Jung spent several years trying to better understand his inner processes, an experience often referred to as his 'confrontation with the unconscious'. It is still insufficiently realised that it brought about a significant change in his psychological type. As a child he was often solitary, but this changed when he went to study medicine in the medical school of the University of Zurich. As a student, he does not appear to have been unusually introverted. While at the Burghölzli, his publications might suggest that he was predominantly a thinking type. His extended experiments with active imagination appear to have changed this: his introversion became more marked, and he became primarily an intuition type, with thinking as an auxiliary function.[1]

According to Jung, introverted intuition is characterised by a tendency to focus not on an inner experience per se (for example, a sensation or feeling), but on the image that *causes* the experience. He takes psychogenic vertigo as his example. An introverted *intuition* type will perceive instinctively 'the inner image that gave rise to [it]'—that is, its 'cause'. The example he gives is 'the image of a tottering man pierced through the heart by an arrow' (1921, par. 656). This is both psychological and medical nonsense. There are a great many possible 'causes' of psychogenic vertigo: they include sudden change of position, fluid fluctuations in the inner ear, anxiety, depression, injury, shock, vomiting, dehydration, and too much alcohol. An image of a tottering man is *not* a possible cause of vertigo, psychogenic or otherwise. An introverted intuition type might experience such an image either simultaneously with or even *slightly before* the attack of vertigo, but in neither case can it be described as a 'cause'. Such an image would be better described as an autonomous *association*.

Jung was an experienced psychiatrist. If he made such a mistake, there must be a reason and the most likely reason is that introverted intuition just happened to be his own type. He could be objective about other types, but not his own. He continues: 'introverted intuition perceives all the background processes of consciousness with almost the same distinctness as extraverted sensation registers external objects' (1921, par. 657). He concedes that such a type 'makes himself and his life symbolic—adapted, it is true, to the inner and eternal meaning of events, but unadapted to present-day reality' (1921, par. 662).

Even while experimenting with active imagination, Jung never entirely lost his footing in everyday reality, but as the introductions to *Symbols of Transformation* and *Memories, Dreams, Reflections* both illustrate, from this time forward he consciously made his life symbolic. He wanted to believe that the introverted intuition type is a seer—i.e. that he had an intuitive knowledge of the effective cause not only of *physical conditions*, but also of *future events*. One is reminded of *Animal Farm*: Jung considered all psychological types to be equal, but when it came to his own type, he seemed to believe that introverted intuition is a little more equal than others. Introverted intuition types may experience images that *seem* to anticipate physical events. It is far more probable that the 'background processes of consciousness' that they experience are more directly related to their own myth (i.e. their image of themselves) than to 'the inner and eternal meaning of [outer] events'.

In his writing, there are at least two Jungs. One is cautious, level-headed, and professional. For example, 'The psychologist should constantly bear in mind that his hypothesis is no more at first than the expression of his own subjective premise and can therefore never lay immediate claim to general validity' (1930, p. 85). And again: 'I cannot let myself presuppose that my peculiar temperament, my own attitude to intellectual problems, is universally valid' (1938, par. 149; cf. 1935, par. 275). His prolonged reflections on psychological typology taught him that his 'subjective premises' determined not only his interests, but also his way of understanding these interests. One of his greatest contributions to psychoanalysis is his readiness not only to concede, but to *insist* that psychology is an inherently plural discipline (see Shamdasani 2003, p. 77).

There is, however, another Jung, and this second Jung very often forgets that his views are an expression of his own psychological type. And when he forgets this, he begins to make dogmatic, reductive, and sweeping statements—faults interestingly close to those for which he criticised Freud (e.g. 1965, p. 150). For example, when he wishes that others would learn how to *see* correctly, he means that he wishes they would 'see' in the same way as he does—that is, he wishes they shared his dominant typological tendencies. In 'Introduction to the Religious and Psychological Problems of Alchemy' he writes:

> *I* did not attribute a religious function to the soul, I merely produced the facts which prove that the soul is *naturaliter religiosa*, i.e. possesses a religious function. [. . .] With a truly tragic delusion these theologians fail to see that it is not a matter of proving the existence of the light, but of blind people who do not know that their eyes could see. It is high time we realized that it is pointless to praise the light and preach it if nobody can see it. It is much more needful to teach people the art of seeing.
>
> (1944, par. 14)

Many Jungians might consider this view a core issue in Jung's thinking; it is, however, a claim *most likely* to have been made by an introverted intuition type. There are many people who would find it impossible to accept, not because they are 'blind', but because their own psychological type would make it difficult for them to understand its premise. Not all Jung's claims are quite as generally valid as he sometimes liked to think they were (see Shamdasani 2003, pp. 83–84). He often forgets his own insistence that the way he 'sees' is an expression of his 'subjective premise'—that is, his psychological type.

As we shall see, the poems attributed to Alberto Caeiro suggest that there might be a far greater gap between making one's life symbolic and assuming full responsibility for one's individual personality than Jung realised.

Alberto Caeiro

The defining characteristic of the poems of Alberto Caeiro is his certainty that he too knows how to see. In '*A espantosa realidade das coisas*' (7–11–15; 1969, pp. 234–235), he declares: 'I'm not even a poet: I see' (2006, pp. 58–59).[2] In a related poem, he writes much the same: 'Our only wealth is seeing' (2006, p. 16; 1969, p. 208). Caeiro wants us to forget how we habitually interpret the world through our associations so as to learn how to see what we are looking at *as it really is*—and *only* as it is.

In '*O meu olhar é nítido como um girassol*' (8–3–14; 1969, pp. 204–205), he presents himself as someone unusually observant:

> My gaze is as attentive as a sunflower.
> I am in the habit of walking along roads
> Looking to my right and to my left,
> And sometimes looking behind me . . .
> And what I see at every moment
> Is something I have never seen before,
> And I am very good at looking at things . . .
> I know how to have the inner wonder
> That a newly born infant has so as
> To confirm that it really has been born . . .

I feel at every moment that I am being born
Into the eternal novelty of the World . . .
I believe in the World as I do in a marigold:
Because I see it.

(1998, p. 48; 2006, p. 11)[3]

Caeiro assures us that he is 'very good at looking at things', and yet, as this poem illustrates, he sees *little or nothing* of the outer world. Because of the simile in the first line, we assume he is walking in the countryside, but as we do not know what lies either to right or to left of him, he might just as well be in the streets of Lisbon. He does not 'see' the objective properties of what he is looking at; he only reflects on the sensations they arouse in him. Everything he refers to in his poems belongs to the outer world, and yet what he sees in the outer world is merely a trigger for his *reflection* about the nature and implications of his various sensations—that is, Caeiro's concern is not with the object itself, but with registering the nature of the way he 'feels' whenever he becomes aware of a new 'sensation', and this always makes him feel as if he is in the process of 'being born /Into the eternal novelty of the World'.

This insight is developed in '*A espantosa realidade das coisas*' (7–11–15; 1969, pp. 234–235):

The astonishing reality of things
Is my constant discovery.
Everything is what it is,
And it is hard to explain to another how happy this makes me,
And how much it suffices me. [. . .]
Sometimes I begin to look at a stone.
I don't begin by thinking about whether it has feelings.
I don't effuse by calling it my sister.
Rather, I like it because it is a stone,
I like it because it feels nothing,
I like it because it has no relation to me whatsoever.

(2006, pp. 58–59)

Jungian theory helps us to specify what is at issue here. An *extraverted* sensation type would have noted and commented on the stone's shape, its density, its texture, its colour, the precise nature and quality of its grain or some other *physical* property of the specific stone at which he was looking. But even when he is looking at something specific, Caeiro never sees *any* of its unique qualities. He has no patience with the fancifulness of St Francis: he feels no relation, of *any* kind, to a stone. Indeed, in spite of his claim, his poems are not really about 'seeing'—at least, *not* in the usual sense of seeing something in the outer world. Caeiro is so captivated by the 'astonishing reality' of his *inner* sensations that he never really sees the 'reality of *things*'. His poems may appear to be extraverted; closer consideration suggests they are introverted. And what they insist on is that we *see* each object as it is, without embellishing it in any way, and that we reflect only on the vivid impression that it makes on us.

For Caeiro, to know something is to enjoy the quality of the sensory impression that it makes. He wants to replace 'thinking' with *immediate sensory experience*. 'To think a flower is to see and smell it,/And to eat a fruit is to know its meaning' (2006, p. 23)—that is, to think about the beauty of a rose or the taste of a peach is to lose one's grip on the immediacy of the sensory experience each presents. And yet, although he recognises that one cannot represent immediate experience in words, this is precisely what Pessoa is doing. Caeiro's poems seek to explore a kind of experience that lies outside the domain of language. As he asserts in '*Leram-me hoje S. Francisco de Assis*' (21–5–17; 1994, p. 133):

> Water is water and this is why it is beautiful. [. . .]
> And since it is water, it is best to call it water,
> Or, better still, not to call it anything,
> But to drink it, to feel it on one's wrists, to look at it,
> And to do this without calling it anything.
>
> (2006, p. 64)

He writes both in order to articulate his sensory responses with visceral immediacy and to 'help mistaken men to feel /The truly real existence of flowers and of rivers' (2006, p. 34), i.e. to share his learning process with others. And what holds for objects that occupy space also holds for time.

In *Primeiro prenúncio de trovoada de depois de amanhã* (10–7–30; 1969, p. 245), Caeiro reflects on the sight of dark steely clouds lowering threateningly. Whenever we see such clouds, we instinctively associate them with coming rain. Caeiro is asking us not to make any such association, nor to admire them for their beauty. To do either is to distract one from the specific sensory experience. One is reminded of Jung's insistence on keeping separate the domains of the aesthetic and the psychological (1922, par. 97ff.). Caeiro, like Jung, wants us to reflect on the immediate impression aroused by an image and to learn how these relate to our own personality:

> The first white clouds hanging low in the dull sky . . .
> The first indication of the day after tomorrow's thunderstorm.
> The day after tomorrow's thunderstorm?
> I am certain of it, but the certainty is a lie.
> To be certain is not to be seeing.
> The day after tomorrow doesn't exist.
>
> (2006, p. 80)

Caeiro believes that we must take every experience as it is, but he is more consistent than Jung. He suggests that as soon as we begin to consciously reflect on a future possibility, we begin to introduce associations that radically distort the experience in question. The same holds for reflections on time past: 'To remember is not to see' (2006, p. 40). As he writes in '*Vive, dizes, no presente*' (19–7–20; 1969, pp. 244–245):

> I want things that exist, not the time that measures them . . .
> I don't want to include time in my way of being.
>
> (2006, p. 77)

Caeiro seeks the elimination of *all* temporal considerations so as to reflect on the *reality* only of the present moment. This is less easy than one might imagine it to be. All we know of the world comes from what we perceive of it, and everything that we see and think about is deeply coloured by our instinctive associations and projected notions. Whatever we consider, whatever we look at, we immediately associate it with ideas and/or images that stem from our cultural tradition, our education, our reading, perhaps most of all, our convictions. Our thoughts and views are almost entirely conditioned by the views of the various groups to which we belong. At every stage of our personal development, we demonstrate a surprising willingness to merely copy and imitate. Significant changes come much more slowly than we like to think. It is human nature, moreover, to harness our perceptions-cum-associations to a purpose. We read the world for information that will help us toward an objective. This was true of hunter gatherers; it remains true of everyone today, whatever their occupation. A Jungian thirst for meaning is only one variant of this. Caeiro wants us to recover a sense of perception *without* such a purpose, without any such thirst. He seeks to understand the nature of his sensations as they present themselves to him—that is, before being coloured by any association or thought.

The poem that best illustrates the difficulty of achieving the focus that Caeiro desires is the paradoxical '*O Tejo é mais belo que o rio que corre pela minha aldeia*' (7–3–14; 1969, pp. 215–216):

> The Tagus is more beautiful than the river that flows through my
>   village,
> But the Tagus is not more beautiful than the river that flows
>   through my village
> Because the Tagus is not the river that flows through my village.
> [. . .]
> The river of my village doesn't make one think of anything.
> Whoever stands on its bank is only standing on its bank.
>
> (1998, p. 55)

When Pessoa-Caeiro looks at the Tagus, he is inevitably reminded of the river's historical associations. He recalls the great age of Portuguese maritime exploration, trade, and colonisation, of Vasco de Gama, Magellan, and Camões. As also suggested by *Message* (1934), the only collection of poems he published in his lifetime, Pessoa is deeply moved by such associations. But Caeiro is *not* Pessoa. When *he* looks at a river, he wants to see just the river. Hence his preference for the river of his village; and he is, of course, careful not to tell us which village. When he looks at the river that flows through his village, he sees it as it is. As he writes in '*Só a Natureza é divina, e ela não é divina*' (1969, pp. 218–219): 'things have neither name nor personality: / They just are' (1998, p. 30). And everything else, he suggests, is association and projection.

Our associations are mostly instinctual: as such, they stem from the unconscious. So, too, do *all* our projections, which are often coloured by our cultural, social, religious and personal convictions as processed by our psychological type. We tend to assume that experience is neutral, and that it becomes significant only if it conjures associations for us. If a devout Christian and a devout Hindu visit a church and a temple together, the cross on the altar will carry more resonance for the Christian, the statue of Shiva will harbour more resonance for the Hindu. There is good reason to assume that our deepest associations *add* value to an experience. Jung accepted this assumption.

Caeiro, however, questions it:

> The only mystery of the Universe is what we add to it, not what
> it lacks.
> We read too much into things—and this leads to error and doubt.
> (1998, p. 80; 1969, p. 238)

His poems suggest that in order to see and understand something as it is, we must stop ourselves from projecting extraneous ideas into it. We must learn to see without allowing even our most instinctive associations to colour our perception. Caeiro wants us to recover, by means of thought, a world that exists *prior* to thought.

A lesson in unlearning

Caeiro and Jung see the world differently because they belong to different psychological types. '*O que nós vemos das cousas são as cousas*' (13–3–14; 1969, pp. 217–218) illustrates Caeiro's way of seeing. This is how he describes what he considers to be the correct way of seeing:

> The important thing is to know how to see,
> To know how to see without recourse to thinking,
> To know how to see when seeing

And how not to think when seeing
Nor to see when thinking.
But this (alas, even our souls are clothed!),
This calls for deep study,
A lesson in unlearning . . .

(1998, p. 57)

For Caeiro, one must learn to see with the concentration expected of a Zen Buddhist. One must prevent one's mind from being distracted by any association. No thought must intrude into the experience. As Descartes discovered when he set out on a comparable objective in the mid-seventeenth century, this is easier said than done. Caeiro realises that he will have to engage in 'deep study'—take an extensive 'lesson in unlearning'—in order to see as he wishes to see.

Caeiro is especially suspicious of those who couch their experiences in poetical or mystical metaphors. '*Tu, místico, vês uma significação em todas as cousas*' (12–4–19; 1969, p. 233) might have been written to challenge the claims of an introverted intuition type such as Jung:

You who are a mystic see a meaning in everything.
For you everything has a veiled significance.
There is something hidden in everything you see.
What you see, you always see in order to see something else. [. . .]
Whereas I, because I have eyes only for seeing,
See an absence of meaning in everything.
This is why I love myself, because to be a thing is not to mean
anything.
To be a thing is not to be open to interpretation.

(1998, p. 88)

He is suspicious of the mystic because the mystic assumes that his way of seeing reflects a universal truth. He wants us to 'learn' to be less eager to find significance, for all claims about significance stem from subjective tendencies related not only to one's culture, but also to one's psychological type. He is not claiming that either life or the world is meaningless; he is merely insisting that the meaning we give to our experience is our own construct.

Pessoa, like Jung, was fascinated by all forms of mystical experience. Alberto Caeiro, his heteronym, has no patience with Pessoa's interest in things spiritual and mystical. In '*Há metafísica bastante em não pensar em nada*', he asks scornfully:

The mystery of things? As if I know what constitutes a mystery!
The only mystery is that some people think about mystery. [. . .]

> The only inner meaning of things
> Is that they have no inner meaning of any kind.
>
> (1998, pp. 49, 50)

Jung's theory that the unconscious compensates consciousness helps to explain how the poet (Pessoa) and his poetic persona (Caeiro) can hold such radically different views. A personification of an aspect of his unconscious insists on a view diametrically opposed to the conscious viewpoint. In Jungian terms, the heteronym is urging Pessoa to abandon his quest to discover the mystery of things and to see the world as it is; to become better rooted in it, to connect with it.

The irony, of course, is that Caeiro's insistence is in itself very close to a form of mysticism, almost all forms of which value unmediated experience. The difference is that the mystic assumes there is a 'truth' at the end of his sustained attention. He has a system to arrive at such a truth. In contrast, Caeiro wants no meaning of any kind to be attached to his perceptions. He regards mystic poets as 'sick philosophers' (2006, p. 31). He wants to experience each thing as it is, without any sense of its relation to anything else, for as soon as we begin to make connections between two different things, we begin to generalise. And all such generalisations are 'a disease of our own ideas' (1998, p. 65).

Whereas Jung would have tried to understand the significance of the projection for the individual, Pessoa wishes to stop himself from making any projections. He wants to understand the significance of his experience *before* he unintentionally colours it with his instinctive associations. This is how Caeiro expresses this sentiment in '*Nao basta abrir a janela*' (4–23; 1969, p. 231):

> It isn't enough just to open the window
> To see the fields and the river. [. . .]
> It is also necessary not to hold any kind of philosophy.
> With philosophy there are no trees, there are only ideas.
> There is only each one of us, like a cave.
>
> (1998, p. 75)

We think that by opening a window we see the tree, or field, or river as each of these really is, but in Caeiro's poem, the window frame is a metaphor for all our deeply ingrained perceptual tendencies. Opening the window is not enough; our projections and associations still constitute a 'frame' for everything that we perceive. In order to 'see' as Caeiro would like us to see, we would have to block all these tendencies, prevent them from directing our thoughts, so as to have a direct, unmediated relation to what we are looking at. Autonomous and habitual associations imprison us. Unless we free ourselves from them, all that we see can be likened to the shadows that Plato's prisoners see on the walls of the cave and mistake for reality.

Our projections and associations determine our way of seeing: they define us. In Caeiro's view, they imprison us. For all our projections and associations harbour a way of seeing, an ideology, a theoretical system—including those that stem from a study of Jungian psychology. This is why we must undergo a 'lesson in unlearning'.

In modest harmony with nature

In 1977, James Yandell gave a talk on 'The Imitation of Jung: An Exploration of the Meaning of 'Jungian'. His subject was the tension between 'being 'Jungian' and being 'oneself'. If one models one's professional practices and one's process of individuation on Jung's writings, in what sense, he asks, can one claim to be oneself? Correspondingly, if individuation means becoming oneself, in what sense might one also be described as a Jungian?

Yandell concluded his classic talk with a quotation from Basho: 'I do not seek to follow in the footsteps of the men of old; I seek the things they sought.' We might all be on the same quest, but each of us must pursue it 'out of his own need and in his own way' (Yandell, p. 37). This might seem as level-headed as one could wish. It is, I believe, more problematic than Yandell intended. In the first place, if one seeks the 'things' that Jung sought, there is a very strong chance that one will pursue these things in a similar way to him. For all his brilliance, Hillman never quite managed to sidestep this difficulty. If one's automatic tendency is to associate everything one experiences with analogous patterns from religion, ritual, mythology, or folklore, and one then invests these associations with an essentially 'Jungian' interpretation, how can one be sure one is discovering one's own truth? In other words, is it not a little worrying that, in spite of Jung having identified so many very different and yet equally valid psychological types, his ideas suggest only one kind of individuation? Is it not more likely that each different type will need not only a different path, but a different goal?

Jungian literature tends to situate experience in relation to that of Jung. It is insufficiently realised that the classic image of individuation outlined in introductions to Jung's ideas is largely based on the way that an introverted intuition type experiences the unconscious. On his good days, Jung recognises this: he did all he could to prevent his admirers from responding to his ideas as if they were a model to be followed. He claimed that when he set out to interpret a dream, he always began by reminding himself that he had 'no idea what this dream means' (1945, par. 533). He insisted that his writings do not constitute a theory (1952, par. 1507). In 'The Tavistock Lectures' he writes: 'Never apply any theory' (1935, par. 248). In 1924 he writes: 'There simply is not and cannot be any [Jungian] treatment, and even if there could be, one would be on the surest road to failure' (1924, par. 203; cf. 1937, par. 79). Jung was always uncomfortable with any use of the adjective 'Jungian' to describe either his ideas or their application. Even so, he could never entirely free himself from his own subjective tendencies. He admits that he applied just enough 'theory' to induce both in himself and in his patient 'a way of looking at the illness' that might produce positive results (1941, par. 218). Unsurprisingly, this 'way of looking' corresponded to the instinctive tendencies of an introverted intuition type.

This may be illustrated by his visit to the Pueblo Indians of New Mexico in early 1925 (Bair, p. 334ff.). He was deeply impressed by their beliefs and traditions, especially by the power of their conviction in their relation to the sun. He concludes:

> I then realized on what the 'dignity', the tranquil composure of the individual Indian, was founded. It springs from his being a son of the sun; his life is cosmologically meaningful, for he helps the father and preserver of all life in his daily rise and descent.
>
> (1965, p. 252)

Jung tells us that from this visit he learned that: 'Knowledge does not enrich us; it removes us more and more from the mythic world in which we were once at home by right of birth' (p. 252). This is exactly the kind of statement one might expect from an introverted intuition type, who instinctively yearns for the 'mythic world' in which he feels at home. However, the significance given to the 'mythic world' by the introverted intuition type is not a natural, but a *human* construct.

This is why Caeiro seeks to experience an even *earlier* epoch in the history of the world: a world as he imagines it was before human beings began to live in such a 'mythic world'. In '*Bendito seja o mesmo sol de outras terras*' (1969, p. 223), he seeks to recover the experience of

> [. . .] the true and primitive Man
> Who saw the sun rise and did not yet worship it.
> For this is natural—more natural
> Than worshipping gold and God,
> And art and moral principles.
>
> (1998, p. 61)

Caeiro wants us to see the world, and everything in it, exactly and only *as it is*, without *any* archetypal associations or any kind of interpretation, for these cannot help but distort, and thus falsify, the nature of the experience.

It might seem that Caeiro's views and Jung's are incompatible. The insistence that 'Things have no inner meaning' would seem to negate the foundation of Jungian psychology. And yet I am not sure this is so. There is much about Jungian psychology that Caeiro would have discarded as evidence of a 'sick' philosophy: for example, Jung's insistence on meaning, his interest in archetypal images, his adherence to the myth of the hero, etc. But in spite of these differences, it might be that Caeiro's poems nonetheless have something useful to contribute to post-Jungian theory.

Jungians interpret the goal of individuation in a variety of ways. At one end of the spectrum are those who understand it as a kind of initiation into an inner world not so very different from that of a shaman; at the other end are those who see it as a balanced consciousness about one's place in a larger social reality. But wherever they stand along this scale there is a tendency to think that individuation results in some kind of enlarged consciousness, even wisdom. It is just such a tendency that Caeiro insists we must 'unlearn' if we are to understand ourselves as we truly are, and not as we would like ourselves both to be and to be seen.

Pessoa was just as interested in exploring his unconscious tendencies as Jung, but because he was an introverted *thinking* type, he had a very different experience of his unconscious. Jung experienced his unconscious in imaginal narratives such as those he records in *The Red Book* (1914–1930), which he describes as his personal myth. Pessoa experienced his unconscious in sensations and feelings, upon which he endlessly reflects. Whereas Jung believed he had a 'centre of consciousness' that had been expanded as a result of his heroic quest, Pessoa could never ascertain the existence of such a centre: he attributed all his experiences to one or other of his various heteronyms. Whereas Jung—presumably because the introverted intuition type is always seeking the numinous—often writes as if he thought of himself as a seer, Pessoa never regarded himself as special. He describes his activity of writing poems simply as his way of 'being alone' (1998, p. 45), and the products of this activity as his 'crochet', i.e. his way of passing the time (1998, p. 205; 2001b, pp. 20–21).

Whereas for Jung, individuation signals assuming responsibility for being the specific individual one is, for Pessoa it means exploring as many different aspects of one's personality as one can identify. In a letter written in January 1935, the year of his death, he admits:

> I do not evolve, I simply JOURNEY. [. . .] I continuously change personality, I keep enlarging (and here there is a kind of evolution) my capacity to create new characters, new forms of pretending that I understand the world or, more accurately, that the world can be understood. That is why I've likened my path to a journey rather than to an evolution. I haven't risen from one floor to another; I've moved, on a level plane, from one place to another.
>
> (2001a, p. 263; 1974, p. 101)

Pessoa's journey has many of the hallmarks of what Jungians call the process of individuation. He engages regularly with the personifications of his unconscious tendencies: Caeiro is only one of his many heteronyms. Pessoa reflects on what each of his heteronyms has to say, assumes responsibility for it and learns from each encounter, but he makes no fuss about it. He does not pretend that he has done anything heroic. He never asserts that he has explored the deeper significance of anything. He makes no claim about having had a richer or deeper or more meaningful journey than anyone else. He hasn't 'risen from one floor to another' as in some kind of ladder, or spiral of perfection. He has kept a journal of his voyage, that is all.

If Pessoa's individuation reads as very different from the textbook outlines of the pattern that Jungian individuation is said to take, it must also be noted that it does not differ very much from some of Jung's more measured thoughts about its outcome. One of Jung's most important statements on individuation is found in a letter of 1956, to Henry Murray, who had asked him to explain exactly what he understood by an individuated person. Because Murray had been the partner of Christiana Morgan, who supplied the material for Jung's *Visions Seminars*, and he was at the time an eminent Professor of Psychology at Harvard University, Jung gave him a carefully considered answer. An individuated person, what he writes will be exactly like anyone else:

> his feelings, thoughts, etc. are just anybody's feelings, thoughts, etc.—quite ordinary, as a matter of fact, and not interesting at all, unless you happen to be particularly interested in that individual and his welfare. [. . .] He will be 'in modest harmony with nature'. As Zen Buddhism says: first mountains are mountains and the sea is the sea. Then mountains are no more mountains, the sea is no more the sea, and in the end the mountains will be the mountains and the sea will be the sea. [. . .] The criterion is consciousness.
>
> (1976, p. 324; cf. 1939, par. 884n.)

This definition reminds us that as long as we are consciously or unconsciously measuring our experience against a Jungian model, the 'Mountains are no more mountains'; they are mountains *seen through Jungian spectacles*. Jung had little patience with those of his followers who saw everything in terms of his ideas. In their enthusiasm, they insist on attributing the most arcane and erudite archetypal meanings to their every experience. Everything they see reminds them of something else—and their every experience seems to confirm Jung's insights. Such Jungians are truly Jungian.

And yet, Jung was forever reminding his followers that the objective of every analysis is to help the analysand to stand on their own feet. He wanted each and every one of his patients to discover their own unique way of seeing the world. This means casting off the support that Jungian theory provides, as if it were a pair of crutches, in order to make room for the individuality of the subject's own experience. Caeiro's poems remind us that if we want to travel our own journey, at the end of the day we have to recover our ability to see the mountains only as mountains; to see them, in other words, without *any* of the archetypal trappings with which Jungians like to colour them. To see them as they are—as just mountains.

Jungians never forget that their individual experience is rooted in their collective identity—and collective identity can very easily transform individuals into tribal creatures. We may inherit some aspects of our collective identity (for example, being European or female), but other aspects (such as an interest in the ideas of Jung), although probably determined by unconscious inclination, are nonetheless shaped by consciousness. In other words, such aspects always rest on something that we *add* to our immediate experience, all too often by way of a tacit adoption of an ideology or set of concerns that sets us apart from others, and which therefore lead to inevitable spirals of conflict with those who hold different views.

Pessoa was just as fascinated by his inner world as Jung. In their works, both men emphasise the need to assume responsibility for one's inner world. Caeiro's poems illustrate, and unusually clearly, the familiar distinction between the poet (Pessoa) and his narrative voice (Caeiro). Pessoa recognises this; indeed, he exploits it. Pessoa realises that Caeiro is an autonomous aspect of his personality, and that it is important for him to understand exactly how Caeiro relates to him. He articulates Caeiro's thoughts in successive poems, curious to know where they will lead. New Criticism used to insist that a poem should stand alone, on its own intrinsic merits; that neither context nor biography is relevant to its significance (see Wellek, 1978). From an aesthetic point of view, this may be a valid perspective. Analytical psychology provides another. It suggests that Caeiro's poems *need* to be read as one side—and the less expected side—of a conscious dialogue between the poet and one of his many unconscious personae. That they demonstrate a point of view so very different from Pessoa's own views seems to illustrate Jung's contention that the unconscious compensates consciousness.

From a Jungian perspective, there is no difficulty in understanding the possible psychological significance of Caeiro's poems for Pessoa. Fernando Pessoa very often carried his introverted thinking to excess. Caeiro was prompting him to connect with the real world in which he lives and to become an intrinsic part of it. As he writes in 'My gaze is clear like a sunflower':

> The world wasn't made for us to think about it
> (To think is to have sore eyes)
> But to look at it and to be in agreement.
>
> (1998, p. 48)

Caeiro was urging Pessoa to see the mountain not through his exaggerated thinking function but to see it only as mountain—to see it as it is in order to be 'in modest harmony' with it. This is his 'lesson in unlearning'.

Nevertheless, Caeiro's poems also carry a collective significance, one from which we all can learn. They remind us that we all tend to lean a little too heavily on the set of beliefs around which we have chosen to construct not only our personality, but also our lives. And too often we cling to these in very much the same way as a child who holds on to its mother in a crowded place, unnecessarily afraid to take full responsibility for our own individuality. If we model our ideas and individuation on those of Jung, we may very well miss discovering our own.

As a thinking type, Pessoa tended not to focus very sharply on what he saw; he was too busy trying to understand it, as if by thinking he could discover some secret to his experience. What Caeiro prompts him to do is to *connect* with the world around him, to really 'see' everything around him, and at all times. In other words, to see, identify with, and respond to the world with a simplicity that knows nothing of any system of thought, whether Zen Buddhism or Jungian psychology; to know

> [. . .] that, wherever you are,
> There is no mystery anywhere in the world
> And that everything is worthwhile.
>
> (2006, p. 20)

Living in a changing world

Caeiro's poems remind us that if members of *any* collective group are to discover their individuality, they have to 'unlearn' their tribal habits. For Jungians, this means learning to see, as Caeiro urges Pessoa to see—that is, to see the world and everything in it *without* the window frame of Jungian theory; *without* a Jungian lens; above all, to be able to discuss it *without* a Jungian jargon and without that all-too-human tendency to assume that a Jungian view is somehow superior to any other.

The earth has been undergoing constant and often violent change for over four billion years. Over the last two decades, some aspects of this change have accelerated alarmingly. The planet is being exploited more ruthlessly and mindlessly than ever before, and stress is becoming an increasingly intrusive part of everyday human experience. A large number of very different factions are involved in trying to correct both these imbalances, and each and every faction believes that it—and it alone—has the key to solving these issues. The clamour of their indignation has done little to improve either situation.

In October 1957, Jung wrote to Martin Flinker:

> Improbable as this may sound, it is only the individual who is qualified to fight against the threat today of international mass-mindedness. In this very unequal-looking struggle the individual does not by any means occupy a lost outpost if he succeeds in seriously getting down to the old Christian injunction to see the beam in his own eye and not worry about the mote in his brother's.
>
> (1976, pp. 396–397)

This is one of his essential beliefs. In 1933, he had written: 'The great events of world history are, at bottom, profoundly unimportant. In the last analysis, the essential thing is the life of the individual' (1933, par. 315). I doubt if many Jungians today could entirely agree with the first part of this view; there *are* issues that can only be improved by concerted collective action. Even so, individuality appears to be under more ferocious and subtle attack than ever before. The combination of globalisation and marketing is threatening not only national and regional, but also individual identity. Society is becoming increasingly impatient with those who do not belong to an identifiable and accepted tribe.

Significant innovation and lasting change are almost always brought about by an individual, and individuation is about discovering our individual identity. As long as we remain Jungians, our tribal identity will ensure that we are at odds with the representatives of a great many other tribes. The greatest challenge facing us today is to learn how to truly respect all those who think differently from ourselves. Our task is to discover that part of our identity that lies deeper than any tribal affiliation, that is at once part of our collective heritage and yet also essentially individual. Only in this way might we come face to face with who we really are. Only in this way do we stand a chance of finding a way to live 'in agreement'—'in modest harmony'—with all those whose different traditions, intellectual affiliations, and typological tendencies give them a very different experience of the world from our own.

Notes

1 Although Jung described himself as an introverted thinking-intuition type (Shamdasani 2003, p. 76), it is unlikely that thinking was Jung's dominant function; in his writings, his argument is often buried by the accumulation of his associated ideas. The suggestion that he was an intuition type is more persuasive (e.g. McLynn 1996, p. 263; Tacey 2006, p. 13). According to Jung, introverted intuition types are always moving 'from image to image, chasing after every possibility in the teeming womb of the unconscious'; they are always in search of a numinous possibility (cf. 1921, par. 658). So arresting are these possibilities that they tend to assume they are always on the brink of discovering some hitherto unrecognised truth (cf. pars 661–662). In other words, they are always looking for an elusive but ultimate 'meaning'.

2 The poems attributed to Alberto Caeiro fall into three categories: poems Pessoa intended for a collection to be called *The Keeper of Sheep*; poems for a collection called *The Shepherd in Love*, which he kept meaning to complete; and *Uncollected Poems*. Most of those quoted above come from *The Keeper of Sheep*. I have retained Portuguese titles to facilitate reference. Pessoa often dated his poems; where this is known, I have included the date in *d-m-y* format. In most cases I have given a reference to the translation used by Richard Zenith and to the original Portuguese (wherever possible to the excellent if now outdated single-volume editions by Maria Aliete Galhoz). The poems can also be found on the invaluable 'Arquivo Pessoa' website.

3 Although the translations of Caeiro's poems are my own, the appended reference is to the same passage in excellent translations by Richard Zenith for Grove (1998) and Penguin (2006). Inevitably, they have influenced mine.

References

Bair, D. (2003). *Jung: A biography*. Boston: Little, Brown & Co.

Jung, C. G. (1914–1930). *The red book*, ed. S. Shamdasani. New York: Norton & Philemon Foundation, 2009.

—— (1921). Psychological types, *CW* 6.

—— (1922). On the relation of analytical psychology to poetry, *CW* 15.

—— (1924). Analytical psychology and education, *CW* 17.

—— (1930). Psychology and literature, *CW* 15.

—— (1933). The meaning of psychology for modern man, *CW* 10.

—— (1935). The Tavistock lectures, *CW* 18.

—— (1937). Psychology and religion, *CW* 11.

—— (1938). Psychological aspects of the mother archetype, *CW* 9.i.

—— (1939). Foreword to Suzuki's 'Introduction to Zen Buddhism, *CW* 11.

—— (1941). Psychotherapy today, *CW* 16.

—— (1944). Introduction to the religious and psychological problems of alchemy, *CW* 12.

—— (1945). On the nature of dreams, *CW* 8.

—— (1952). Religion and psychology: A reply to Martin Buber, *CW* 18.

—— (1965). *Memories, dreams, reflections*, ed. A. Jaffé. New York: Random House/Vintage.

—— (1976). *Letters, vol. 2: 1951–1961*, ed. G. Adler. London: Routledge & Kegan Paul.

—— (1978). Jung in America. *Spring*, pp. 37–53.

McLynn, F. (1996). *Jung: A biography*. London, Bantam.

Pessoa, F. (current). *Archivo Pessoa*. http://arquivopessoa.net.

—— (1969). *Obra poética*, ed. M. A. Galhoz. 3rd edn. Rio de Janeiro: Nova Aguilar.

—— (1974). *Obras em prosa*, ed. M. A. Galhoz. Rio de Janeiro: Nova Aguilar.

—— (1994). *Poemas completos de Alberto Caeiro*, ed. T. S. Cunha. Lisbon: Presença.

—— (1998). *Fernando Pessoa & Co.: Selected poems*, tr. R. Zenith. New York: Grove.

—— (2001a). *The selected prose of Fernando Pessoa*, tr. R. Zenith. New York: Grove.

—— (2001b). *The book of disquiet*, tr. and ed. R. Zenith. London: Penguin.

—— (2006). *A little larger than the entire universe: Selected poems*, tr. R. Zenith. London: Penguin.

—— (2010). *Forever someone else: Selected poems*, tr. R. Zenith. 2nd bilingual edition. Lisbon: Assírio & Alvim.

Shamdasani, S. (2003). *Jung and the making of modern psychology: The dream of a science*. Cambridge: Cambridge University Press.

Tacey, D. (2006). *How to read Jung*. New York: Norton.

Wellek, R. (1978). The new criticism: Pro and contra. *Critical Inquiry* 4[4]. pp. 611–624.

Yandell, J. (1977). *The imitation of Jung: An exploration of the meaning of 'Jungian'*. St Louis, MO: The Centerpoint Foundation.

INDEX

Note: page numbers in italic type refer to Figures.